500 best sauces, salad dressings, marinades & more

George Geary

Robert
ROSE

For complete cataloguing information, see page 343.

Disclaimer
The recipes in this book have been carefully tested by our kitchen and our tasters. To the best of our knowledge, they are safe and nutritious for ordinary use and users. For those people with food or other allergies, or who have special food requirements or health issues, please read the suggested contents of each recipe carefully and determine whether or not they may create a problem for you. All recipes are used at the risk of the consumer.

We cannot be responsible for any hazards, loss or damage that may occur as a result of any recipe use.

For those with special needs, allergies, requirements or health problems, in the event of any doubt, please contact your medical adviser prior to the use of any recipe.

Editor: Carol Sherman
Recipe Editor: Jennifer MacKenzie
Copy Editor: Jo Calvert
Indexer: Gillian Watts
Design and Production: Kevin Cockburn/PageWave Graphics Inc.
Photography: Colin Erricson
Food Styling: Kathryn Robertson
Prop Styling: Charlene Erricson

Interior Photography (in order of appearance): © iStockphoto.com/mantonis (Cabernet Sauvignon Vinaigrette), © iStockphoto.com/ALEAIMAGE (Traditional Mayonnaise), © iStockphoto.com/Mark Fairey (Country Ketchup), © iStockphoto.com/JoanVicent (Coarse Brown Mustard), © iStockphoto.com/KCline Photography (Mango Lime Chutney), ©iStockphoto.com/MentalArt (Tarragon Pickle Relish), © iStockphoto.com/JackJelly (Basic Brown Sauce), © Robert Rose (Hollandaise Sauce), © iStockphoto.com/kivoart (Garden Fresh Pesto Sauce), © Robert Rose (Spaghetti Anchovy Puttanesca), © iStockphoto.com/Cathleen Clapper (All-American BBQ Sauce), © iStockphoto.com/Robyn Mackenzie (Guacamole), © iStockphoto.com/Stieglitz (South-of-the-Border Salsa), © iStockphoto.com/MBPHOTO (Milk Chocolate Sauce), © Robert Rose (Rich Caramel Sauce), © iStockphoto.com/Fertnig Photography (Crème Anglaise)

We acknowledge the financial support of the Government of Canada through the Book Publishing Industry Development Program (BPIDP) for our publishing activities.

Published by Robert Rose Inc.
120 Eglinton Avenue East, Suite 800, Toronto, Ontario, Canada M4P 1E2
Tel: (416) 322-6552 Fax: (416) 322-6936

Printed and bound in Canada.

1 2 3 4 5 6 7 8 9 CPL 17 16 15 14 13 12 11 10 09

Contents

To Neil.
You're the best.

Acknowledgments

I could never have created this book without "my team" of family and friends, and I thank you all from the bottom of my heart: My parents, who are always ready to help at a moment's notice and are always saying how proud you are of me — I am the proudest of you. My sisters, Monica and Pattie, my two roses, for always putting up with this thorn. Neil, always ready to step in when someone does not show up, to clean my dishes at the eleventh hour, to take me to the airport before the sun comes up and to pick me up hours after it goes down — thank you for being you. Jonathan, for all the years of friendship. Sean and Chris at Sephno Systems, for keeping my media going. The entire staff at Corona Tuscany Starbucks, for always having my drink ready, and asking about my latest project. My two main gals at United (ONT) Airlines, Robin and Reena, for always smiling at 4 a.m. when I am flying off to who knows where (I am glad you know where I am going) — you both make traveling so much easier.

My recipe testers, friends and colleagues: Teri, for being my longest-running student and always laughing, even in France. Carol Ann, for support and ideas. The "craft group" that often gathers at the house for recipe testing, cooking and crafts — Buzz, Chris, Don, Eilena, Jack, Jeff, Sean and Ted. Nancie McDermott, Phillis Carey, Denise Vivaldo, Cathy Thomas and Tim Haskell, for being the best colleagues. Annette, Josephine and Val at the Los Angeles County Fair, for prepping, selling and working so hard, and for keeping me grounded in Pomona every September. The Yorba Linda Danish Cultural Center for bringing in this "Non-Dan" into your group, and every one of my students at the center. Placenta, La Mirada and Anaheim parks and recreation groups, for giving this teacher a chance. My second hand in the kitchen, Adrianna Hymann, for knowing exactly how to make everything look great, even under pressure. Erika and Sara at Holland America Line for believing in me, putting me on your "Dam" ships, and letting me share my love of food around the world.

Karen Tripson, my personal copy editor, for being a friend and a colleague for years — I cherish your friendship and direction. Lisa Ekus-Staffer, for being a great friend for so long and now my literary agent — I wish we weren't 3,000 miles apart. Bob Dees, my publisher and friend, for putting up with all of my jokes, rants and raves for six books now — thank you for trusting and investing in me. Carol Sherman, for making me laugh and keeping my voice for five books now. Jennifer MacKenzie, for testing and editing recipes and giving her guidance. Jo Calvert, for careful copy editing and asking all the right questions. The entire staff at PageWave Graphics, including Kevin Cockburn, Andrew Smith, Joseph Gisini and Daniella Zanchetta, for making this book a piece of art. And, finally, all of my students, and the cooking schools and directors across the globe, for welcoming me into their kitchens.

Introduction

When I completed my first book, *125 Best Cheesecake Recipes*, in 2002, I phoned my colleague Cathy Thomas. Cathy is the food editor of the Orange County Register, a newspaper in Southern California where I live. She wanted to do a photo spread of some of the cheesecakes I had created for the book and my home. She came over with a photographer, and we had a great time. When Cathy opened my refrigerator, though, she was surprised not to find any salad dressings. I told her that I like to make my own simple, fast dressings, and that's when it clicked — I couldn't remember ever seeing a huge salad-dressing cookbook in print.

When we began working on this book, we expanded on dressings to include their saucy cousins, as well as condiments, salsas and rubs. It just made sense. After researching commercial varieties, and finding so many unrecognizable ingredients listed on their labels, I realized how reassuring it is to know exactly what goes into the dressings and sauces I serve and enjoy. Homemade versions don't keep as long as their commercial counterparts, but there's no doubt they taste better. Sample just one, and you will toss those ancient jars and bottles huddled in your fridge — and start fresh. It's easy and it's fast. Now get dressed and sauced!

Tools and Equipment

Many of the tools you'll need will have other uses in your kitchen and will last a long time, so it's worth purchasing quality equipment the first time.

Hand Tools

Salad (herb) spinner

I was skeptical when these came on the market a few years back. Now I use them every time I make salad. Place your salad greens in the "colander" part of the spinner. Wash your salad greens, and shake off excess water. Place colander into bowl of the spinner, place lid on and, depending on the model, pump the top. The spinner, using centrifugal force, forces the water into the bottom of the spinner bowl. There are smaller versions available for fresh herbs.

Rubber spatulas

A rubber spatula is the perfect tool for scraping a bowl clean. It also allows for the most thorough mixing of ingredients, the least waste when turning ingredients into the baking pan and an easy cleanup. The new silicone spatulas, which are heatproof to 800°F (427°C), are ultra-efficient because they can go from the mixing bowl to the stovetop. Commercial-quality spatulas are more flexible and durable than grocery-store brands.

Balloon whisk

To achieve perfectly beaten egg whites or whipped cream, use a sturdy whisk. They come in many sizes for different jobs. If you buy only one whisk, select a medium-size one.

Liquid measuring cups

The most accurate way to measure liquid ingredients is with a glass or Pyrex measuring cup with a pouring spout. They are widely available in sizes ranging from 1 cup (250 mL) to 8 cups (2 L). Place the measure on a flat surface and add the liquid until it reaches the desired level. When checking for accuracy, bend over so that your eye is level with the measure. (Angled liquid measures are now available that allow you to measure ingredients without bending — the markings are inside the cup for easy viewing.) Pyrex cups can also be used in the microwave to melt butter and heat water.

Dry measuring cups

The most accurate way to measure dry ingredients is with nesting metal measuring cups. They usually come in sets of four to six cups, in sizes ranging from $\frac{1}{4}$ cup (50 mL) to 1 cup (250 mL). Spoon the dry ingredient into the appropriate cup, then level it off by sliding the flat end of a knife or spatula across the top of the cup. Brown sugar and shortening need to be packed firmly into the cup for correct measurement.

Measuring spoons

The most accurate measuring spoons are metal. You'll need a set of sturdy spoons ranging from $\frac{1}{8}$ tsp (0.5 mL) to 1 tbsp (15 mL) to measure small amounts of both liquid and dry ingredients.

Mixing bowls

A nested set of small, medium and large mixing bowls will be used countless times. Having the right size bowl for the job, whether it's beating an egg white or whipping a quart (1 L) of cream, helps the cooking process. Ceramic, glass and stainless-steel bowls all have their merits, but I think stainless steel is the most versatile.

Microplane zester/grater

A Microplane zester/grater with a handle is the best tool for quickly removing zest from lemons and other citrus fruits. To use it, rub the Microplane over the skin so you can see the zest. Do not zest any of the white pith, as it has a bitter taste. The Microplane is also good for grating hard cheeses and chocolate.

Garlic press

A garlic press is the fastest way to turn a clove of garlic into small bits. When you use a garlic press, your crushed garlic will have a stronger flavor, because of the release of oils, than garlic minced with a knife.

Electric Equipment
Handheld mixer

A handheld mixer is great for small jobs. It allows easy access around the bowl when you're beating egg whites or whipping cream. It also makes it easier to mix ingredients in pots that are on the stove.

Food processor

Select a sturdy processor that is large enough to handle the volume of ingredients in the recipes you use most often. My 11-cup (2.75 L) Cuisinart has worked well for me over many years.

Common Ingredients

Oils

I use a variety of oils, some to add flavor and some to balance the acidity in foods that I'm preparing. If you don't have the oil that's called for in any recipe, use another type. You may create a new sauce or dressing.

Canola oil

Produced in Canada, canola oil is low in saturated fatty acids, and is the healthiest of all commonly used cooking oils. It is pressed from canola seeds grown mainly in Canada and the northern States. You can use canola oil in any recipe calling for soybean or vegetable oil.

Corn oil

There is little to no taste in this oil. I use it when I am relying on flavor from other ingredients in my recipe.

Hot chile oil

This is a neutral-flavored oil infused with chile peppers.

Olive oils

I try to keep only a few bottles of oil on hand, so it keeps fresh. When you're choosing oil, always check the expiration date on the bottle — the fresher the better. The U.S. Department of Agriculture and the International Olive Oil Council use different designations and descriptions for basic olive oil types but here's a general description of the types available:

- *Extra virgin olive oil:* From the cold first pressing of the olives, this oil has no more than 0.8% acidity.
- *Extra light virgin olive oil:* This is "light" in flavor not in calories.
- *Virgin olive oil:* Smooth in taste, this oil has no more than 2% acidity.
- *100% pure olive oil:* This is the lowest grade of olive oil.
- *Herbed olive oil:* This describes olive oil that has been infused with fresh herbs for a few weeks.

Nut oils

These oils exhibit a slight taste and aroma of the nuts from which they were extracted.

Sesame oil

Cold-pressing the seeds for this oil results in a light cooking oil. When the oil is pressed from toasted sesame seeds, it has a stronger flavor and darker color, and is often used for garnishing.

Soybean oil

A byproduct of processing soybean meal, this oil has a flavor that's light and delicate. Soybean oil can be substituted for the canola or vegetable oil called for in recipes.

Vegetable oil

Most oils labeled "vegetable" are soybean or canola oil, or a blend of different oils. Corn and olive oil blends may also contain vegetable oil.

Vinegars

For the recipes in this book, I call for an array of vinegars. You may interchange them and create a different, but likely successful, result. The word "vinegar" derives from the Old French *vin aigre*, which means "sour wine."

Apple cider vinegar

Also labeled as cider vinegar, this is made from apple cider.

Balsamic vinegar

Traditionally manufactured in Modena, Italy, from concentrated grape juice, this is a very dark brown. The finest examples have been aged in successive casks made of various types of woods. True balsamic vinegars are aged

4 to 12 years; some are aged up to 100 years, and will be priced as a rare antique. It is said that every winemaker should start a cask of balsamic vinegar upon the birth of each daughter, to be part of her dowry in 18 years and the gift of a lifetime of balsamic vinegar for the new family.

Fruit vinegars

These vinegars are made from fruit wines, and the vinegars are more commonly produced in Canada, Europe and Asia than in America.

Herb vinegars

These are flavored with a fresh herb such as tarragon, thyme or oregano. You can make your own by infusing a light, mild tasting vinegar, such as white wine vinegar, with a fresh herb for a few weeks.

Malt vinegar

Made from aged, malted barley, this light brown vinegar is used in chutneys.

Rice vinegar

A popular ingredient in Asian cuisines, rice vinegar is found in an array of shades, from white and colorless to red to black. I prefer the white, which is available natural or seasoned. The natural is light in color and mild in taste, while seasoned rice vinegar contains sake, salt and sugar.

Wine vinegars

Made from wine, these have a smoother flavor than apple cider vinegar. Their varying prices reflect the quality of the wines used, but all are valued for the delicate flavors they impart. They include red wine vinegar, Cabernet Sauvignon vinegar, Champagne vinegar, white wine vinegar and sherry wine vinegar.

Other Ingredients

Capers

Pickled buds from the plant of the same name, which grows wild throughout the Mediterranean, capers are prized for their salty flavor.

Chili sauce

You can find so many types of chili sauce. Any thick, flavorful version will add body in a recipe, but the best is the one you make yourself (see Bold Chili Sauce, page 125).

Dill pickles

I like using crunchy dill pickles when I cook, but you can replace them with pickle relish to save time chopping.

Hoisin sauce

This sweet and spicy Chinese dipping sauce is found in the "international" section of the supermarket. Traditional hoisin sauce is made with sweet potatoes, but today's varieties are made with fermented soybeans with sweet potatoes added for texture.

Horseradish

Part of the mustard and wasabi family, horseradish is available prepared in jars and as a fresh root that you can grate and mix with vinegar or cream.

Hot pepper sauce

I like to use a plain hot pepper sauce, such as Tabasco, that's available in small bottles and keeps for a long time.

Ketchup

Make a batch of ketchup when you have a garden filled with too many tomatoes — you will never use the bottled varieties again. In a pinch, of course, store-bought ketchup is fine to cook with.

Mayonnaise

I have a number of recipes for homemade mayonnaise. You can always save time by using a manufactured brand, but if you make mayonnaise from scratch, you will never go back. I guarantee it.

Mustards

You can find many varieties of mustards on store shelves. It's so easy, I tend to make my own versions. All are interchangeable, but sometimes you want the special zest of whole grains or flavored mustard.

Pimentos

These roasted red peppers are commonly found in jars and stuffed into the centers of some Spanish green olives.

Plum jam

Thickened plums, this jam is sometimes sweetened. You can substitute a berry jam.

Soy sauce

This is made with fermented soybeans. I like to use the reduced-sodium variety as typical soy sauce adds too much salt to the dish. Check the label to make sure the sauce is made from soybeans and not just additives and colorings.

Teriyaki sauce

This sweet sauce contains soy sauce, mirin and a sweetener. I like the common bottled varieties found in the "international" sections of major supermarkets.

Tomatoes, fresh and canned

To substitute fresh for canned or vice versa, here is a quick chart:

- 2½ lbs (1.25 kg) fresh Roma (plum) tomatoes produce 3 cups (750 mL) tomato purée — halve and seed uncooked tomatoes, then pass them through the fine plate of a food mill.
- 1½ lbs (750 g) diced fresh Roma (plum) tomatoes are equivalent to a 28 oz (796 mL) can diced tomatoes — dice the tomatoes or crush them to the thickness you need.
- 2 lbs (1 kg) cooked fresh Roma (plum) tomatoes are equivalent to a 28 oz (796 mL) can stewed tomatoes.

Tomato paste

You can find paste in small cans and in tubes. If your recipe calls for a entire can, use that. I use the tube paste when I only need a little bit for a recipe, then seal it up and keep it refrigerated and ready for the next use.

White miso

This soybean product is available in paste or powder form in Asian markets. Use it to make a beverage or soup, or to add flavor.

Worcestershire sauce

Originally made in Worcester, England, by two chemists, John Lea and William Perrins, this sauce is a fermented liquid condiment with sweet overtones. It's mainly used in sauces and on steaks. You can make your own (see Worcestershire Sauce, page 142) or buy the prepared version.

Sugars
Brown sugar

When measuring brown sugar, lightly pack it into a measuring cup. Unless a recipe is specific, you can interchange dark or light brown sugar.

Granulated sugar

Granular (white) sugar is the most common form. Choose pure sugarcane sugar, rather than sugar made from beets. I find the crystals of the cane sugar work better because they dissolve more easily in recipes.

Liquid Sugars

Liquid sugars come in a variety of flavors, and can be used to add sweetness to vinaigrettes. Store in a cool, dry place for the longest shelf life.

Corn syrup

Corn syrup is made from cornstarch and is available in light (white) and dark (golden) varieties. Use the dark version when its color isn't a problem and the caramel flavor is an asset to the recipe. Both types are used as table syrups and in frosting, candy and jam.

Honey

Made by bees from flower nectar, honey is a natural sugar. That doesn't mean it has fewer calories, though; it actually has more. Because it is sweeter than other liquid sweeteners, use less honey when substituting it for them.

Molasses

Made from sugarcane or sugar-beet syrup, molasses is available in three grades: light (fancy), dark (cooking) and blackstrap. Light molasses is typically used as table syrup, while dark molasses provides the distinctive, sweet flavor of gingerbread and Boston baked beans. Blackstrap molasses is slightly more nutritious than the other versions, and is not commonly used in baking.

Pure maple syrup

This is made by boiling sap collected from maple trees in the spring. I use only pure maple syrup. I find that the imitation syrups, which are a mixture of corn syrup and maple extracts, have a strange aftertaste.

Dairy Products

Cheese

Hard/semihard cheese

Buy chunks of fresh cheese and shred or grate it yourself to ensure the best quality and save the expense of ready-made grated cheese. Varieties used for the recipes in this book include:

- *Asiago cheese* is an Italian cheese with the characteristics of Parmesan and Romano, and can be interchanged for them in recipes.
- *Cheddar* is a firm, ripened cheese that can be mild to sharp in flavor. In color, it ranges from white to orange (which gets its color from annatto, a natural dye). It is popularly served plain with crackers, cooked in casseroles and sauces, or shredded as a garnish.
- *Parmesan* is ripened for 2 or more years to a hard, dry state, which makes it perfect for grating or shaving. The rich, sharp flavor of the premium-aged versions imported from Italy is easily distinguished from that of the grocery-store brands of grated cheese.
- *Romano* is named after Rome, where it's been manufactured for more than 2,000 years. Romano cheese is a dry cheese that needs to be grated. It is made from sheep's milk (pecorino romano) or goat's milk (caprino romano).

Soft cheese

Soft cheese can be used in small chunks, which will melt in hot liquids such as pasta sauce. Varieties used for the recipes in this book include:

- *Cottage cheese* is a fresh cow's milk cheese that comes in small, medium and large curds with various fat contents. The moisture content is high. The creamed style has extra cream added and extra calories as a result. Cottage cheese is drained to become other styles of cheese, of which the driest version is farmer's cheese.
- *Cream cheese* is made from cow's milk. It contains 33% fat and less than 55% moisture. Whipped cream cheese, which is soft because it has air whipped into it, has slightly fewer calories, but is not recommended in these recipes. Nonfat cream cheese, of course, has no calories from fat. Use it on a bagel or sandwich, but not in these recipes.
- *Goat cheese* is derived from goat's milk. Fresh goat cheese is very soft, like cream cheese; aged goat cheese is firmer, and is often labeled chèvre.
- *Mascarpone* is an Italian double- or triple-cream cheese that can be easily spread. The delicate, buttery texture is delicious with fruit, but it is very versatile as a cooking ingredient, and is found in both savory and sweet recipes.
- *Neufchâtel cheese* is a reduced-fat cream cheese. It contains 23% fat, so it has fewer calories. In recipes, it can be substituted for regular cream cheese.
- *Provolone* is an Italian cow's milk cheese made from whole milk, and has a smooth skin. It is aged for up to a year, or even more, to create its mild, smoky flavor. It is good for cooking. The varieties that are aged the longest are firm enough to grate.

Blue Cheese

Blue cheese is aptly named for the blue veins running through it — a result of being treated with molds and ripened. This aging process intensifies the flavor of the cheese, which is popular in salads and salad dressings, and with fruit. It is also used in cooking. The texture is firm enough for crumbling. My favorite brands are Maytag from Iowa, and Point Reyes from Northern California. Well-known international blue cheeses include Gorgonzola from Italy, Stilton from England and Roquefort from France. In the European Union, blue cheeses are protected by designation of origin, which means they can only bear the place names if they are manufactured there. All are interchangeable, some are stronger than others.

Sour cream

Made from cream, this contains 12 to 16% butterfat. Its tang comes from the lactic acid.

Butter

I use unsalted butter so I know how much salt is going into any recipe. If I am making an all-butter recipe (such as compound butter), I use one of the higher-fat European or Irish butters found in specialty-food stores.

Buttermilk

Buttermilk is lower in fat than regular milk because the fat has been removed to make butter. It has a thick and sour taste. If you don't have buttermilk, you can add 1 tbsp (15 mL) lemon juice to 1 cup (250 mL) whole milk, and use it instead.

Yogurt

Produced by the bacterial fermentation of milk, yogurt is available in an array of flavors. You can also find soy yogurt, made from soy milk.

Yogurt cheese

To make yogurt cheese, place 3 cups (750 mL) plain yogurt in a cheesecloth-lined strainer set over a bowl, then let it drain overnight in the refrigerator. Makes about 1½ to 1¾ cups (375 to 425 mL).

Heavy cream

Heavy cream is 36% or more butterfat. It is also known as whipping cream or table cream. If you can find cream that has only been pasteurized and not ultra-pasteurized, you will have a more flavorful product. Freeze any unused cream that is close to its expiry date. It won't make nice whipped cream, but is fine for other purposes.

Butterfat in Milk Products

Percentage of Butterfat	Product
82 to 85%	European butters
80%	U.S. butters
40%	Manufacturing cream
36%	Heavy cream
30 to 35%	Whipping cream
25%	Medium cream
18 to 30%	Light or table cream
10.5 to 18%	Half-and-half cream
3.25%	Whole milk
2%	Reduced, partly-skimmed or 2% milk
1.5 to 1.8%	Semi-skimmed milk
1%	Low-fat or 1% milk
0.0 to 0.5%	Nonfat or skim milk

Eggs

The recipes in this book were tested using large eggs. In some areas you can purchase a pasteurized liquid egg product (this is not liquid egg substitute), which is a great product for making recipes that call for raw eggs if you have food-safety concerns. Please consult your medical professional prior to making or serving dishes with raw eggs if this is a concern for you.

Produce

Whenever I can, I like to shop at my local farmer's market so I can buy in season from the source. If it is not possible, I go to the grocery store, but only purchase enough for a few days. It is assumed all produce with inedible peels and pits are peeled and pitted before using unless otherwise specified.

Fruit

In most of these recipes you can substitute a similar type of fruit if the specified fruit is out of season or hard to find.

Avocado

There are many varieties of avocado. The Hass variety is a large avocado with a slightly bumpy skin. Because the flesh is creamy and flavorful, I prefer Hass avocados.

Berries

At the supermarket, look for firm berries that have been stored in a refrigerator, or buy berries from a local source. Refrigerate them as soon as you get home. For every hour the berries are out of the refrigerator, you will lose 1 day of freshness.

Citrus Fruits

All citrus fruits are interchangeable, so if your region does not have one of the fruits called for in a recipe, by all means substitute another. The amount of zest and juice yielded by a citrus fruit depends on the weight and thickness of the rind. Choose fruits that feel heavy.
- *Citrus zest (orange, lemon or lime):* Use a Microplane (see page 7) to zest the fruits.

- *Clementine:* The clementine season is very short, and in my market you have to buy them by the case. You can substitute tangerines.
- *Dried peel (orange, lemon or lime):* You can find this in spice stores.
- *Lemon juice:* I joke in classes about why lemon juice comes in a green bottle — so you can't see the brown liquid. Real lemon juice should be light in color. Squeeze a fresh lemon, instead, whenever possible.
- *Lime juice:* Fresh limes are best. You do not need to purchase the expensive key lime juice, regular lime juice will do.
- *Orange juice:* If I don't have fresh oranges on hand, I use frozen orange juice concentrate from a can, then dilute it according to the package directions, unless the recipe calls for concentrate. It's the same and less expensive than juice from a carton.

Mangos

Ripe mangos feel firm in your hand, but yield slightly to gentle pressure. For attractive slices: cut the flesh in half along each side of the pit and separate. Invert to slice lengthwise, then cut off the skin.

Pears or apples

Buy whatever is in season. The fruit will be fresher and also less expensive. My favorites are Bosc or Bartlett pears and Rome, Granny Smith or McIntosh apples.

Asian pears

These are crisp like an apple, but not as sweet. They bruise so easily, they are usually wrapped individually with netting.

Tomatillos

These look like unripe tomatoes, each surrounded by a papery husk. Pull off the husks, then wash the stickiness off the tomatillo skins under cool water.

Vegetables

Garlic

Look for a tight bulb. Most U.S. garlic is harvested in the late spring or early summer. In Canada, garlic is harvested from mid- to late-summer. When you buy garlic at any other time of year, it's likely to have been in cold storage or imported from China.

To roast garlic: Preheat oven to 400°F (200°C). Cut off and discard about 1/4 inch (0.5 cm) from the top of the bulb, then drizzle it with 1 tsp (5 mL) oil. Wrap in foil and roast until golden brown and very soft, 30 to 35 minutes. Let it cool, then turn it upside down and press out the cloves.

Gingerroot

Use the edge of a spoon to scrape off the outer layer, then slice, mince or grate on a Microplane or ginger grater.

Mushrooms

Never submerge mushrooms in water — they are like sponges and all of the soil on the surface will be sucked into their pores. Instead, brush the mushrooms with a moistened towel. When selecting button mushrooms, make sure the area between each stem and cap is tight. If they are separating, that's a sign of age.

Root vegetables

These are harvested when they're ready to eat. Look for crisp and firm radishes, leeks and jicama.

Herbs

In recent years, major grocery stores have begun to carry fresh herbs at good prices, a luxury when there's a few feet of snow on the ground. Dried herbs are more intensely flavored than fresh. If you must substitute dried for fresh, use half as much dried as the fresh herb called for. Dried herbs go stale quickly, especially if they're finely ground. Keep dried herbs in airtight containers in a cool, dry, dark place. Once they lose their aroma, be ruthless and discard them.

Here is a list of the herbs used in the recipes and tips on how to chop them. I wash fresh herbs and dry them in a salad spinner (see page 6), then roll them in moist paper towel and put that inside a plastic bag which goes into the refrigerator.

- *Basil:* Use only the leaves. To chiffonade: stack the leaves with the largest on the bottom. Roll them up tightly, jelly-roll fashion, then finely slice across the roll. This prevents the basil from being bruised in the cutting, and prematurely darkening.
- *Chives:* Place the chives in a row, then finely slice across their blades.
- *Cilantro:* Also known as Mexican or Chinese parsley, it is used in salsas and has a distinctive taste. If you want, you can substitute Italian flat-leaf parsley.
- *Dill:* Remove the light feathery leaves, discarding any of the thicker stems, and chop.
- *Mint:* There are many types of mint, but the most commonly available are wintergreen and spearmint. Remove all the leaves and discard the stems, then chop.
- *Oregano:* Remove the leaves and any flowers and discard the stems, then chop.
- *Parsley:* Since the parsley with the very curly leaves lacks flavor, I use Italian flat-leaf parsley, instead.
- *Sage:* The soft velvety leaves contain the flavor. Remove them and discard the stems, then chop.

- *Tarragon:* Hold the top of the stem and strip off the leaves with your other hand; discard the stem and any brown leaves, then chop.
- *Thyme:* Remove the leaves and chop.

Chiles

Chiles are a powerful flavor enhancer for sauces, rubs and salad dressings. In most cases, they're interchangeable. For the best texture in any dish, substitute a fresh chile for another fresh chile, or dried for dried. The names can be confusing and may vary if the chiles are dried, canned and or fresh.

I am asked all the time which chiles are the hottest. In 1912, chemist Wilber Scoville, created a scale designating the heat level of different chiles by measuring the capsaicin that makes the chiles hot. Bell peppers are 0 and the hottest, Naga Jolokia, which I do not use, measures more than 1,000,000 heat units. Select chiles that fit your desire for more or less heat.

Chiles	Scoville Heat Scale
Fresh	
Banana	0 to 250
Anaheim	500 to 1,500
New Mexico	500 to 1,500
Poblano	1,250 to 2,500
Jalapeño	5,000 to 10,000
Serrano	10,000 to 25,000
Habanero	100,000 to 500,000
Dried	
Ancho (dried poblano)	1,500 to 2,500
Guajillo	2,000 to 4,500
Chipotle	5,000 to 10,000
Serrano	10,000 to 25,000
Habanero	100,000 to 500,000

Spices and Ground Herbs

Spices go stale all too quickly, especially those that are finely ground. The shelf life of herbs and spices is highly variable. Generally, whole spices may stay flavorful and fragrant for up to 4 years and ground spices for up to 2 years; ground herbs (such as oregano) may stay flavorful and fragrant for up to 6 months to 2 years, with proper storage. If they have lost their intense fragrance, they are probably past their prime.

For the best flavor, purchase whole spices and grind them as you need them. When you're purchasing ground spices, I recommend buying them from one of the sources I list on page 343. They grind their spices daily, and you cannot get any that are fresher. Keep spice containers tightly sealed, and store them in a cool, dry, dark place.

Patty Erd from the Spice House in Chicago suggests that you sprinkle dried-out herbs on the coals of your barbecue to harvest their last bit of flavor while you grill.

- *Adobe seasoning:* This blend of spices has a flavorful, smoked-chile taste, but it's not fiery hot.
- *Bouquet garni (also known as herb bouquet):* It typically includes thyme, oregano, savory and bay leaves that are tied together with string or wrapped in cheesecloth. A bouquet garni allows you to cook herbs in a packet, so you can remove them easily before serving the dish.
- *Chile pequín powder:* You may purchase whole, dried chile de arbol peppers and grind them yourself. You can also buy ready-made powder.
- *Dry mustard:* It comes in three different heat levels — regular yellow, mild yellow and hot.
- *Mustard seeds* come in three different types — brown, regular yellow and hot yellow.

- *Herbes de Provence:* This blend is used in French Provençal cooking. Grown in the region, these herbs include rosemary, thyme, tarragon, basil, savory, fennel, marjoram and lavender.
- *Dried onion flakes and minced dried garlic:* I get asked why I use dried instead of fresh. Using dried onion flakes or minced dried garlic produces an intense flavor you can not achieve by using fresh.
- *Dried red and/or green bell pepper flakes:* Concentrated, finely diced red and/or green bell peppers yield a fresh taste and flavor when soaked in liquid. If dried flakes are not available, replace them with twice as much minced fresh bell pepper.

Seasoning

Seasonings are spices and herbs blended to create a balanced flavor all in one jar.

- *Dried tomato powder:* This is made of the sweetest red tomatoes, dried and ground into a fine powder (see Sources, page 343).
- *Italian seasoning:* This blend includes oregano, basil, marjoram, thyme and rosemary.
- *Paprika:* I like Hungarian the best, but other types — such as Californian, Spanish or North African — are also fine to use. Some are hot and some are sweet.
- *Taco seasoning:* This is a blend of paprika, salt, dried onion flakes, tomato powder, cumin, garlic, oregano, black pepper, cocoa powder and allspice.
- *Tandoori seasoning:* This blend includes coriander, cumin, sweet Hungarian paprika, garlic, ginger, cardamom and saffron.

Spices and Extracts

- *Allspice:* Versatile, this adds flavor in baking, as well as in jerk and some grilling seasonings.

- *Cinnamon:* Currently you can find about five different types of cinnamon on the market. I like the Vietnamese cassia cinnamon for its sweet, strong flavor.
- *Ground ginger:* This powder from China is best finely ground.
- *Vanilla:* Use a pure vanilla extract, and preferably one that has been cold-processed in water and ethyl alcohol, then aged, instead of by cooking and steeping the extract out of the pods. Pure vanilla extract has a distinctive flavor and aroma.

Salt and Pepper

Lately, it seems, there are so many different types of salts and peppers on the market. They have been around for a long time, but recently they've become widely available. To keep it simple, I use only a few types.

- *Kosher salt, coarse and fine:* This refined rock salt is available coarse-grained or finely ground.
- *Sea salt, coarse and fine:* Most sea salt is coarse-grained, but some finely ground varieties are available. There are many kinds of sea salt, each reflecting the unique environment from which it was harvested.
- *Black peppercorns:* I like to grind my pepper fresh each time. I have a number of pepper grinders, set differently for coarse or fine grinds.
- *Szechwan peppercorns:* Not really peppercorns at all, but marketed that way, these dried berries are spicy, fragrant and a must for Asian recipes.
- *White pepper, coarse and fine:* Finely ground white pepper has traditionally been used in Western cooking for white sauces, cream soups, fish dishes and other foods in which specks of black pepper would be unattractive. Coarse white pepper is the size and type of pepper preferred in Southeast

Asia where it is generously sprinkled on meat (especially beef and pork) before grilling, broiling or stir-frying.

Wine

Many salad dressings call for wine. If you like the wine to drink, you will like it to cook with. Sometimes I create recipes just to use up a leftover cup of wine.

Liqueurs

I purchase the well-known brands of liqueurs. They are not that much more expensive than the store brands and are better quality.

Nuts and Seeds

Nothing can ruin a recipe more than rancid nuts, so I purchase mine from a specialty store that has a high turnover. You should refrigerate or freeze shelled nuts that won't be used right away. I package the leftovers in vacuum-pack bags and freeze them, then defrost and toast them before use — with great results.

To toast nuts: Preheat oven to 350°F (180°C). Spread in a single layer on a rimmed baking sheet and bake, checking a few times to make sure they don't burn, until fragrant, 10 to 12 minutes (some nuts may require longer baking times). Let cool before chopping. Nuts provide nutrition, including a generous serving of "good" monounsaturated fat. Because of the fat content, they have the corresponding calories, too. I only keep nuts for 3 months.

Chocolate

Anyone that knows me knows I have a problem. I am addicted to chocolate, and certainly have my fair share daily. I am in heaven every time I visit Belgium. I try to use European brands. Belgian and French chocolates are smoother and richer than their American counterparts.

- *Unsweetened chocolate:* Made without sugar, this is pure chocolate liquor that has been cooled and formed into bars.
- *Milk chocolate:* This contains at least 10% chocolate liquor and 12% milk solids.
- *Semisweet and bittersweet chocolate:* These chocolates can be switched in most recipes without any change to the outcome other than the taste. Semisweet chocolate must contain at least 15 to 35% chocolate liquor, while bittersweet must contain at least 35%. Today you can find some extremely bitter varieties (80 to 95%), which are best used only when unsweetened chocolate is needed.
- *Cocoa powder:* I use Dutch-process cocoa powder. It is processed with alkali, which neutralizes the cocoa powder's natural acidity. The resulting cocoa powder is darker and richer — some are brick red.
- *White chocolate:* Not really a chocolate, white chocolate is a mixture of cocoa butter, milk solids, vanilla and lecithin. It does not contain chocolate liquor. Choose white chocolate that's made with cocoa butter and not tropical oils, such as palm kernel, coconut and cottonseed, which create an "off" taste.

Different Types of Lettuce

When I was growing up, salad was always iceberg lettuce with a few tomatoes thrown in. Today the variety of lettuce and packaged blends is amazing. Packaged blends are great for one salad or to try new lettuce. If you eat salad a few times a week, though, you can purchase all of the lettuce separately and save a bundle.

Lettuce is divided into four categories by farmers and growers.

1. *Crisphead:* Iceberg is a crisphead. The leaves are thin, light green and very densely packed as they are in a cabbage. Crisphead lettuce is known for its crispy texture and mild flavor, and is grown in cold-weather areas.
2. *Romaine:* This tall lettuce has ridged leaves tightly packed together. The leaves are dark green on the outside and get lighter toward the center. Hearts of romaine are the light leaves, and are sold in packages of two, three or more.
3. *Butterhead:* Small in size, its leaves are not packed. These are tender, with a smooth and light texture; the flavor is "buttery" and mild. Boston and Bibb are common types.
4. *Loose-leaf:* The leaves are loose and attached at the base. Oak leaf is a common type.

Varieties of Lettuce

- *Arugula:* Sometimes called rocket or roquette. This has flat leaves with long stems that look like dandelion leaves and has a peppery taste. It's normally paired with other varieties to balance out the taste.
- *Belgian endive:* Also called French endive. Related to chicory and escarole, this bullet-shaped lettuce has tightly packed leaves that are yellow or white, crisp and slightly bitter. Keep it tightly wrapped to prevent it from turning green.
- *Chicory:* Also called curly endive. This lettuce is slightly bitter, with darker outer leaves and paler or even yellow leaves toward the center. The ragged leaves are on long thin stems.

- *Escarole:* Another member of the chicory family, this lettuce has broad wavy leaves and a milder taste than chicory.
- *Oak leaf:* The varieties are named after their colors — from red to dark green or bronze — and have curly or ruffled leaves.
- *Radicchio:* This variety looks like red cabbage, but it's actually related to chicory Because of its steep cost, the soft leaves are used only for a accents in salads. A small head of radicchio goes a long way.
- *Watercress:* The tender stalks and small dark green leaves have a peppery flavor, reflecting the mustard family they belong to. Use watercress quickly.

Packaged Salads

You will find many different brands and sizes of packaged blends in your grocer's produce department. If you need more lettuce or want to save money, make your own blends. Here's a sampling of blends to make:
- *American:* iceberg, romaine, carrots, cabbage and radishes
- *European:* romaine, iceberg, radicchio, endive and leaf lettuce
- *Field greens:* loose-leaf lettuce, curly endive, radicchio and carrots
- *Italian blend:* romaine and radicchio
- *Mediterranean blend:* escarole, loose-leaf lettuce, radicchio and endive
- *Spring mix:* baby lettuce, endive and mustard greens
- *Baby spinach:* a blend of small spinach leaves

Selection, Storage and Use

Lettuce is a very delicate vegetable so care should be taken when selecting and storing it. When choosing your leaves be sure that they are fresh and crisp, with no signs of wilting, or dark spots on the edges.

Lettuce keeps well in plastic bags in the crisper section of the refrigerator. Iceberg lettuce keeps the best, lasting around 2 weeks, while romaine, keeps about 10 days, and butterhead types and endives last approximately 4 days. The very delicate greens don't last very long, so it's best to buy only as much as you need at one time and use them immediately. I like to purchase mine at the farmers' market, directly from the growers. Farmers' market greens typically last longer than grocery-store purchases.

Salad greens should not be stored near fruits (such as apples) that produce ethylene gases, as this will increase brown spots on the lettuce leaves and hasten spoilage. Greens that are bought in bunches should be checked for insects. Those leaves that have roots should be placed, root down, in a glass of water with a bag over the leaves, and stored in the refrigerator.

Remove any brown, slimy or wilted leaves. For all lettuce types, you should thoroughly wash and "dry" the leaves to remove any dirt or lingering insects. If you eat lettuce often, it's wise to invest in a salad spinner. Simply rinse the leaves, then use the spinner to remove the excess water.

In addition to their most common use in salads, certain lettuce varieties can be braised, steamed, sautéed and even grilled to create wonderful and different taste treats. Try halving a head of radicchio or romaine lengthwise, then brush on some extra virgin olive oil and grill the halves, cut-side down, until they soften and just begin to brown — absolutely delicious.

Salad Dressings

Lower-Fat Dressings

Vinaigrettes

Homemade vinaigrette makes fresh greens from a grocery store or farmers' market really pop. They are the simplest dressings to make. You don't need special equipment — a bowl and a whisk are sufficient. In many cases you can put all of the ingredients into a jar, then cover and shake it for a few seconds. The main components of vinaigrette are acid (such as vinegar or lemon juice), flavorings (such as herbs and garlic) and oil. Oil is slowly whisked into the other ingredients until the mixture emulsifies (thickens).

Many ingredients may be in your pantry already. Some oils and vinegars may seem expensive, but they have a long shelf life and can be used in many recipes. Think of them as valuable tools that can create new flavors for your family and make any salad a standout instead of just a side dish.

Most of these dressings work well with lighter lettuce such as butterhead or European blends. Refrigerate any unused portion of vinaigrette in a covered container or bottle for up to 1 week, unless otherwise stated.

You may double or triple any of the dressings. Most of the recipes will make a sufficient amount for 4 to 8 servings. I want your dressing to be fresh so make only what you need. For vinaigrettes, shake vigorously to blend the oils with the other ingredients. For the creamy dressings, just stir to combine.

Emulsifying

Many of these recipes direct you to whisk until emulsified. You've probably noticed that some store-bought vinaigrettes separate and have to be shaken to blend them before use. This is what you are doing when you pour oil into the other ingredients while whisking. You want to whisk vigorously so the dressing becomes thicker and cloudy. The whisking also causes the fat globules to break up into small drops that disperse in the vinegar so the mixture looks blended. Honey, mustard and egg are the classic ingredients in emulsified dressings. I also instruct you to pour in the oil in a steady stream, because you want the other ingredients to incorporate slowly with the oil. If you add all of the oil at once, it just sits on top and won't emulsify. When it sits, it separates; if you refrigerate any leftover dressing, shake it prior to use.

Apple Cider Vinaigrette

Makes 1 cup (250 mL)

This vinaigrette can be served warm. Simply microwave the dressing for 15 seconds and it's perfect for a wilted spinach salad.

Tip

You should take about 45 seconds to incorporate the oil to ensure it gets emulsified with the other ingredients. If you pour too fast it will float on top.

2 tbsp	balsamic vinegar	25 mL
2 tbsp	apple cider vinegar	25 mL
1 tbsp	liquid honey	15 mL
½ tsp	sea salt	2 mL
¾ cup	vegetable or peanut oil	175 mL

1. In a bowl, whisk together balsamic and cider vinegars, honey and salt. While whisking, pour in oil in a thin steady stream until emulsified.

Cabernet Sauvignon Vinaigrette

Makes 1 cup (250 mL)

When I have a few tablespoons of wine left, I use it to create my salad dressing for the next day.

2 tbsp	Cabernet Sauvignon wine	25 mL
2 tbsp	Cabernet Sauvignon vinegar	25 mL
½ tsp	dried oregano	2 mL
½ tsp	dried onion flakes	2 mL
¾ cup	soybean oil	175 mL

1. In a bowl, whisk together wine, vinegar, oregano and onion flakes. Whisk in oil.

Champagne Vinaigrette

Makes 1 cup (250 mL)

*Use a dry rosé Champagne
for this dressing and
you'll have a light pink
vinaigrette — perfect for
Valentine's Day.*

2 tbsp	dry Champagne	25 mL
2 tbsp	Champagne vinegar	25 mL
1/4 tsp	garlic salt	1 mL
1/4 tsp	onion salt	1 mL
1/4 tsp	granulated sugar	1 mL
1/8 tsp	sea salt	0.5 mL
1/8 tsp	ground white pepper	0.5 mL
3/4 cup	light extra virgin olive oil	175 mL

1. In a bowl, whisk together Champagne, vinegar, garlic salt, onion salt, sugar, sea salt and white pepper. Whisk in oil.

Chenin Blanc Vinaigrette

Makes 1 cup (250 mL)

*Here's a light sharp
vinaigrette to dress any salad.*

Tip
Dried red or green bell
peppers are concentrated
small diced bell peppers that
yield a fresh taste and flavor.
They are available in bulk
food and spice stores. If you
can't find them, use a double
amount of diced fresh bell
peppers instead.

2 tbsp	Chenin Blanc wine	25 mL
2 tbsp	white wine vinegar	25 mL
1 tsp	dried onion flakes	5 mL
1 tsp	dried red bell peppers (see Tip, left)	5 mL
1/2 tsp	dried basil	2 mL
1/2 tsp	ground ginger	2 mL
3/4 cup	soybean oil	175 mL

1. In a bowl, whisk together wine, vinegar, onion flakes, dried red bell peppers, basil and ginger. Whisk in oil.

Cilantro and Lime Vinaigrette

Makes 1 cup (250 mL)

It's great on salad, but I also like to drizzle this over grilled fish.

½ cup	apple juice	125 mL
¼ cup	extra virgin olive oil	50 mL
¼ cup	white wine vinegar	50 mL
2 tbsp	finely chopped fresh cilantro	25 mL
1 tsp	grated lime zest	5 mL
2 tsp	freshly squeezed lime juice	10 mL
1 tsp	granulated sugar	5 mL
	Salt and freshly ground black pepper	

1. In a bowl, whisk together apple juice, oil, vinegar, cilantro, lime zest and juice and sugar. Season with salt and pepper to taste.

Crushed Blueberry Vinaigrette

Makes 1½ cups (375 mL)

This vinaigrette is sweet and tangy, with a beautiful purple hue from the blueberries.

Tip
The blueberries quickly break down and lose their appeal, so this vinaigrette can only be kept in the refrigerator for up to 2 days.

⅓ cup	white wine vinegar	75 mL
2 tbsp	granulated sugar	25 mL
2 tsp	Dijon Mustard (page 120) or store-bought	10 mL
⅔ cup	soybean oil	150 mL
½ cup	fresh or frozen blueberries, crushed	125 mL

1. In a bowl, whisk together vinegar, sugar and mustard. While whisking, pour in oil in a thin steady stream until emulsified. Toss in crushed blueberries.

Honey Poppy Seed Vinaigrette

Makes ¾ cup (175 mL)

This colorful dressing, with its blue poppy seeds, looks great on light green lettuce leaves.

Tip
Valued for their color and sweetness, blue poppy seeds aren't always available in stores. If you can't find them, check out online retailers (see Sources, page 343) or use regular poppy seeds.

3 tbsp	white wine vinegar	45 mL
2 tbsp	liquid honey	25 mL
1 tbsp	blue poppy seeds (see Tip, left)	15 mL
½ cup	peanut oil	125 mL

1. In a bowl, whisk together vinegar, honey and poppy seeds. While whisking, pour in oil in a thin steady stream until emulsified.

Hot Bacon Vinaigrette

Makes ¾ cup (175 mL)

In the 1970s — when salad bars were all the rage — hot bacon dressing was very popular. This is one of the best dressings to use on spinach.

¼ cup	white wine vinegar	50 mL
2 tbsp	real bacon bits	25 mL
2 tsp	freshly squeezed lemon juice	10 mL
1 tsp	dried onion flakes	5 mL
1 tsp	dried red bell peppers (see Tip, page 24)	5 mL
¼ cup	corn oil	50 mL
¼ cup	soybean oil	50 mL

1. In a bowl, whisk together vinegar, bacon bits, lemon juice, onion flakes and red bell peppers. Whisk in corn and soybean oils.
2. In a small saucepan, heat vinaigrette over low heat for 2 minutes, or microwave for 3 to 4 seconds prior to use.

Italian Herb Vinaigrette

Makes 1 cup (250 mL)

*This vinaigrette is a
full-flavor dressing made with
simple pantry ingredients.*

2 tbsp	white wine vinegar	25 mL
2 tbsp	balsamic vinegar	25 mL
1 tbsp	dried basil	15 mL
1 tbsp	dried rosemary	15 mL
2 tsp	Dijon Mustard (page 120) or store-bought	10 mL
¾ cup	light extra virgin olive oil	175 mL

1. In a bowl, whisk together white wine and balsamic vinegars, basil, rosemary and mustard. While whisking, pour in oil in a thin steady stream until emulsified, about 45 seconds.

Lemon Dijon Vinaigrette

**Makes 1¼ cups
(300 mL)**

*I like to drizzle this
vinaigrette on salads made
with fresh shrimp.*

2 tbsp	white wine vinegar	25 mL
2 tbsp	balsamic vinegar	25 mL
1 tsp	grated lemon zest	5 mL
2 tbsp	freshly squeezed lemon juice	25 mL
2 tbsp	granulated sugar	25 mL
2 tbsp	liquid honey	25 mL
2 tsp	Dijon Mustard (page 120) or store-bought	10 mL
⅔ cup	soybean oil	150 mL

1. In a bowl, whisk together white wine and balsamic vinegars, lemon zest and juice, sugar, honey and mustard. While whisking, pour in oil in a thin steady stream until emulsified.

Lemon Mint Cilantro Chile Vinaigrette

Makes 1 cup (250 mL)

Here's a vinaigrette that adds a little heat and spice.

1 tsp	grated lemon zest	5 mL
3 tbsp	freshly squeezed lemon juice	45 mL
2 tbsp	granulated sugar	25 mL
1 tbsp	finely chopped fresh mint	15 mL
1 tbsp	finely chopped fresh cilantro	15 mL
1	jalapeño pepper, seeded and finely chopped	1
½ cup	soybean oil	125 mL

1. In a bowl, whisk together lemon zest and juice, sugar, mint, cilantro and jalapeño. Whisk in oil.

Lucca Vinaigrette

Makes 1 cup (250 mL)

This vinaigrette reminds me of Lucca, a little village in Tuscany where I ate a fantastic salad.

2 tbsp	white wine vinegar	25 mL
2 tbsp	balsamic vinegar	25 mL
1 tsp	Dijon Mustard (page 120) or store-bought	5 mL
1 tsp	grated lemon zest	5 mL
⅔ cup	soybean oil	150 mL
2 tbsp	pine nuts, toasted and finely chopped	25 mL

1. In a bowl, whisk together white wine and balsamic vinegars, mustard and lemon zest. While whisking, pour in oil in a thin steady stream until emulsified. Toss in pine nuts.

Old Venice Italian Vinaigrette

When you taste this dressing, you might think you're eating in a small trattoria beside a Venetian canal.

2 tbsp	white wine vinegar	25 mL
2 tbsp	balsamic vinegar	25 mL
2 tsp	Dijon Mustard (page 120) or store-bought	10 mL
2 tsp	minced garlic	10 mL
2 tsp	dried onion flakes	10 mL
1 tsp	hot pepper flakes	5 mL
1 tsp	freshly ground black pepper	5 mL
1/4 cup	soybean oil	50 mL
1/4 cup	canola oil	50 mL

1. In a bowl, whisk together white wine and balsamic vinegars, mustard, garlic, onion flakes, hot pepper flakes and black pepper. While whisking, pour soybean and canola oils in a thin steady stream until emulsified.

Orange Blossom Vinaigrette

Makes 1¼ cups (300 mL)

The aroma of this vinaigrette reminds me of orange blossoms that bloom not far from my home in Southern California.

Tip
If you can't find orange vinegar, add 2 tsp (10 mL) each white wine vinegar and orange juice.

2 tbsp	white wine vinegar	25 mL
2 tbsp	orange vinegar (see Tip, left)	25 mL
1/4 cup	freshly squeezed orange juice	50 mL
2 tsp	minced dried shallots	10 mL
1 tsp	dried thyme	5 mL
1/2 tsp	ground white pepper	2 mL
1/2 tsp	sea salt	2 mL
3/4 cup	extra virgin olive oil	175 mL

1. In a bowl, whisk together white wine and orange vinegars, orange juice, shallots, thyme, pepper and salt. Whisk in oil.

Orange Cinnamon Vinaigrette

Makes 1 cup (250 mL)

Add a spiced citrus zing to your greens.

2 tsp	grated orange zest	10 mL
½ cup	freshly squeezed orange juice	125 mL
¼ cup	sunflower oil	50 mL
¼ cup	natural rice vinegar	50 mL
1 tsp	ground cinnamon	5 mL
	Salt and freshly ground black pepper	

1. In a bowl, whisk together orange zest and juice, oil, vinegar and cinnamon. Season with salt and pepper to taste.

Parmesan Vinaigrette

Makes 1 cup (250 mL)

Freshly grate your cheese to create a flavorful dressing.

¼ cup	sherry wine vinegar	50 mL
1 tsp	minced dried garlic	5 mL
1 tsp	dried oregano	5 mL
1 tsp	dried basil	5 mL
¼ cup	freshly grated Parmesan cheese	50 mL
¼ cup	extra virgin olive oil	50 mL
¼ cup	canola oil	50 mL

1. In a bowl, whisk together vinegar, garlic, oregano, basil and cheese. Whisk in olive and canola oils.

Peach Citrus Vinaigrette

The combination of mint and peach makes this a perfect summertime dressing.

Tip
Since the peach is uncooked, it will eventually brown, so this vinaigrette only keeps for up to 2 days in the refrigerator.

½ cup	sherry wine vinegar	125 mL
1	small ripe peach, puréed	1
1 tsp	dried mint	5 mL
1 tsp	dried cilantro	5 mL
½ tsp	grated lemon zest	2 mL
½ cup	canola oil	125 mL
¼ cup	extra virgin olive oil	50 mL

1. In a bowl, whisk together vinegar, peach purée, mint, cilantro and lemon zest. While whisking, pour in canola and olive oils in a thin steady stream until emulsified.

Pomegranate Vinaigrette

This red vinaigrette is perfect for Christmas dinner.

½ cup	sherry wine vinegar	125 mL
½ cup	pomegranate seeds, crushed	125 mL
1 tbsp	liquid honey	15 mL
½ tsp	sea salt	2 mL
½ tsp	ground white pepper	2 mL
¾ cup	soybean oil	175 mL

1. In a bowl, whisk together vinegar, pomegranate seeds, honey, salt and pepper. While whisking, pour in oil in a thin steady stream until emulsified.

Radda Vinaigrette

Makes 1¼ cups (300 mL)

Radda is the beautiful village in Tuscany that is home to the Chianti wineries.

¼ cup	sherry wine vinegar	50 mL
¼ cup	Chianti wine	50 mL
2 tsp	dried Italian seasoning	10 mL
½ cup	canola oil	125 mL
¼ cup	extra virgin olive oil	50 mL

1. In a bowl, whisk together vinegar, wine and Italian seasoning. Whisk in canola and olive oils.

Raspberry Vinaigrette

Makes 1¾ cups (425 mL)

A spring salad will burst with flavor when dressed with this vinaigrette made with fresh berries.

Tip
Vinaigrette keeps for up to 2 days in the refrigerator.

¼ cup	white balsamic vinegar	50 mL
¼ cup	Chablis wine	50 mL
1 tbsp	granulated sugar	15 mL
2 tsp	sea salt	10 mL
1 tsp	ground white pepper	5 mL
½ cup	soybean oil	125 mL
¼ cup	canola oil	50 mL
½ cup	raspberries, crushed	125 mL

1. In a bowl, whisk together vinegar, wine, sugar, salt and pepper. Whisk in soybean and canola oils. Toss in raspberries

Red Balsamic Vinaigrette with Kalamata Olives

Makes 1¼ cups (300 mL)

I enjoyed a similar dressing on the Greek island of Santorini. It's such a perfect dressing for Greek salads, I just had to get the recipe for you.

2 tbsp	red wine vinegar	25 mL
2 tbsp	balsamic vinegar	25 mL
1 tsp	Dijon Mustard (page 120) or store-bought	5 mL
1 tsp	chopped fresh thyme	5 mL
1 tsp	chopped fresh oregano	5 mL
¾ cup	soybean oil	175 mL
¼ cup	kalamata olives, pitted and finely chopped	50 mL

1. In a bowl, whisk together red wine and balsamic vinegars, mustard, thyme and oregano. While whisking, pour in oil in a thin steady stream until emulsified. Toss in chopped olives.

Roasted Garlic Vinaigrette

Makes 1½ cups (375 mL)

This dressing makes roasting the garlic worthwhile.

Tip

To roast garlic: Preheat oven to 400°F (200°C). Cut about ¼ inch (0.5 cm) off the top of the bulb and drizzle with 1 tsp (5 mL) olive oil. Wrap in foil and roast until golden brown and very soft, 30 to 35 minutes. Let cool, turn upside down and press cloves out of bulb.

¼ cup	white wine vinegar	50 mL
¼ cup	freshly grated Parmesan cheese	50 mL
1 tsp	dried oregano	5 mL
½ cup	canola oil	125 mL
¼ cup	extra virgin olive oil	50 mL
1	medium head garlic, roasted and puréed (see Tip, left)	1

1. In a bowl, whisk together vinegar, cheese and oregano. Whisk in canola and olive oils. Whisk in roasted garlic. Refrigerate in a bottle with a tight-fitting lid for at least 2 hours to fully infuse the vinaigrette with garlic flavor.

Roasted Red Pepper Vinaigrette

Makes 1¼ cups (300 mL)

This vinaigrette is sweet with flavor and bold with color.

¼ cup	red wine vinegar	50 mL
¼ cup	minced roasted red bell peppers	50 mL
1 tsp	minced dried garlic	5 mL
1 tsp	dried oregano	5 mL
1 tsp	dried basil	5 mL
½ tsp	dried thyme	2 mL
½ tsp	hot pepper flakes	2 mL
½ cup	canola oil	125 mL
¼ cup	extra virgin olive oil	50 mL

1. In a bowl, whisk together vinegar, red peppers, garlic, oregano, basil, thyme and hot pepper flakes. Whisk in canola and olive oils.

Sandwich Dressing

Makes 1 cup (250 mL)

Here's the perfect juicy dressing to accompany subs, torpedoes and hoagies.

Tip
Refrigerate this dressing in a squirt bottle, so it's easy to squeeze out over sandwich fillings.

¼ cup	red wine vinegar	50 mL
¼ cup	freshly squeezed lemon juice	50 mL
2 tsp	Dijon Mustard (page 120) or store-bought	10 mL
2 tsp	minced dried garlic	10 mL
2 tsp	dried onion flakes	10 mL
¼ cup	soybean oil	50 mL
¼ cup	extra virgin olive oil	50 mL

1. In a bowl, whisk together vinegar, lemon juice, mustard, garlic and onion flakes. While whisking, pour in soybean and olive oils in a thin steady stream until emulsified.

Sherry Vinaigrette

I like to pour this tart vinaigrette onto fresh garden tomatoes.

¼ cup	sherry wine vinegar	50 mL
¼ cup	freshly grated Romano cheese	50 mL
1 tbsp	Dijon Mustard (page 120) or store-bought	15 mL
1 tsp	minced dried shallots	5 mL
½ cup	canola oil	125 mL
¼ cup	extra virgin olive oil	50 mL

1. In a bowl, whisk together vinegar, Romano cheese, mustard and shallots. While whisking, pour in canola and olive oils in a thin steady stream until emulsified.

Smoked Chipotle Vinaigrette

Here's a smoky, spicy dressing that's perfect for a Mexican salad.

¼ cup	red wine vinegar	50 mL
1	chipotle pepper in adobo sauce, drained, seeded and minced	1
2 tsp	Dijon Mustard (page 120) or store-bought	10 mL
2 tsp	minced dried garlic	10 mL
1 tsp	sea salt	5 mL
1 tsp	freshly ground black pepper	5 mL
½ tsp	hot pepper flakes	2 mL
¾ cup	soybean oil	175 mL

1. In a bowl, whisk together vinegar, chipotle, mustard, garlic, salt, pepper and hot pepper flakes. While whisking, pour in oil in a thin steady stream until emulsified.

Stilton Vinaigrette

Makes 1¼ cups (300 mL)

A mild blue cheese from England gives this dressing lots of flavor.

¼ cup	white wine vinegar	50 mL
2 tsp	Dijon Mustard (page 120) or store-bought	10 mL
2 tsp	dried onion flakes	10 mL
1 tsp	freshly ground black pepper	5 mL
¾ cup	soybean oil	175 mL
¼ cup	crumbled Stilton blue cheese	50 mL

1. In a bowl, whisk together vinegar, mustard, onion flakes and pepper. While whisking, pour in oil in a thin steady stream until emulsified. Toss in blue cheese.

White Balsamic Vinaigrette

Makes ¾ cup (175 mL)

Star anise gives this vinaigrette a slight licorice taste, which is partnered with the perfect balance of orange.

Tip

You can grind whole star anise to a powder if you can't find the powdered version.

2 tbsp	white balsamic vinegar	25 mL
2 tbsp	white wine vinegar	25 mL
2 tsp	Dijon Mustard (page 120) or store-bought	10 mL
2 tsp	minced garlic	10 mL
1 tsp	grated orange zest	5 mL
1 tsp	star anise powder (see Tip, left)	5 mL
¼ cup	soybean oil	50 mL
¼ cup	canola oil	50 mL
1 tbsp	extra virgin olive oil	15 mL

1. In a bowl, whisk together balsamic and white wine vinegars, mustard, garlic, orange zest and star anise powder. While whisking, pour in soybean, canola and olive oils in a thin steady stream until emulsified.

International Dressings

Asian All-Purpose Dressing

Makes ³⁄₄ cup (175 mL)

This light summer salad dressing perfectly suits a combination of grated Asian cabbage and carrots.

Tip
Natural rice vinegar, also called unseasoned rice vinegar, has no added sugar or salt and I prefer it over the seasoned variety.

2 tbsp	natural rice vinegar (see Tip, left)	25 mL
1¹⁄₂ tbsp	soy sauce	22 mL
1 tbsp	granulated sugar	15 mL
¹⁄₂ tsp	freshly grated gingerroot	2 mL
1 tbsp	coarsely chopped fresh cilantro	15 mL
¹⁄₂ cup	canola oil	125 mL
1¹⁄₂ tsp	sesame oil	7 mL
3	drops hot chili oil	3

1. In a bowl, whisk together vinegar, soy sauce, sugar, ginger and cilantro. While whisking, pour in canola, sesame oil and hot chili oils in a steady stream until emulsified for 1 minute.

Caesar Dressing

Makes ¹⁄₂ cup (125 mL)

This dressing was made famous by Caesar Cardini at his restaurant in Tijuana, Mexico, in the 1940s. Today his restaurant is gone, but the salad is still served at the same spot by Caesar's Sports Bar and Grill. Romaine lettuce is a good choice for the base.

Tip
This recipe contains raw egg yolks. If you are concerned about the safety of using raw eggs, use pasteurized eggs in the shell or pasteurized liquid whole eggs, instead.

1	egg yolk, at room temperature, or 2 tbsp (25 mL) pasteurized eggs (liquid or in the shell) (see Tip, left)	1
1 tbsp	freshly squeezed lemon juice	15 mL
¹⁄₂ tsp	sea salt	2 mL
6 tbsp	olive oil, divided	90 mL
1	clove garlic, minced	1
¹⁄₂ tsp	Worcestershire Sauce (page 142) or store-bought	2 mL
¹⁄₂ tsp	Dijon Mustard (page 120) or store-bought	2 mL
¹⁄₂ tsp	apple cider vinegar	2 mL
	Freshly ground black pepper	
3 tbsp	freshly grated Parmesan cheese	45 mL

1. In a bowl, whisk together egg yolk, lemon juice, salt and 1 tbsp (15 mL) of the oil. Whisk in garlic, Worcestershire sauce, mustard and vinegar. While vigorously whisking, pour in remaining oil in a thin steady stream until emulsified. Add black pepper and cheese. Because of the egg yolk, this dressing does not store well. Make it fresh and use it right away.

Chasen's French Dressing

This is adapted from a dressing served at Chasen's Restaurant, the famed star-studded Los Angeles establishment that closed its doors in 1995. The restaurant is now a grocery store, which has a few of the original booths preserved, so you can sit where the famous once sat.

¾ cup	red wine vinegar	175 mL
¼ cup	Country Ketchup (page 116) or store-bought	50 mL
1	clove garlic, minced	1
1 tsp	granulated sugar	5 mL
1 tsp	sea salt	5 mL
1 tsp	freshly squeezed lemon juice	5 mL
½ tsp	Worcestershire Sauce (page 142) or store-bought	2 mL
¼ tsp	freshly ground black pepper	1 mL
¼ tsp	dry mustard	1 mL
¼ tsp	hot pepper sauce	1 mL
¼ tsp	ground white pepper	1 mL
½ cup	soybean oil	125 mL
½ cup	extra virgin olive oil	125 mL

1. In a bowl, whisk together vinegar, ketchup, garlic, sugar, salt, lemon juice, Worcestershire sauce, black pepper, mustard, hot pepper sauce and white pepper. While whisking, pour in soybean and olive oils in a thin steady stream until emulsified.

English Stilton Dressing

A rich cream-based dressing laced with blue cheese, this can be used with iceberg or any firm lettuce.

Tip
If you process the blue cheese in the food processor instead of folding it into the dressing, it will become an unattractive gray/blue color.

● **Food processor**

4 oz	cream cheese, softened	125 g
4 oz	small-curd cottage cheese	125 g
1/2 cup	sour cream	125 mL
1/4 cup	Traditional Mayonnaise (page 106) or store-bought	50 mL
1 tbsp	freshly squeezed lemon juice	15 mL
1 1/2 tsp	fresh dill	7 mL
1/2 tsp	dried onion flakes	2 mL
1/2 tsp	whole black peppercorns	2 mL
1/4 tsp	garlic powder	1 mL
2 oz	Stilton blue cheese, crumbled	60 g

1. In a food processor fitted with a metal blade, process cream cheese, cottage cheese, sour cream, mayonnaise, lemon juice, dill, onion flakes, peppercorns and garlic powder until smooth, for 45 seconds. Place in a bowl. Fold in crumbled blue cheese.

Fresh Spicy Ginger Dressing

A kick of a dressing, this pairs well with grated Asian cabbage and carrots.

3 tbsp	white wine vinegar	45 mL
2 tbsp	reduced-sodium soy sauce	25 mL
1 tbsp	granulated sugar	15 mL
1 tbsp	freshly grated gingerroot	15 mL
1/2	jalapeño pepper, seeded and finely minced	1/2
1/4 tsp	cayenne pepper	1 mL
2/3 cup	canola oil	150 mL
2 tsp	sesame oil	10 mL

1. In a bowl, whisk together vinegar, soy sauce, sugar, ginger, jalapeño and cayenne for 1 minute. While vigorously whisking, pour in canola and sesame oils in a thin steady stream until emulsified.

German Dressing

Light and full of flavor, this dressing is delicious with cooked small red potatoes, so it's perfect for German potato salad. Use about 3 pounds (1.5 kg) of potatoes with this amount of dressing.

1/4 cup	tarragon vinegar	50 mL
1 tsp	granulated sugar	5 mL
1 tsp	paprika	5 mL
1/2 tsp	sea salt	2 mL
1/2 tsp	dry mustard	2 mL
1/2 tsp	celery seeds	2 mL
1/4 tsp	freshly ground black pepper	1 mL
3/4 cup	olive oil	175 mL

1. In a bowl, whisk together vinegar, sugar, paprika, salt, mustard, celery seeds and pepper. While vigorously whisking, pour in oil in a thin steady stream until emulsified.

Island Salad Dressing

Makes 1/2 cup (125 mL)

When you're visiting any tropical island, you'll find the hotel buffets feature a dressing used as "sauce" on pineapples or lettuce. Try this dressing on fresh tropical fruits such as pineapple, papaya, mangos and kiwis and sprinkle with toasted shredded coconut.

2 tbsp	freshly squeezed lemon juice	25 mL
2 tbsp	freshly squeezed lime juice	25 mL
2 tbsp	granulated sugar	25 mL
1 tbsp	dark rum	15 mL
1/4 cup	coarsely chopped fresh mint	50 mL

1. In a bowl, whisk together lemon juice, lime juice, sugar, rum and mint.

Japanese Dressing

**Makes ¼ cup
(50 mL)**

I like to marinate Japanese cucumbers in this dressing, but other vegetables — such as carrots, snow peas and radishes or any combination of these all work, as well.

2 tbsp	canola oil	25 mL
1 tbsp	natural rice vinegar (see Tip, page 37)	15 mL
1 tsp	reduced-sodium soy sauce	5 mL
1 tsp	sesame oil	5 mL
Pinch	ground white pepper	Pinch
Pinch	sea salt	Pinch

1. In a bowl, whisk together canola oil, vinegar, soy sauce, sesame oil, salt and white pepper.

Malaysian Dressing

**Makes ¾ cup
(175 mL)**

Toss this dressing with bell peppers, pineapple, golden raisins, bean sprouts and bamboo shoots.

¼ cup	natural rice vinegar (see Tip, page 37)	50 mL
¼ cup	unsweetened pineapple juice	50 mL
3 tbsp	reduced-sodium soy sauce	45 mL
1 tbsp	freshly grated gingerroot	15 mL
	Zest and juice from 1 orange	
1	clove garlic, minced	1
1 tsp	toasted sesame seeds	5 mL

1. In a bowl, whisk together vinegar, pineapple juice, soy sauce, ginger, orange zest and juice, garlic and sesame seeds.

Russian Dressing

**Makes 1¾ cups
(425 mL)**

This dressing enhances an array of firm lettuce leaves, such as romaine, or any type of cabbage.

1 cup	Traditional Mayonnaise (page 106) or store-bought	250 mL
½ cup	Country Ketchup (page 116) or store-bought	125 mL
1 tbsp	finely chopped Italian flat-leaf parsley	15 mL
1½ tsp	dried onion flakes	7 mL
¼ tsp	dry mustard	1 mL
¼ tsp	Worcestershire Sauce (page 142) or store-bought	1 mL
4	drops hot pepper sauce	4

1. In a bowl, blend together mayonnaise, ketchup, parsley, onion flakes, mustard, Worcestershire sauce and hot pepper sauce.

South-of-the-Border Dressing

Makes 1½ cups (375 mL)

This hot spicy dressing is a good match for a Mexican dinner, and is perfect on a taco salad.

Tip
Make sure your avocado is ripe for the best flavor and texture.

- **Food processor**

4 oz	cream cheese, softened	125 g
½ cup	buttermilk	125 mL
½ cup	Traditional Mayonnaise (page 106) or store-bought	125 mL
1	avocado (see Tip, left)	1
2 tsp	fresh dill	10 mL
1 tsp	freshly squeezed lemon juice	5 mL
2	chipotle peppers in adobo sauce, drained	2

1. In a food processor fitted with a metal blade, process cream cheese, buttermilk, mayonnaise, avocado, dill, lemon juice and chipotle peppers until smooth, about 45 seconds.

Sweet-and-Sour Dressing

Makes about ¼ cup (50 mL)

This simple warm dressing is designed for spinach leaves.

5	thick slices bacon	5
⅓ cup	water	75 mL
3 tbsp	cider vinegar	45 mL
1 tsp	granulated sugar	5 mL
½ tsp	paprika	2 mL
¼ tsp	freshly ground black pepper	1 mL
¼ tsp	dry mustard	1 mL

1. In a skillet over medium heat, add bacon and fry until crisp, about 7 minutes. Transfer bacon to a paper towel to drain. Add water, vinegar, sugar, paprika, pepper and mustard to pan. Simmer, stirring, until sugar is dissolved, about 5 minutes. Chop bacon and return to pan, and combine with other ingredients. Serve hot.

Thai Peanut Dressing

Makes 2 cups (500 mL)

I like to use this dressing as a marinade for Thai chicken or with napa cabbage.

½ cup	Smooth Peanut Butter (page 298) or store-bought	125 mL
½ cup	peanut oil	125 mL
¼ cup	white wine vinegar	50 mL
¼ cup	reduced-sodium soy sauce	50 mL
¼ cup	freshly squeezed lemon juice	50 mL
4	cloves garlic, minced	4
2 tsp	cayenne pepper	10 mL
1 tsp	freshly grated gingerroot	5 mL

1. In a bowl, whisk together peanut butter, peanut oil, vinegar, soy sauce, lemon juice, garlic, cayenne and ginger.

Wafu Dressing

Makes 1 cup (250 mL)

A popular vinaigrette in Japan, this dressing tastes great with napa cabbage.

½ cup	Traditional Mayonnaise (page 106) or store-bought	125 mL
2 tbsp	reduced-sodium soy sauce	25 mL
1	clove garlic, minced	1
Pinch	ground ginger	Pinch
2 tbsp	natural rice vinegar (see Tip, page 37)	25 mL
2 tbsp	sesame oil	25 mL
2 tbsp	whole milk	25 mL

1. In a bowl, combine mayonnaise, soy sauce, garlic and ginger. Whisk in vinegar, sesame oil and milk.

Avocado Dressing

**Makes about 2 cups
(500 mL)**

*Here's a dressing with a light
green color that's perfect for
St. Patrick's Day.*

- **Food processor**

4 oz	cream cheese, softened	125 g
½ cup	buttermilk	125 mL
½ cup	Traditional Mayonnaise (page 106) or store-bought	125 mL
1	ripe avocado	1
2 tsp	chopped fresh dill	10 mL
1 tsp	freshly squeezed lemon juice	5 mL

1. In a food processor fitted with a metal blade, process cream cheese, buttermilk, mayonnaise, avocado, dill and lemon juice until smooth, about 2 minutes.

Baja Dressing

**Makes 1½ cups
(375 mL)**

*Use this spicy, zippy dressing
on salad or as a dip for celery
and carrot sticks.*

- **Food processor**

4 oz	cream cheese, softened	125 g
½ cup	buttermilk	125 mL
½ cup	Traditional Mayonnaise (page 106) or store-bought	125 mL
1 tsp	freshly ground black pepper	5 mL
1 tsp	taco seasoning	5 mL
1	chipotle pepper in adobo sauce, drained	1
1 tsp	freshly squeezed lemon juice	5 mL

1. In a food processor fitted with a metal blade, process cream cheese, buttermilk, mayonnaise, black pepper, taco seasoning, chipotle pepper and lemon juice until smooth, about 2 minutes.

Blue Cheese Dressing

**Makes 1½ cups
(375 mL)**

*Here's a rich and fresh
creamy dressing with chunks
of blue cheese.*

● **Food processor**

4 oz	plain yogurt	125 g
½ cup	buttermilk	125 mL
¼ cup	Traditional Mayonnaise (page 106) or store-bought	50 mL
¼ cup	sour cream	50 mL
1 tsp	dried onion flakes	5 mL
½ tsp	garlic salt	2 mL
2 oz	blue cheese, crumbled	60 g

1. In a food processor fitted with a metal blade, process yogurt, buttermilk, mayonnaise, sour cream, onion flakes and garlic salt until smooth, about 2 minutes. Transfer to a small bowl and fold in blue cheese.

Buffalo Blue Cheese Dressing

**Makes 1½ cups
(375 mL)**

*As well as a classic salad
dressing, it's a dandy dipping
sauce for Buffalo wings.*

● **Food processor**

4 oz	cream cheese, softened	125 g
½ cup	buttermilk	125 mL
¼ cup	Traditional Mayonnaise (page 106) or store-bought	50 mL
1 tsp	dried onion flakes	5 mL
½ tsp	garlic salt	2 mL
½ tsp	hot pepper sauce	2 mL
¼ tsp	hot pepper flakes	1 mL
2 oz	blue cheese, crumbled	60 g

1. In a food processor fitted with a metal blade, process cream cheese, buttermilk, mayonnaise, onion flakes, garlic salt, hot pepper sauce and hot pepper flakes until smooth, about 2 minutes. Transfer to a small bowl and fold in blue cheese.

Cajun Spice Dressing

Makes 1 cup (250 mL)

I had a similar dressing in New Orleans one spring day.

- Food processor

4 oz	cream cheese	125 g
½ cup	Traditional Mayonnaise (page 106) or store-bought	125 mL
¼ cup	buttermilk	50 mL
½ tsp	hot pepper flakes	2 mL
½ tsp	dried onion flakes	2 mL
½ tsp	paprika	2 mL
½ tsp	garlic salt	2 mL
¼ tsp	caraway seeds	1 mL
3	drops hot pepper sauce	3

1. In a food processor fitted with a metal blade, process cream cheese, mayonnaise, buttermilk, hot pepper flakes, onion flakes, paprika, garlic salt, caraway seeds and hot pepper sauce until smooth, about 2 minutes.

Catalina Dressing

Makes 1½ cups (375 mL)

There are many Catalina dressings on the market, but this homemade version has much more fresh flavor.

½ cup	canola oil	125 mL
⅓ cup	Country Ketchup (page 116) or store-bought	75 mL
¼ cup	granulated sugar	50 mL
¼ cup	diced onion	50 mL
¼ cup	cider vinegar	50 mL
1½ tsp	sea salt	7 mL
½ tsp	chili powder	2 mL
½ tsp	celery seeds	2 mL
¼ tsp	dry mustard	1 mL
⅛ tsp	paprika	0.5 mL

1. In a bowl, whisk together oil, ketchup, sugar, onion, vinegar, salt, chili powder, celery seeds, mustard and paprika.

Celery Seed Dressing

**Makes 2 cups
(500 mL)**

*Try this dressing as a sauce
for crab cakes.*

● **Food processor**

4 oz	cream cheese, softened	125 g
1/2 cup	canola oil	125 mL
1/3 cup	County Ketchup (page 116) or store-bought	75 mL
1/4 cup	white wine vinegar	50 mL
1/4 cup	granulated sugar	50 mL
1 tsp	sea salt	5 mL
1/2 tsp	dried onion flakes	2 mL
1/4 tsp	celery seeds	1 mL
1/8 tsp	paprika	0.5 mL

1. In a food processor fitted with a metal blade, process cream cheese, oil, ketchup, vinegar, sugar, salt, onion flakes, celery seeds and paprika until smooth, about 2 minutes.

Cracked Black Peppercorn Dressing

**Makes 1¹/₂ cups
(375 mL)**

*This peppery dressing livens
up salad served with a steak
dinner.*

● **Food processor**

4 oz	cream cheese, softened	125 g
1/2 cup	buttermilk	125 mL
1/2 cup	Traditional Mayonnaise (page 106) or store-bought	125 mL
1 tsp	whole black peppercorns	5 mL
1 tsp	sea salt	5 mL
1 tsp	freshly squeezed lemon juice	5 mL
1/2 tsp	Hungarian paprika	2 mL

1. In a food processor fitted with a metal blade, process cream cheese, buttermilk, mayonnaise, black peppercorns, salt, lemon juice and paprika until smooth, about 2 minutes.

Cracked Peppercorn and Parmesan Dressing

Makes 1½ cups (375 mL)

Szechwan peppercorns add a punch to this dressing.

Tip
You can replace the Szechwan peppercorns with whole black peppercorns.

• **Food processor**

4 oz	cream cheese, softened	125 g
¼ cup	buttermilk	50 mL
¼ cup	Bold Chili Sauce (page 125) or store-bought	50 mL
¼ cup	Traditional Mayonnaise (page 106) or store-bought	50 mL
1 tsp	Szechwan peppercorns	5 mL
½ tsp	dried onion flakes	2 mL
¼ cup	freshly grated Parmesan cheese	50 mL

1. In a food processor fitted with a metal blade, process cream cheese, buttermilk, chili sauce, mayonnaise, peppercorns and onion flakes until smooth, about 2 minutes. Transfer to a bowl and fold in Parmesan cheese.

Creamy Asiago Dressing

Makes 1 cup (250 mL)

Asiago cheese is an Italian cheese with a flavor that's similar to Cheddar and Romano combined.

• **Food processor**

3 oz	cream cheese, softened	90 g
½ cup	Traditional Mayonnaise (page 106) or store-bought	125 mL
¼ cup	half-and-half (10%) cream	50 mL
1 tbsp	Country Ketchup (page 116) or store-bought	15 mL
½ tsp	dried dill	2 mL
½ tsp	garlic powder	2 mL
½ cup	shredded Asiago cheese	125 mL

1. In a food processor fitted with a metal blade, process cream cheese, mayonnaise, cream, ketchup, dill and garlic powder until smooth, about 2 minutes. Transfer to a bowl and fold in Asiago cheese.

Creamy California Dressing

Makes 1 cup (250 mL)

I developed this dressing using the Hass variety of avocado that was first cultivated in Southern California.

• **Food processor**

3 oz	cream cheese, softened	90 g
1/2 cup	Traditional Mayonnaise (page 106) or store-bought	125 mL
1/2	ripe avocado	1/2
2 tsp	olive oil	10 mL
1 tsp	sea salt	5 mL
1/2 tsp	hot pepper flakes	2 mL

1. In a food processor fitted with a metal blade, process cream cheese, mayonnaise, avocado, oil, salt and hot pepper flakes until smooth, about 2 minutes.

Creamy Curried Dressing

Makes 1 1/4 cups (300 mL)

When serving an Asian dinner, try this dressing on cabbage.

1 cup	Traditional Mayonnaise (page 106) or store-bought	250 mL
1/4 cup	buttermilk	50 mL
1 tbsp	freshly squeezed lemon juice	15 mL
1 tsp	mild curry powder	5 mL
1/2 tsp	dried onion flakes	2 mL
1/4 tsp	freshly ground black pepper	1 mL
1/4 tsp	sea salt	1 mL

1. In a bowl, whisk together mayonnaise, buttermilk, lemon juice, curry powder, onion flakes, black pepper and salt.

Creamy Dill Dressing

Makes 1 cup (250 mL)

Try this dressing on fried fish pieces.

● **Food processor**

4 oz	cream cheese, softened	125 g
¼ cup	small-curd cottage cheese	50 mL
¼ cup	buttermilk	50 mL
1 tsp	fresh dill	5 mL
½ tsp	dried onion flakes	2 mL
¼ tsp	freshly ground black pepper	1 mL
¼ tsp	sea salt	1 mL

1. In a food processor fitted with a metal blade, process cream cheese, cottage cheese, buttermilk, dill, onion flakes, pepper and salt until smooth, about 2 minutes.

Creamy French Honey Dressing

Makes 1 cup (250 mL)

I devoured a dressing similar to this in Cannes, France, one spring.

½ cup	Traditional Mayonnaise (page 106) or store-bought	125 mL
¼ cup	olive oil	50 mL
1 tbsp	liquid honey	15 mL
1 tbsp	freshly squeezed lemon juice	15 mL
2 tsp	prepared horseradish	10 mL
2 tsp	Bold Chili Sauce (page 125) or store-bought	10 mL
2	cloves garlic, minced	2
1 tsp	sea salt	5 mL
½ tsp	dry mustard	2 mL
½ tsp	paprika	2 mL
¼ tsp	freshly ground black pepper	1 mL
⅛ tsp	cayenne pepper	0.5 mL

1. In a bowl, whisk together mayonnaise, oil, honey, lemon juice, horseradish, chile sauce, garlic, salt, mustard, paprika, pepper and cayenne.

Creamy Ginger Spice Dressing

Makes 1½ cups (375 mL)

Fresh ginger heightens the flavor of this dressing.

• **Food processor**

8 oz	cream cheese, softened	250 g
¼ cup	buttermilk	50 mL
¼ cup	small-curd cottage cheese	50 mL
1 tbsp	freshly grated gingerroot	15 mL
½ tsp	tandoori seasoning	2 mL
¼ tsp	sea salt	1 mL

1. In a food processor fitted with a metal blade, process cream cheese, buttermilk, cottage cheese, ginger, tandoori seasoning and salt until smooth, about 2 minutes.

Creamy Italian Dressing

Makes 1 cup (250 mL)

Here's a dressing that can be made quickly with pantry items you most likely have on hand.

½ cup	Traditional Mayonnaise (page 106) or store-bought	125 mL
¼ cup	balsamic vinegar	50 mL
¼ cup	light olive oil	50 mL
1 tbsp	dried basil	15 mL
2 tsp	Dijon Mustard (page 120) or store-bought	10 mL
1 tsp	dried rosemary	5 mL

1. In a bowl, whisk together mayonnaise, vinegar, oil, basil, mustard and rosemary.

Creamy Poppy Seed Dressing

Makes 1 cup (250 mL)

This is a hearty dressing to keep on hand.

Tip

Valued for their color and sweetness, blue poppy seeds aren't always available in stores. If you can't find them, check out online retailers (see Sources, page 343) or use regular poppy seeds.

- **Food processor**

4 oz	cream cheese, softened	125 g
1/4 cup	Traditional Mayonnaise (page 106) or store-bought	50 mL
3 tbsp	white wine vinegar	45 mL
2 tbsp	peanut oil	25 mL
2 tbsp	liquid honey	25 mL
1 tbsp	blue poppy seeds (see Tip, left)	15 mL

1. In a food processor fitted with a metal blade, process cream cheese, mayonnaise, vinegar, peanut oil, honey and poppy seeds until smooth, about 2 minutes.

Creamy Roma Dressing

Makes 1 1/2 cups (375 mL)

Here's a dressing that's light red with a burst of flavor.

- **Food processor**

4 oz	cream cheese, softened	125 g
1/2 cup	Traditional Mayonnaise (page 106) or store-bought	125 mL
1/4 cup	buttermilk	50 mL
1 tbsp	freshly squeezed lemon juice	15 mL
1/2 tsp	hot pepper flakes	2 mL
1/2 tsp	dried onion flakes	2 mL
1/4 cup	diced, seeded Roma (plum) tomatoes	50 mL

1. In a food processor fitted with a metal blade, process cream cheese, mayonnaise, buttermilk, lemon juice, hot pepper flakes and onion flakes until smooth, about 2 minutes. Transfer to a bowl and fold in tomatoes.

Creamy Two-Cheese Italian Dressing

Makes 1¼ cups (300 mL)

This dressing blends two of my favorite Italian cheeses — Parmesan and Romano.

• **Food processor**

4 oz	cream cheese, softened	125 g
¼ cup	Traditional Mayonnaise (page 106) or store-bought	50 mL
1 tbsp	balsamic vinegar	15 mL
1 tbsp	light olive oil	15 mL
1 tbsp	dried basil	15 mL
2 tsp	Dijon Mustard (page 120) or store-bought	10 mL
1 tsp	dried rosemary	5 mL
¼ cup	freshly grated Parmesan cheese	50 mL
¼ cup	freshly grated Romano cheese	50 mL

1. In a food processor fitted with a metal blade, process cream cheese, mayonnaise, vinegar, oil, basil, mustard and rosemary until smooth, about 2 minutes. Transfer to a bowl and fold in Parmesan and Romano cheeses.

Creamy Zesty Chipotle Dressing

Makes 1 cup (250 mL)

Be forewarned — this is a red-hot dressing. I like to use it for a bold flavor.

• **Food processor**

4 oz	cream cheese, softened	125 g
½ cup	Traditional Mayonnaise (page 106) or store-bought	125 mL
¼ cup	plain yogurt	50 mL
½ tsp	hot pepper flakes	2 mL
½ tsp	dried onion flakes	2 mL
2	chipotle peppers in adobo sauce, drained	2
⅛ tsp	sea salt	0.5 mL
⅛ tsp	freshly ground black pepper	0.5 mL

1. In a food processor fitted with a metal blade, process cream cheese, mayonnaise, yogurt, hot pepper flakes, onion flakes, chipotle peppers, salt and black pepper until smooth, about 2 minutes.

Crushed Pecan Blue Cheese Dressing

**Makes about
2 cups (500 mL)**

*Pecans are the perfect nuts
to go with the blue cheese in
this dressing.*

• **Food processor**

4 oz	cream cheese, softened	125 g
½ cup	buttermilk	125 mL
¼ cup	Traditional Mayonnaise (page 106) or store-bought	50 mL
¼ cup	small-curd cottage cheese	50 mL
1 tsp	dried onion flakes	5 mL
½ tsp	garlic salt	2 mL
½ tsp	hot pepper sauce	2 mL
2 oz	blue cheese, crumbled	60 g
¼ cup	pecans, toasted and crushed	50 mL

1. In a food processor fitted with a metal blade, process cream cheese, buttermilk, mayonnaise, cottage cheese, onion flakes, garlic salt and hot pepper sauce until smooth, about 2 minutes. Transfer to a bowl and fold in blue cheese and pecans.

Cucumber Garlic Creamy Dressing

**Makes 2 cups
(500 mL)**

*Use this creamy dressing as a
dip for radishes or any other
root vegetables.*

• **Food processor**

1	cucumber, peeled, seeded and cut into 4 pieces	1
4 oz	cream cheese, softened	125 g
½ cup	canola oil	125 mL
½ cup	red wine vinegar	125 mL
⅓ cup	Country Ketchup (page 116) or store-bought	75 mL
⅓ cup	granulated sugar	75 mL
2	cloves garlic, minced	2
1 tsp	sea salt	5 mL
½ tsp	dried onion flakes	2 mL
¼ tsp	celery seeds	1 mL
⅛ tsp	Hungarian paprika	0.5 mL

1. In a food processor fitted with a metal blade, process cucumber and cream cheese until smooth, about 2 minutes.
2. Add oil, vinegar, ketchup, sugar, garlic, salt, onion flakes, celery seeds and paprika and process until smooth, about 45 seconds.

Feta Cheese Dressing

**Makes 1½ cups
(375 mL)**

*This fast and easy dressing
has a zip of feta.*

● **Food processor**

4 oz	cream cheese, softened	125 g
¼ cup	balsamic vinegar	50 mL
¼ cup	light olive oil	50 mL
2 tsp	Dijon Mustard (page 120) or store-bought	10 mL
1 tsp	dried rosemary	5 mL
4 oz	feta cheese, crumbled	125 g

1. In a food processor fitted with a metal blade, process cream cheese, vinegar, oil, mustard and rosemary until smooth, about 2 minutes. Transfer to a bowl and fold in feta cheese.

French Honey Dressing

**Makes about
1¾ cups (425 mL)**

*Lavender makes this dressing
très French.*

● **Food processor**

¾ cup	extra virgin olive oil	175 mL
4 oz	cream cheese, softened	125 g
¼ cup	freshly squeezed lemon juice	50 mL
2 tbsp	Traditional Mayonnaise (page 106) or store-bought	25 mL
2 tbsp	liquid honey	25 mL
2	cloves garlic, minced	2
2 tsp	Bold Chili Sauce (page 125) or store-bought	10 mL
1 tsp	sea salt	5 mL
½ tsp	dry mustard	2 mL
½ tsp	Hungarian paprika	2 mL
¼ tsp	freshly ground black pepper	1 mL
¼ tsp	dried lavender	1 mL
⅛ tsp	cayenne pepper	0.5 mL

1. In a food processor fitted with a metal blade, process oil, cream cheese, lemon juice, mayonnaise, honey, garlic, chili sauce, salt, mustard, paprika, black pepper, lavender and cayenne until smooth, about 2 minutes.

Fresh Orange French Dressing

This dressing will make your taste buds pop!

¾ cup	olive oil	175 mL
½ cup	Traditional Mayonnaise (page 106) or store-bought	125 mL
¼ cup	freshly squeezed orange juice	50 mL
¼ cup	liquid honey	50 mL
3	cloves garlic minced	3
1 tsp	sea salt	5 mL
1 tsp	Hungarian paprika	5 mL
1 tsp	Spicy or Bold Chili Sauce (pages 124 and 125) or store-bought	5 mL
½ tsp	dry mustard	2 mL
¼ tsp	ground white pepper	1 mL

1. In a bowl, whisk together oil, mayonnaise, orange juice, honey, garlic, salt, paprika, chili sauce, mustard and pepper.

Golden Honey Mustard Dressing

So rich, this dressing is surprisingly quick and easy to make.

1 cup	Traditional Mayonnaise (page 106) or store-bought	250 mL
¼ cup	buttermilk	50 mL
2 tbsp	liquid honey	25 mL
1 tbsp	Honey Stone-Ground Mustard (page 122) or store-bought	15 mL
1 tsp	sea salt	5 mL

1. In a bowl, whisk together mayonnaise, buttermilk, honey, mustard and salt.

Green Goddess Dressing

Makes 2¼ cups (550 mL)

I've updated this dressing that was all the rage in the 1960s.

2 cups	Traditional Mayonnaise (page 106) or store-bought	500 mL
4	anchovy fillets, minced	4
1	green onion, chopped	1
1 tbsp	chopped Italian flat-leaf parsley	15 mL
1 tbsp	tarragon vinegar	15 mL
2 tsp	chopped fresh chives	10 mL
1 tsp	chopped fresh tarragon	5 mL

1. In a bowl, stir together mayonnaise, anchovies, green onion, parsley, vinegar, chives and tarragon until blended.

Lime Cilantro Cream Dressing

Makes 1¼ cups (300 mL)

This zippy lime dressing has a touch of cilantro.

- **Food processor**

4 oz	cream cheese, softened	125 g
¼ cup	buttermilk	50 mL
¼ cup	Traditional Mayonnaise (page 106) or store-bought	50 mL
¼ cup	plain yogurt	50 mL
½ tsp	grated lime zest	2 mL
¼ cup	freshly squeezed lime juice	50 mL
1 tsp	dried cilantro	5 mL
½ tsp	dried onion flakes	2 mL

1. In a food processor fitted with a metal blade, process cream cheese, buttermilk, mayonnaise, yogurt, lime zest and juice, cilantro and onion flakes until smooth, about 2 minutes.

Louis Dressing

Makes ¾ cup (175 mL)

Since this dressing is so good as a dipping sauce for cooked shrimp, I've named it after Louis sauce, a traditional seafood sauce.

½ cup	Traditional Mayonnaise (page 106) or store-bought	125 mL
¼ cup	Bold Chili Sauce (page 125) or store-bought	50 mL
2	green onions, chopped	2
1	green chile pepper, minced	1

1. In a bowl, combine mayonnaise, chili sauce, green onions and chile pepper.

Louisiana French Dressing

Makes 2 cups (500 mL)

Louisiana has strong French roots as you can taste in the flavors of many of its recipes, including this one.

- **Food processor**

1 cup	Traditional Mayonnaise (page 106) or store-bought	250 mL
¾ cup	extra virgin olive oil	175 mL
¼ cup	freshly squeezed lemon juice	50 mL
2	cloves garlic, minced	2
2 tsp	Bold Chili Sauce (page 125) or store-bought	10 mL
1 tsp	sea salt	5 mL
1 tsp	Hungarian paprika	5 mL
½ tsp	dry mustard	2 mL
½ tsp	cayenne pepper	2 mL
¼ tsp	freshly ground black pepper	1 mL

1. In a food processor fitted with a metal blade, process mayonnaise, oil, lemon juice, garlic, chile sauce, salt, paprika, mustard, cayenne and black pepper until smooth, about 2 minutes.

Maple Balsamic Dressing

Makes 1 cup (250 mL)

Maple syrup makes a wonderful natural sweetener for salad dressings.

● **Food processor**

4 oz	cream cheese, softened	125 mL
¼ cup	balsamic vinegar	50 mL
¼ cup	light olive oil	50 mL
2 tbsp	pure maple syrup	25 mL
1 tbsp	dried basil	15 mL
1 tsp	dried rosemary	5 mL

1. In a food processor fitted with a metal blade, process cream cheese, vinegar, oil, maple syrup, basil and rosemary until smooth, about 2 minutes.

Marriott's Creamy Peppercorn Dressing

Makes 4 cups (1 L)

One of my first jobs was in the banquet kitchen of the Anaheim Marriott Hotel in California, where I learned so much about quality and production. This was my favorite dressing, which I enjoyed every day on my lunch salad. When I asked, the company was happy to share the recipe with you.

Tip

To make onion juice: In a food processor fitted with metal blade, process 1 sweet onion until puréed, about 2 minutes. Press the juice through a fine-mesh strainer, discarding solids.

Variation

Add 4 oz (125 g) blue cheese when you add the Parmesan.

● **Food processor**

4 cups	Traditional Mayonnaise (page 106) or store-bought	1 L
¼ cup	onion juice (see Tip, left)	50 mL
1½ tbsp	apple cider vinegar	22 mL
1½ tbsp	whole black peppercorns	22 mL
1½ tsp	Worcestershire Sauce (page 142) or store-bought	7 mL
1½ tsp	freshly squeezed lemon juice	7 mL
1 tsp	hot pepper sauce	5 mL
1	clove garlic, minced	1
⅓ cup	freshly grated Parmesan cheese	75 mL

1. In a food processor fitted with a metal blade, process mayonnaise, onion juice, vinegar, peppercorns, Worcestershire sauce, lemon juice, hot pepper sauce and garlic until peppercorns are ground, for 45 seconds. Transfer to a bowl and fold in Parmesan. Dressing keeps well, covered and refrigerated, for up to 3 weeks.

Oahu Dressing

Makes about 1½ cups (375 mL)

I first had this dressing in Oahu, Hawaii on my first visit to the islands. Here it is for you.

● **Food processor**

4 oz	cream cheese, softened	125 g
½ cup	plain yogurt	125 mL
2 tbsp	unsweetened pineapple juice	25 mL
2 tbsp	liquid honey	25 mL
½ cup	macadamia nuts, toasted and chopped	125 mL
¼ cup	flaked sweetened coconut	50 mL

1. In a food processor fitted with a metal blade, process cream cheese, yogurt, pineapple juice and honey until smooth, about 2 minutes. Transfer to a bowl and fold in macadamia nuts and coconut.

Pecan Pesto Dressing

Makes 1¾ cups (425 mL)

Basil and pecans come together to make a very flavorful dressing.

● **Food processor**

½ cup	packed fresh basil	125 mL
2 tbsp	extra virgin olive oil	25 mL
4 oz	cream cheese, softened	125 g
½ cup	buttermilk	125 mL
¼ cup	Traditional Mayonnaise (page 106) or store-bought	50 mL
1 tsp	dried onion flakes	5 mL
½ tsp	garlic salt	2 mL
¼ cup	pecans, toasted and finely chopped	50 mL

1. In a food processor fitted with a metal blade, pulse basil and oil about 10 times. Add cream cheese, buttermilk, mayonnaise, onion flakes and garlic salt and process until smooth, about 2 minutes. Transfer to a bowl and fold in pecans.

Ranch Dressing

Makes 1 cup (250 mL)

This is the best all-purpose creamy herb dressing to use with vegetables, chicken and salads.

½ cup	buttermilk	125 mL
½ cup	sour cream	125 mL
1 tbsp	granulated sugar	15 mL
1½ tsp	dried bell peppers (see Tip, page 24)	7 mL
1 tsp	sea salt	5 mL
1 tsp	garlic salt	5 mL
1 tsp	dried onion flakes	5 mL
½ tsp	dried basil	2 mL
½ tsp	dried thyme	2 mL
½ tsp	dried parsley	2 mL
½ tsp	freshly ground black pepper	2 mL

1. In a bowl, whisk together buttermilk, sour cream, sugar, bell peppers, salt, garlic salt, onion flakes, basil, thyme, parsley and black pepper, about 45 seconds.

Red French Tomato Dressing

Makes 1 cup (250 mL)

Paris has so many bistros. I had lunch one summer that served a zesty dressing like this one.

Tip
Dried tomato powder is made of the sweetest red tomatoes, dried and ground into a fine powder. It adds a nice fresh tomato flavor without adding moisture to the dressing (see Sources, page 343).

½ cup	Traditional Mayonnaise (page 106) or store-bought	125 mL
¼ cup	freshly squeezed lemon juice	50 mL
¼ cup	extra virgin olive oil	50 mL
2	cloves garlic, minced	2
2 tsp	Bold Chili Sauce (page 125) or store-bought	10 mL
1 tsp	sea salt	5 mL
1 tsp	dried tomato powder (see Tip, left)	5 mL
½ tsp	dry mustard	2 mL
½ tsp	Hungarian paprika	2 mL
¼ tsp	freshly ground black pepper	1 mL

1. In a bowl, whisk together mayonnaise, lemon juice, oil, garlic, chili sauce, salt, tomato powder, mustard, paprika and pepper.

Roasted Garlic Dressing

Makes ¾ cup (175 mL)

This dressing is perfect for garlic lovers.

● **Food processor**

4 oz	cream cheese, softened	125 g
¼ cup	Traditional Mayonnaise (page 106) or store-bought	50 mL
8	cloves garlic, roasted (see Tip, page 33)	8
½ tsp	Hungarian paprika	2 mL
½ tsp	sea salt	2 mL
¼ tsp	hot pepper flakes	1 mL

1. In a food processor fitted with a metal blade, process cream cheese, mayonnaise, garlic, paprika, salt and hot pepper flakes until smooth, about 2 minutes.

Roasted Honey Garlic Dressing

Makes 1 cup (250 mL)

This dressing is one of my sister's favorites.

● **Food processor**

4 oz	cream cheese, softened	125 g
¼ cup	sour cream	50 mL
¼ cup	buttermilk	50 mL
8	cloves garlic, roasted (see Tip, page 33)	8
2 tsp	liquid honey	10 mL
1 tsp	dried onion flakes	5 mL
½ tsp	sea salt	2 mL
¼ tsp	hot pepper flakes	1 mL

1. In a food processor fitted with a metal blade, process cream cheese, sour cream, buttermilk, garlic, honey, onion flakes, salt and hot pepper flakes until smooth, about 2 minutes.

Roquefort Dressing

Makes 1 cup (250 mL)

The blue cheese for this dressing is cured in the caves of Roquefort, France.

½ cup	Traditional Mayonnaise (page 106) or store-bought	125 mL
¼ cup	buttermilk	50 mL
1½ tsp	Worcestershire Sauce (page 142) or store-bought	7 mL
¼ tsp	garlic powder	1 mL
2 oz	Roquefort cheese, crumbled	60 g

1. In a bowl, whisk together mayonnaise, buttermilk, Worcestershire sauce and garlic powder until smooth. Fold in Roquefort cheese.

Sesame Ginger Dressing

Makes ¾ cup (175 mL)

If you're having Chinese food, serve a salad with this dressing.

½ cup	Traditional Mayonnaise (page 106) or store-bought	125 mL
¼ cup	buttermilk	50 mL
1½ tsp	liquid honey	7 mL
2 tsp	Worcestershire Sauce (page 142) or store-bought	10 mL
1 tsp	freshly grated gingerroot	5 mL
1 tsp	sesame seeds	5 mL
¼ tsp	garlic powder	1 mL

1. In a bowl, whisk together mayonnaise, buttermilk, honey, Worcestershire sauce, ginger, sesame seeds and garlic powder until smooth.

Spicy Hot Love Dressing

Makes 1½ cups (375 mL)

This dressing is so simple, you're fated to fall for it.

1 cup	Traditional Mayonnaise (page 106) or store-bought	250 mL
¼ cup	sour cream	50 mL
¼ cup	plain yogurt	50 mL
1 tsp	hot pepper flakes	5 mL
½ tsp	cayenne pepper	2 mL

1. In a bowl, combine mayonnaise, sour cream, yogurt, hot pepper flakes and cayenne until smooth.

Tarragon Cream Dressing

Makes 1 cup (250 mL)

Toss this dressing with romaine leaves then top it all with chopped red onions.

½ cup	Traditional Mayonnaise (page 106) or store-bought	125 mL
¼ cup	plain yogurt	50 mL
¼ cup	buttermilk	50 mL
1 tbsp	dried tarragon	15 mL
2 tsp	reduced-sodium soy sauce	10 mL
¼ tsp	garlic powder	1 mL

1. In a bowl, whisk together mayonnaise, yogurt, buttermilk, tarragon, soy sauce and garlic powder until smooth.

Thousand Island Dressing

Makes 1¾ cups (425 mL)

This is the "secret sauce" that's found on fast food hamburgers.

• **Food processor**

1	hard-boiled egg	1
1 cup	Traditional Mayonnaise (page 106) or store-bought	250 mL
¼ cup	Bold Chili Sauce (page 125) or store-bought	50 mL
¼ cup	pimento-stuffed olives	50 mL
1	sweet pickle, cut in half	1
1½ tsp	dried onion flakes	7 mL
1½ tsp	freshly squeezed lemon juice	7 mL
1 tsp	dried parsley	5 mL
⅛ tsp	sea salt	0.5 mL
⅛ tsp	freshly ground black pepper	0.5 mL

1. In a food processor fitted with a metal blade, pulse egg, mayonnaise, chili sauce, olives, pickle, onion flakes, lemon juice, parsley, salt and black pepper until desired texture. For a chunky dressing, pulse about 10 times; for a smooth dressing, process about 1 minute. Refrigerate for at least 1 hour to allow the flavors to develop.

Tomato Basil Dressing

Makes ½ cup (125 mL)

When serving an Italian pasta dish, toss the accompanying salad with this dressing.

● **Food processor**

4 oz	cream cheese, softened	125 g
2 tbsp	Traditional Mayonnaise (page 106) or store-bought	25 mL
2	cloves garlic, minced	2
2 tsp	Bold Chili Sauce (page 125) or store-bought	10 mL
1 tsp	sea salt	5 mL
1 tsp	dried tomato powder (see Tip, page 61)	5 mL
1 tsp	dried basil	5 mL
½ tsp	Hungarian paprika	2 mL
¼ tsp	freshly ground black pepper	1 mL

1. In a food processor fitted with a metal blade, process cream cheese, mayonnaise, garlic, chili sauce, salt, tomato powder, basil, paprika and pepper until smooth, about 2 minutes.

Wasabi Sour Cream Dressing

Makes ¾ cup (175 mL)

Use this dressing with grated cabbages and carrots.

½ cup	Traditional Mayonnaise (page 106) or store-bought	125 mL
¼ cup	sour cream	50 mL
1½ tsp	liquid honey	7 mL
1 tsp	Worcestershire Sauce (page 142) or store-bought	5 mL
¼ tsp	wasabi powder	1 mL

1. In a bowl, whisk together mayonnaise, sour cream, honey, Worcestershire sauce and wasabi powder.

Zesty Tomato Onion Dressing

**Makes ½ cup
(125 mL)**

*Hearty dishes are
complemented by this zesty
dressing.*

- **Food processor**

4 oz	cream cheese, softened	125 g
2 tbsp	Traditional Mayonnaise (page 106) or store-bought	25 mL
2	cloves garlic, minced	2
1 tbsp	dried onion flakes	15 mL
2 tsp	Spicy Chili Sauce (page 124) or store-bought	10 mL
1 tsp	sea salt	5 mL
1 tsp	dried tomato powder (see Tip, page 61)	5 mL
½ tsp	Hungarian paprika	2 mL
¼ tsp	freshly ground black pepper	1 mL

1. In a food processor fitted with a metal blade, process cream cheese, mayonnaise, garlic, onion flakes, chili sauce, salt, tomato powder, paprika and pepper until smooth, about 2 minutes.

Lower-Fat Dressings

"Lower fat" does not need to mean less flavor. I think salads are some of the easiest dishes in which you can achieve optimal flavors with lower-fat ingredients. Use a tasty lower-fat dressing and watch what you top your salads with. Try carrot shavings, instead of grated cheeses, and a few toasted nuts in place of croutons.

Lemon Herb Dressing

Makes ½ cup (125 mL)

Use butterhead lettuce with this dressing.

¼ cup	white wine vinegar	50 mL
1 tbsp	grated lemon zest	15 mL
3 tbsp	freshly squeezed lemon juice	45 mL
2	cloves garlic, minced	2
1 tsp	chopped fresh tarragon	5 mL
1 tsp	chopped fresh rosemary	5 mL
½ tsp	Dijon Mustard (page 120) or store-bought	2 mL
⅛ tsp	garlic salt	0.5 mL
⅛ tsp	freshly ground black pepper	0.5 mL

1. In a bowl, whisk together vinegar, lemon zest and juice, garlic, tarragon, rosemary, mustard, salt and pepper until blended.

Lemon Yogurt Dressing

Makes 2½ cups (625 mL)

Here's a fresh simple dressing.

Tip

To make yogurt cheese: Place 3 cups (750 mL) plain yogurt in a cheesecloth-lined sieve set over a bowl. Place in the refrigerator and let it drain overnight (discard the liquid).

1½ cups	yogurt cheese (see Tip, left)	375 mL
1 cup	buttermilk	250 mL
2 tbsp	white wine vinegar	25 mL
2	cloves garlic, minced	2
1 tsp	dried dill	5 mL
1 tsp	grated lemon zest	5 mL
⅛ tsp	sea salt	0.5 mL
⅛ tsp	freshly ground black pepper	0.5 mL

1. In a bowl, whisk together yogurt cheese, buttermilk, vinegar, garlic, dill, lemon zest, salt and pepper until blended.

Miso Dressing

A bowl of miso soup begins the day in Japan, then reappears in soups, sauces, marinades and as an energizing afternoon beverage. Derived from fermented soybeans, miso is very nutritious. Try this dressing over chopped napa cabbage.

⅓ cup	white miso	75 mL
⅓ cup	natural rice vinegar (see Tip, page 37)	75 mL
⅓ cup	granulated sugar	75 mL
3 tbsp	dry mustard	45 mL
1 tsp	freshly squeezed lemon juice	5 mL

1. In a bowl, whisk together miso, vinegar, sugar, mustard and lemon juice until blended.

Parmesan Dressing

This dressing may be lower in fat, but it has lots of flavor.

1⅓ cups	1% milk	325 mL
1 tsp	cider vinegar	5 mL
⅓ cup	Low-Fat No-Egg Mayonnaise (page 111) or store-bought	75 mL
⅓ cup	plain yogurt	75 mL
¼ tsp	white wine vinegar	1 mL
1 tsp	Dijon Mustard (page 120) or store-bought	5 mL
½ tsp	dried parsley	2 mL
¼ tsp	sea salt	1 mL
¼ tsp	freshly ground black pepper	1 mL
¼ tsp	granulated sugar	1 mL
⅛ tsp	garlic powder	0.5 mL
¾ cup	freshly grated Parmesan cheese (about 3 oz/90 g)	175 mL

1. In a bowl, whisk together milk and cider vinegar. Set aside until it thickens, about 2 minutes. Whisk in mayonnaise, yogurt, white wine vinegar, mustard, parsley, salt, pepper, sugar and garlic powder. Toss in Parmesan cheese. Refrigerate in a sealed container for 2 hours prior to use.

Peppercorn Dressing

*You can also use this dressing
as a low-cal dipping sauce for
celery or vegetables.*

- **Food processor**

⅓ cup	Low-Fat No-Egg Mayonnaise (page 111) or store-bought	75 mL
⅓ cup	plain yogurt	75 mL
2 tbsp	white wine vinegar	25 mL
1 tsp	whole black peppercorns	5 mL
½ tsp	dried parsley	2 mL
¼ tsp	dried tarragon	1 mL
¼ tsp	sea salt	1 mL
¼ tsp	freshly ground black pepper	1 mL
¼ tsp	granulated sugar	1 mL
⅛ tsp	garlic powder	0.5 mL

1. In a food processor fitted with a metal blade, process mayonnaise, yogurt, vinegar, peppercorns, parsley, tarragon, salt, pepper, sugar and garlic powder until smooth, about 2 minutes. Refrigerate in a sealed container for 2 hours prior to use.

Raspberry Yogurt Dressing

Makes 1 cup (250 mL)

*Dip fresh berries into this
yogurt dressing for a sweet
treat.*

1 cup	raspberry-flavored yogurt	250 mL
2 tbsp	white wine vinegar	25 mL
2	cloves garlic, minced	2
1 tsp	dried tarragon	5 mL
⅛ tsp	sea salt	0.5 mL
⅛ tsp	freshly ground black pepper	0. 5 mL

1. In a bowl, whisk together yogurt, vinegar, garlic, tarragon, salt and pepper until blended.

Tarragon Buttermilk Dressing

Makes ⅔ cup (150 mL)

This dressing is so good, you'll think you're eating a rich, full-calorie dressing.

⅓ cup	Low-Fat No-Egg Mayonnaise (page 111) or store-bought	75 mL
⅓ cup	buttermilk	75 mL
1 tsp	Dijon Mustard (page 120) or store-bought	5 mL
1 tsp	dried tarragon	5 mL
¼ tsp	sea salt	1 mL
¼ tsp	freshly ground black pepper	1 mL
⅛ tsp	garlic powder	0.5 mL

1. In a bowl, whisk together mayonnaise, buttermilk, mustard, tarragon, salt, pepper and garlic powder. Refrigerate in a sealed container for 2 hours prior to use.

Balsamic Vinaigrette

Makes 1 cup (250 mL)

Here's a light and easy vinaigrette.

½ cup	balsamic vinegar	125 mL
3 tbsp	Low-Fat No-Egg Mayonnaise (page 111) or store-bought	45 mL
3 tbsp	hot water	45 mL
3 tbsp	freshly squeezed orange juice	45 mL
¼ tsp	dried basil	1 mL
¼ tsp	dried oregano	1 mL
¼ tsp	sea salt	1 mL
¼ tsp	granulated sugar	1 mL

1. In a bowl, whisk together vinegar, mayonnaise, hot water, orange juice, basil, oregano, salt and sugar. Refrigerate in a sealed container for 2 hours prior to use.

Blue Cheese Dressing

Makes 2 cups (500 mL)

This dressing is creamy yet light in calories.

Variation
Use any feta or Gorgonzola, instead of the blue cheese.

1⅓ cups	1% milk	325 mL
1 tsp	cider vinegar	5 mL
⅓ cup	Low-Fat No-Egg Mayonnaise (page 111) or store-bought	75 mL
⅓ cup	plain yogurt	75 mL
1 tsp	white wine vinegar	5 mL
1 tsp	Dijon Mustard (page 120) or store-bought	5 mL
½ tsp	dried parsley	2 mL
¼ tsp	dried tarragon	1 mL
¼ tsp	sea salt	1 mL
¼ tsp	freshly ground black pepper	1 mL
¼ tsp	granulated sugar	1 mL
⅛ tsp	garlic powder	0.5 mL
4 oz	blue cheese, crumbled	125 g

1. In a bowl, combine milk and cider vinegar. Let stand until thickened, about 2 minutes. Whisk in mayonnaise, yogurt, white wine vinegar, mustard, parsley, tarragon, salt, pepper, sugar and garlic powder. Toss in blue cheese. Refrigerate in a sealed container for 2 hours prior to use.

Chile and Lime Dressing

Makes 1 cup (250 mL)

Try this dressing as a dip with baked corn chips.

1	can (4½ oz/127 mL) chopped green chiles, drained	1
¼ cup	chopped fresh cilantro	50 mL
1 tsp	grated lime zest	5 mL
¼ cup	freshly squeezed lime juice	50 mL
¼ cup	hot water	50 mL
2	cloves garlic, minced	2
2 tsp	liquid honey	10 mL
1 tsp	freshly ground black pepper	5 mL

1. In a bowl, whisk together chiles, cilantro, lime zest and juice, hot water, garlic, honey and pepper until blended. Refrigerate in a sealed container for 2 hours prior to use.

Citrus Vinaigrette

Makes ½ cup (125 mL)

Drizzle this vinaigrette on freshly sliced pears.

¼ cup	white wine vinegar	50 mL
1 tbsp	grated lemon zest	10 mL
2 tbsp	freshly squeezed lemon juice	25 mL
2 tbsp	freshly squeezed orange juice	25 mL
1 tbsp	canola oil	15 mL
1	clove garlic, minced	1
½ tsp	Dijon Mustard (page 120) or store-bought	2 mL
⅛ tsp	garlic salt	0.5 mL
⅛ tsp	freshly ground black pepper	0.5 mL

1. In a bowl, whisk together vinegar, lemon zest and juice, orange juice, oil, garlic, mustard, garlic salt and pepper until blended.

Buttermilk Dressing

Makes ¾ cup (175 mL)

Here's a lighter version of the popular dressing.

½ cup	buttermilk	125 mL
¼ cup	Low-Fat No-Egg Mayonnaise (page 111) or store-bought	50 mL
1 tbsp	white wine vinegar	15 mL
2 tsp	Dijon Mustard (page 120) or store-bought	10 mL
1 tsp	chopped fresh chives	5 mL
1	clove garlic, minced	1
½ tsp	granulated sugar	2 mL
¼ tsp	sea salt	1 mL
¼ tsp	freshly ground black pepper	1 mL

1. In a bowl, whisk together buttermilk, mayonnaise, vinegar, mustard, chives, garlic, sugar, salt and pepper until blended.

Creamy Yogurt Herb Dressing

Makes ½ cup (125 mL)

The plum sauce adds a hint of sweetness.

Variation
Replace the plum sauce with strawberry jam.

½ cup	plain yogurt	125 mL
1 tbsp	balsamic vinegar	15 mL
1 tsp	plum sauce	5 mL
½ tsp	onion powder	2 mL
¼ tsp	dried tarragon	1 mL
¼ tsp	dried Italian seasoning	1 mL
⅛ tsp	sea salt	0.5 mL

1. In a bowl, whisk together yogurt, vinegar, plum sauce, onion powder, tarragon, Italian seasoning and salt until blended. Refrigerate in a sealed container for 2 hours prior to use.

Cucumber Dressing

Makes 1¼ cups (300 mL)

Napa cabbage perfectly suits this dressing.

- **Food processor**

1 cup	plain nonfat yogurt	250 mL
½	cucumber, peeled, seeded and cut into chunks	½
1 tsp	freshly squeezed lemon juice	5 mL
1 tsp	fresh dill	5 mL
1	clove garlic	1
½ tsp	sea salt	2 mL
½ tsp	ground white pepper	2 mL

1. In a food processor fitted with a metal blade, process yogurt, cucumber, lemon juice, dill, garlic, salt and white pepper until smooth, about 1 minute.

Fat-Free Honey Dijon Dressing

Makes ¾ cup (175 mL)

I like to use this dressing as a dip for baked chicken pieces.

¼ cup	Dijon Mustard (page 120) or store-bought	50 mL
¼ cup	white wine vinegar	50 mL
5 tbsp	liquid honey	75 mL
2 tbsp	instant skim milk powder	25 mL
1 tsp	onion powder	5 mL
½ tsp	dry mustard	2 mL

1. In a bowl, whisk together mustard, vinegar, honey, milk powder, onion powder and dry mustard until blended. Refrigerate in a sealed container for 2 hours prior to use.

Fat-Free Zesty Herb Dressing

Makes 1 cup (250 mL)

I like to use this as a coleslaw dressing for shredded cabbages and carrots.

⅔ cup	hot water	150 mL
¼ cup	white wine vinegar	50 mL
1 tbsp	chopped fresh dill	15 mL
1 tsp	granulated sugar	5 mL
¼ tsp	garlic powder	1 mL
¼ tsp	dry mustard	1 mL
¼ tsp	freshly ground black pepper	1 mL

1. In a bowl, whisk together hot water, vinegar, dill, sugar, garlic powder, dry mustard and pepper until blended. Refrigerate in a sealed container for 2 hours prior to use.

Honey Basil Vinaigrette

Make this speedy dressing with a few simple ingredients.

¼ cup	balsamic vinegar	50 mL
2 tbsp	liquid honey	25 mL
¼ tsp	dried basil	1 mL
¼ tsp	dried oregano	1 mL
¼ tsp	sea salt	1 mL
¼ tsp	freshly ground black pepper	1 mL

1. In a bowl, whisk together vinegar, honey, basil, oregano, salt and pepper until smooth. Refrigerate in a sealed container for 2 hours prior to use.

Honey Mustard Dressing

Makes 1 cup (250 mL)

Here's a sweet dressing with a hit of tartness from the mustard.

¼ cup	Dijon Mustard (page 120) or store-bought	50 mL
¼ cup	liquid honey	50 mL
¼ cup	white wine vinegar	50 mL
2 tbsp	instant skim milk powder	25 mL
1 tsp	onion powder	5 mL
½ tsp	dry mustard	2 mL
¼ cup	canola oil	50 mL

1. In a bowl, whisk together mustard, honey, vinegar, milk powder, onion powder and dry mustard. While vigorously whisking, pour in oil in a thin steady stream until smooth.

Shallot Dressing

Makes 1¼ cups (300 mL)

A light drizzle of this dressing is perfect for butterhead lettuce.

⅔ cup	warm water	150 mL
1 tsp	arrowroot powder	5 mL
¼ cup	minced shallots	50 mL
¼ cup	sherry wine vinegar	50 mL
1 tbsp	Dijon Mustard (page 120) or store-bought	15 mL

1. In a bowl, whisk together warm water and arrowroot until smooth. Whisk in shallots, vinegar and mustard.

Creamy Herb Dressing

Makes 2¼ cups (550 mL)

Here's a thick dressing with a light pink color.

Tip
Make sure you drain the cottage cheese or you will have a watery dressing.

- **Food processor**

1	red bell pepper, seeded and chopped	1
2 cups	nonfat cottage cheese, drained (see Tip, left)	500 mL
¼ cup	fresh basil	50 mL
3	cloves garlic, minced	3
1 tbsp	freshly squeezed lemon juice	15 mL
1 tbsp	chopped fresh chives	15 mL
½ tsp	sea salt	2 mL
¼ tsp	freshly ground black pepper	1 mL

1. In a food processor fitted with a metal blade, process bell pepper, cottage cheese, basil, garlic, lemon juice, chives, salt and pepper until smooth.

Tomato Vinaigrette

Makes 1 cup (250 mL)

I like to pour this vinaigrette over cooked asparagus.

2	Roma (plum) tomatoes, seeded and diced	2
2 tbsp	white wine vinegar	25 mL
1/2 tsp	dried basil	2 mL
1/2 tsp	dried thyme	2 mL
1/2 tsp	Dijon Mustard (page 120) or store-bought	2 mL

1. In a saucepan over low heat, bring tomatoes, vinegar, basil, thyme and mustard to a light boil, stirring, about 4 minutes. Use vinaigrette warm or cool.

Low-Fat Paris Dressing

Makes 1/4 cup (50 mL)

A full-flavor version of my Paris dressing.

2 tbsp	freshly squeezed lemon juice	25 mL
1 tbsp	olive oil	15 mL
2 tsp	white wine vinegar	10 mL
1/4 tsp	sea salt	1 mL
1/4 tsp	granulated sugar	1 mL
1/8 tsp	mild dry mustard	0.5 mL
1/8 tsp	freshly ground black pepper	0.5 mL

1. In a bowl, whisk together lemon juice, oil, vinegar, salt, sugar, mustard and pepper until smooth.

Olive Vinaigrette

**Makes ⅓ cup
(75 mL)**

*Here's a perfect vinaigrette to
try on Greek salads.*

¼ cup	balsamic vinegar	50 mL
3 tbsp	pitted and finely chopped Niçoise olives	45 mL
1 tbsp	liquid honey	15 mL
1½ tsp	prepared mustard	7 mL
1 tsp	finely chopped fresh cilantro	5 mL
1 tsp	finely chopped shallots	5 mL

1. In a bowl, whisk together vinegar, olives, honey, mustard, cilantro and shallots until blended.

Ranch Buttermilk Dressing

**Makes 2 cups
(500 mL)**

*Here's a flavorful
lower-calorie version of
this popular dressing.*

1⅓ cups	nonfat milk	325 mL
2 tsp	cider vinegar	10 mL
⅔ cup	Low-Fat No-Egg Mayonnaise (page 111) or store-bought	150 mL
4 tsp	white wine vinegar	20 mL
1 tsp	Dijon Mustard (page 120) or store-bought	5 mL
¾ tsp	dried dill	3 mL
½ tsp	dried parsley	2 mL
½ tsp	minced dried garlic	2 mL
¼ tsp	sea salt	1 mL
¼ tsp	freshly ground black pepper	1 mL
¼ tsp	granulated sugar	1 mL

1. In a bowl, combine milk and vinegar. Let stand until it thickens, about 3 minutes. Whisk in mayonnaise, vinegar, mustard, dill, parsley, dried garlic, salt, pepper and sugar until smooth.

Sesame Orange Dressing

Makes 1 cup (250 mL)

Serve this dressing with shredded cabbage and orange segments.

⅓ cup	warm water	75 mL
¼ cup	natural rice vinegar (see Tip, page 37)	50 mL
¼ cup	sesame oil	50 mL
2 tsp	freshly squeezed orange juice	10 mL
1 tsp	apple juice concentrate	5 mL
1 tsp	reduced-sodium soy sauce	5 mL
1½ tsp	Dijon Mustard (page 120) or store-bought	7 mL
¼ tsp	garlic powder	1 mL
¼ tsp	onion powder	1 mL
⅛ tsp	cayenne pepper	0.5 mL

1. In a bowl, combine warm water, vinegar, sesame oil, orange juice, apple juice concentrate, soy sauce, mustard, garlic powder, onion powder and cayenne until blended.

Yogurt Dressing

Makes 2½ cups (625 mL)

I like using this dressing on Greek salads or in lamb sandwiches.

Tip

To make yogurt cheese: Place 3 cups (750 mL) plain yogurt in a cheesecloth-lined sieve set over a bowl. Place in the refrigerator and let it drain overnight (discard the liquid).

1½ cups	yogurt cheese (see Tip, left)	375 mL
1 cup	buttermilk	250 mL
2 tbsp	white wine vinegar	25 mL
2	cloves garlic, minced	2
1 tsp	dried dill	5 mL
⅛ tsp	sea salt	0.5 mL
⅛ tsp	freshly ground black pepper	0.5 mL

1. In a bowl, combine yogurt cheese, buttermilk, vinegar, garlic, dill, salt and pepper until blended.

Zesty Oil-Free Dressing

Makes ³⁄₄ cup (175 mL)

Use this dressing on salads, or drizzle it on sandwiches for a lower-calorie sub.

¼ cup	freshly squeezed lemon juice	50 mL
¼ cup	cider vinegar	50 mL
¼ cup	unsweetened apple juice	50 mL
½ tsp	dried oregano	2 mL
½ tsp	dry mustard	2 mL
½ tsp	onion powder	2 mL
½ tsp	dried basil	2 mL
⅛ tsp	dried thyme	0.5 mL
⅛ tsp	dried rosemary	0.5 mL

1. In a bowl, whisk together lemon juice, vinegar, apple juice, oregano, mustard, onion powder, basil, thyme and rosemary until smooth.

Garlic Caesar Dressing

Makes ¼ cup (50 mL)

Here's a lower-fat version for Caesar salads.

5	cloves garlic, finely minced	5
1 tbsp	freshly squeezed lemon juice	15 mL
2 tsp	balsamic vinegar	10 mL
1 tsp	red wine vinegar	5 mL
1 tsp	warm water	5 mL
½ tsp	dry mustard	2 mL
2	drops hot pepper sauce	2

1. In a bowl, combine garlic, lemon juice, balsamic and red wine vinegars, warm water, mustard and hot pepper sauce until blended.

Complete Salads and Accompaniments

Complete Salads

I've put together a set of my favorite salads for this chapter, complete with dressings. Many grocery stores are now combining all the salad makings in one package, but you can do it yourself. Not only will you save money, but — I assure you — these salads will become family favorites.

Caprese Salad

Serves 4 to 6

This simple fresh salad from Italy makes a lovely appetizer or side dish.

1 tbsp	red wine vinegar	15 mL
1 tbsp	balsamic vinegar	15 mL
1 tsp	sea salt	5 mL
1/2 tsp	granulated sugar	2 mL
1/2 tsp	freshly ground black pepper	2 mL
1/2 cup	extra virgin olive oil	125 mL
2 lbs	plum tomatoes, sliced	1 kg
1 lb	ball mozzarella, cut into 1/4-inch (0.5 cm) thick slices	500 g
1/2 cup	loosely packed fresh basil chiffonade	125 mL

1. In a bowl, whisk together red wine and balsamic vinegars, salt, sugar and pepper. Whisk in oil.
2. Divide sliced tomatoes and mozzarella evenly onto plates. Drizzle dressing on top. Sprinkle with basil and serve.

Carrot and Raisin Salad

Serves 8

At my elementary school I happily ate carrot and raisin salad every week. Here is my adult variation.

1/2 cup	Traditional Mayonnaise (page 106) or store-bought	125 mL
1 tsp	freshly squeezed lime juice	5 mL
1/2 tsp	sea salt	2 mL
1/2 tsp	freshly ground black pepper	2 mL
4 cups	shredded carrots	1 L
1 cup	golden raisins	250 mL
1	apple, cubed	1
1/2 cup	sliced almonds, toasted	125 mL

1. In a large bowl, whisk together mayonnaise, lime juice, salt and pepper. Add carrots, raisins, apple and almonds and mix to evenly coat. Cover and refrigerate until chilled, for at least 1 hour or for up to 2 days.

Chicken Salad

Serves 6

I created this recipe using an entire deli-roasted chicken. If you have part of a chicken, you can adjust the recipe accordingly.

Tip

If you process the chicken spread too much you will get a creamy consistency. Avoid this by pulsing the mixture as described.

Variation

If you have a fresh herb available — such as tarragon, dill or rosemary — chop and add 2 tbsp (25 mL) to the mixture.

• **Food processor**

1/2 cup	red onion, sliced	125 mL
3	cloves garlic	3
3 oz	cream cheese, softened	90 g
1/3 cup	Traditional Mayonnaise (page 106) or store-bought	75 mL
1/4 tsp	freshly ground black pepper	1 mL
1/4 tsp	sea salt	1 mL
3 lbs	deli roasted chicken, bones and skin removed	1.5 kg
1	large head Boston lettuce	1

1. In a food processor fitted with a metal blade, process onion until finely chopped, about 20 seconds. In the last 5 seconds, add garlic through the feed tube. Add cream cheese, mayonnaise, pepper and salt and pulse about 3 times. Add chicken and pulse 6 times until coarsely chopped.
2. Divide lettuce leaves evenly onto 6 plates. Serve salad on top.

Chinese Chicken Salad

This is my version of take-out Chinese salad. Try it for lunch or dinner. I also use this dressing for an easy marinade for pork or chicken.

Tip

Make the dressing 2 to 3 days ahead to let the flavors develop, then cover and refrigerate it. So they don't get soggy, add the almonds just before serving the salad.

Variation

Try using fresh spinach leaves instead of salad greens for a heartier meal.

4 cups	salad greens	1 L
1 lb	cooked chicken pieces	500 g
Dressing		
¼ cup	cider vinegar	50 mL
2 tbsp	freshly squeezed orange juice	25 mL
2 tbsp	granulated sugar	25 mL
1 tsp	Dijon Mustard (page 120) or store-bought	5 mL
1 tsp	sea salt	5 mL
½ cup	canola oil	125 mL
2 tbsp	poppy seeds	25 mL
2 tbsp	sliced almonds, toasted	25 mL

1. Place 1 cup (250 mL) of greens on each plate. Top with chicken pieces. Set aside.
2. *Dressing:* In a bowl, whisk together vinegar, orange juice, sugar, mustard and salt. While whisking, pour in oil in a thin steady stream until emulsified. Stir in poppy seeds and almonds. Drizzle on salad.

Brown Derby Cobb Salad

Serves 8

The Brown Derby was a celebrated watering hole in Los Angeles, frequented by movie and television stars. This salad was made famous by the restaurant owner, Robert Cobb.

Tip

You can store this dressing for up to 1 week in the refrigerator.

Dressing

¾ cup	red wine vinegar	175 mL
1 tbsp	Worcestershire Sauce (page 142)	15 mL
2 tsp	freshly squeezed lemon juice	10 mL
1 tsp	granulated sugar	5 mL
1 tsp	freshly ground black pepper	5 mL
1 tsp	Dijon Mustard (page 120)	5 mL
¾ tsp	sea salt	3 mL
1	clove garlic, minced	1
1 cup	extra virgin olive oil	250 mL
1 cup	canola oil	250 mL

Salad

4 cups	finely chopped iceberg lettuce (about ½ head)	1 L
2 cups	finely chopped watercress (about ½ bunch)	500 mL
1 cup	chicory, finely chopped (about 1 small bunch)	250 mL
4 cups	finely chopped romaine (about ½ head)	1 L
2	vine-ripened tomatoes, seeded and diced	2
1 lb	cooked boneless skinless chicken breasts, diced	500 g
8 oz	bacon, crisply cooked and crumbled	250 g
1	ripe avocado, diced	1
3	hard-boiled eggs, finely chopped	3
2 tbsp	chopped fresh chives	25 mL
½ cup	crumbled Roquefort cheese	125 mL

1. *Dressing:* In a wide-mouthed jar with a tight-fitting lid, combine vinegar, ¼ cup (50 mL) water, Worcestershire, lemon juice, sugar, pepper, mustard, salt and garlic. Shake for 1 minute. Add olive and canola oils and shake until emulsified, about 1 minute. Use immediately or cover tightly and store in the refrigerator until ready to use. Shake before using.

2. *Salad:* In a large shallow bowl or deep plate, toss together iceberg lettuce, watercress, chicory and romaine with enough of the dressing to coat.

3. Divide salad evenly onto 8 plates. Arrange tomatoes in a strip across middle of greens. Arrange chicken on top. Sprinkle with bacon, avocado, eggs, chives and Roquefort.

Blue Cheese Peanut Coleslaw

The rich bite of blue cheese combined with creamy peanut dressing makes this coleslaw a picnic favorite.

Tip
I like to shred the carrots and cut the cabbage by hand instead of purchasing pre-cut vegetables. It just tastes better this way to me, but if you're in a hurry I understand.

Variation
For a different flavor, you can substitute any cheese for the blue cheese.

1/2 cup	Traditional Mayonnaise (page 106) or store-bought	125 mL
2 tbsp	freshly squeezed lemon juice	25 mL
1/2 tsp	freshly ground black pepper	2 mL
1/2 tsp	sea salt	2 mL
1/4 tsp	granulated sugar	1 mL
1	onion, diced	1
1	green bell pepper, diced	1
2 cups	shredded carrots	500 mL
12 oz	cabbage (about 1/2 head), grated	375 g
4 oz	blue cheese, crumbled	125 g
1	package (8 oz/250 g) unsalted roasted peanuts, crushed	1

1. In a large salad bowl, whisk together mayonnaise, lemon juice, pepper, salt and sugar until blended. Add onion, bell pepper, carrots and cabbage and stir to coat with dressing. Add blue cheese and peanuts. Refrigerate, tightly covered, for at least 1 hour prior to serving or for up to 3 days.

Fast Egg Salad

Serves 4

You can serve this salad on toasted bread or on a bed of greens.

8	hard-boiled eggs	8
1/2	red onion, minced	1/2
1/4 cup	Traditional Mayonnaise (page 106) or store-bought	50 mL
2 tbsp	Dijon Mustard (page 120) or store-bought	25 mL
1 tsp	dried dill	5 mL
1 tsp	Hungarian paprika	5 mL
1/2 tsp	sea salt	2 mL
1/2 tsp	freshly ground black pepper	2 mL

1. In a bowl, using a fork, stir together eggs, onion, mayonnaise, mustard, dill, paprika, salt and pepper until blended. Use immediately or cover and refrigerate for up to 3 days.

Warm German Potato Salad

Serves 8

This salad is great with a large steak or even a roasted chicken.

4 lbs	red potatoes, cut into quarters	2 kg
8 oz	bacon slices	250 g
1 tbsp	all-purpose flour	15 mL
2 tbsp	granulated sugar	25 mL
1/3 cup	water	75 mL
1/4 cup	white wine vinegar	50 mL
1/2 cup	chopped green onions	125 mL
1/2 tsp	sea salt	2 mL
1/2 tsp	freshly ground black pepper	2 mL
1/2 tsp	mustard seeds	2 mL

1. In a large pot of boiling salted water, cook potatoes until tender but still firm, about 15 minutes. Drain and let cool.
2. In a large deep skillet over medium–high heat, cook bacon until evenly browned and crisp. Transfer to a paper towel to drain. Crumble and set aside.
3. Add flour to bacon fat remaining in skillet and cook, stirring, until lightly browned, about 2 minutes. Reduce heat to medium. Add sugar, water and vinegar and cook, stirring, until dressing has thickened, about 5 minutes.
4. Add bacon, potatoes and green onions and stir until coated and heated. Stir in salt, pepper and mustard seeds. Serve warm.

Greek Salad

This light salad is prefect for a spring day.

3 tbsp	extra virgin olive oil	45 mL
1½ tbsp	freshly squeezed lemon juice	22 mL
1	clove garlic, minced	1
½ tsp	dried oregano	2 mL
¼ tsp	sea salt	1 mL
¼ tsp	freshly ground black pepper	1 mL
1	cucumber	1
3	Roma (plum) tomatoes, cut into wedges	3
1	small red onion, cut into rings	1
½	green bell pepper, sliced	½
4 oz	feta cheese, crumbled	125 g
½ cup	kalamata olives, pitted	125 mL
	Freshly ground black pepper	

1. In a bowl, whisk together oil, lemon juice, garlic, oregano, salt and pepper.
2. Cut cucumber in half lengthwise. Scoop out seeds and slice cucumber into half-moons. In a large salad bowl, combine tomatoes, onion, cucumber slices, bell pepper, feta and olives. Pour dressing over top and toss gently to combine just before serving. Garnish with a little freshly ground black pepper.

Panzanella Salad

Serves 8

I've recreated this recipe from the memory of a salad I enjoyed in Tuscany.

Salad

8 oz	bacon	250 g
4 cups	Italian bread, cut into 1-inch (2.5 cm) cubes and dried overnight	1 L
2 tbsp	canola oil	25 mL
3	Roma (plum) tomatoes, seeded and cut into small pieces	3
2	heirloom tomatoes, seeded and cut into small pieces	2
2 cups	chopped romaine lettuce	500 mL

Dressing

1/4 cup	red wine vinegar	50 mL
1/4 tsp	sea salt	1 mL
1/4 tsp	freshly ground black pepper	1 mL
3 tbsp	extra virgin olive oil	45 mL
1 tbsp	shredded fresh mint	15 mL
1 tbsp	shredded fresh basil	15 mL
1 tsp	chopped fresh tarragon	5 mL

1. *Salad:* In a large deep skillet over medium-high heat, cook bacon until evenly browned and crisp. Transfer to a paper towel to drain. Crumble and set aside. In a large bowl, toss bread cubes in bacon drippings from pan to soak up fat.
2. Add canola oil and tomatoes to pan and cook, until tomatoes are browned, about 5 minutes. Set aside.
3. *Dressing:* In a bowl, whisk together vinegar, salt and pepper. Whisk in oil.
4. *Assemble:* In a large bowl, combine tomatoes, bread cubes, bacon and lettuce and toss well with dressing. Garnish with mint, basil and tarragon.

Three-Herb Pasta Salad

Make this pasta salad in the morning so all of the flavors have time to develop by the time you're ready to serve it for lunch or dinner.

Tips

I prefer to use a small round or shell-shaped pasta that is easily coated by the creamy sauce.

Drain pasta and rinse with cool water. Then drain thoroughly and toss with a few sprinkles of olive oil.

- **Food processor**

8 oz	cream cheese, softened	250 g
½ cup	Traditional Mayonnaise (page 106) or store-bought	125 mL
½ cup	buttermilk	125 mL
2 tbsp	freshly squeezed lemon juice	25 mL
1 tbsp	chopped fresh dill	15 mL
1 tbsp	chopped fresh tarragon	15 mL
1 tsp	chopped fresh rosemary	5 mL
1 tbsp	dried onion flakes	15 mL
1 tbsp	freshly ground black pepper	15 mL
½ tsp	garlic powder	2 mL
1 lb	pasta, cooked (see Tips, left)	500 g

1. In a food processor fitted with a metal blade, process cream cheese, mayonnaise, buttermilk and lemon juice until smooth, about 2 minutes. Add dill, tarragon, rosemary, onion flakes, pepper and garlic powder. Process until well blended. Add dressing to cooked pasta and toss. Cover and refrigerate for at least 2 hours prior to serving or for up to 3 days.

Ambrosia Salad

Serves 6 to 8

This typical ambrosia salad is my sister Pattie's favorite. It's a must at every holiday dinner.

1 cup	sour cream	250 mL
1 cup	mini marshmallows	250 mL
1 cup	drained mandarin oranges	250 mL
1 cup	drained crushed pineapple	250 mL
1 cup	sweetened flaked coconut	250 mL

1. In a bowl, combine sour cream, marshmallows, mandarin oranges, pineapple and coconut. Tightly cover and refrigerate for 8 hours prior to serving or for up to 6 days.

All-Summer Potato Salad

Serves 6

This perfect potato salad is suitable for any gathering.

Tip
If you are taking this salad outdoors, be sure to keep it on ice in the cooler, so the mayonnaise doesn't go bad.

1 cup	Traditional Mayonnaise (page 106) or store-bought	250 mL
1 cup	onion, minced	250 mL
½ cup	chopped green onions	125 mL
¼ cup	Dijon Mustard (page 120) or store-bought	50 mL
3 tbsp	natural rice vinegar	45 mL
2 tsp	sea salt	10 mL
1 tsp	chopped fresh tarragon	5 mL
¼ tsp	freshly ground black pepper	1 mL
2	hard-boiled eggs, chopped	2
3 lbs	white fingerling potatoes, cooked and cut into quarters	1.5 kg
2 cups	diced celery	500 mL

1. In a large bowl, whisk together mayonnaise, onion, green onions, mustard, vinegar, salt, tarragon and pepper. Add eggs, potatoes and celery and toss to coat well. Cover and refrigerate for 4 hours prior to serving or for up to 3 days.

Salad Niçoise

Serves 6

This simple salad is served in bistros throughout France.

1	large head Boston lettuce	1
1 lb	green beans, cooked and cooled	500 g
1½ tbsp	minced shallots	22 mL
½ cup	Italian Herb Vinaigrette (page 27) or Red Balsamic Vinaigrette (page 33)	125 mL
¼ tsp	sea salt	1 mL
¼ tsp	freshly ground black pepper	1 mL
4	Roma (plum) tomatoes, cut into wedges	4
4	small fingerling potatoes, cooked and sliced	4
1	can (6 oz/170 g) solid white tuna, drained	1
6	hard-boiled eggs, halved	6
⅓ cup	small black Niçoise olives	75 mL
3 tbsp	minced Italian flat-leaf parsley	45 mL
2 tbsp	capers, drained	25 mL

1. Arrange lettuce leaves on a large serving platter. In a large bowl, toss together beans, shallots, 2 or 3 spoonfuls of vinaigrette, salt and pepper.
2. Baste tomatoes with a spoonful of vinaigrette. Place potatoes in the center of platter and arrange a mound of beans at either end, with tomatoes and small mounds of tuna at strategic intervals. Ring platter with halves of hard-boiled eggs, sunny-side up. Spoon more vinaigrette over all. Scatter with olives, parsley and capers.

Salad Olivier

Serves 6

This salad was invented by a French chef, M. Olivier, who served it in Moscow in the late 1800s. It is known worldwide by many names including Salade Olivier, Russian Salad or Sour Russian Potato Salad.

2½ cups	cubed boneless skinless cooked chicken	625 mL
4	medium boiling potatoes, cooked, peeled and cubed	4
1 cup	frozen peas, cooked	250 mL
2	hard-boiled eggs, coarsely chopped	2
1	small onion, finely chopped	1
1	large carrot, diced	1
2 tbsp	dill pickle relish, drained	25 mL
1 tbsp	capers, drained	15 mL
¾ cup	Traditional Mayonnaise (page 106) or store-bought	175 mL
¼ cup	sour cream	50 mL
1 tbsp	Dijon Mustard (page 120) or store-bought	15 mL
2 tsp	freshly squeezed lemon juice	10 mL
½ tsp	sea salt	2 mL
½ tsp	freshly ground black pepper	2 mL
½ tsp	dried dill	2 mL
1	head Boston lettuce	1
1	large Roma (plum) tomato, cut into small wedges	1
⅛ tsp	Hungarian paprika	0.5 mL

1. In a large bowl, combine chicken, potatoes, peas, hard-boiled eggs, onion, carrot, pickle relish and capers. Fold slightly to mix.
2. In another bowl, whisk together mayonnaise, sour cream, mustard, lemon juice, salt, pepper and dill. Pour over salad and stir gently. Cover and refrigerate for at least 1 hour prior to serving or for up to 4 days.
3. To serve, mound lettuce leaves on a large platter and top with chicken mixture. Garnish with tomato wedges. Sprinkle with paprika.

Green Papaya Salad

Serves 4

This traditional Thai salad is delicious served with grilled fish or chicken.

2	cloves garlic, minced	2
1/4 cup	peanuts, chopped	50 mL
1 tsp	freshly squeezed lemon juice	5 mL
1	tomato, diced	1
1 tbsp	fish sauce	15 mL
1 tbsp	packed brown sugar	15 mL
2 tbsp	roughly chopped fresh cilantro	25 mL
1	large ripe green papaya, peeled and grated	1

1. In a large bowl, combine garlic, peanuts, lemon juice, tomato, fish sauce, brown sugar and cilantro. Toss with green papaya.

Tabbouleh Salad

Serves 6 to 8

This Lebanese staple is a refreshing and healthy summer salad and a wonderful way to use mint.

Tip
If using coarse bulgur, increase the soaking time to 30 minutes.

1/3 cup	fine bulgur (see Tip, left)	75 mL
1 cup	warm water	250 mL
1/4 cup	freshly squeezed lemon juice	50 mL
2	cloves garlic, crushed	2
1/2 tsp	sea salt ·	2 mL
1/2 tsp	freshly ground black pepper	2 mL
1	bunch fresh mint, chopped (about 1 cup/250 mL)	1
4 cups	chopped Italian flat-leaf parsley	1 L
1/2 cup	chopped green onions	125 mL
3	tomatoes, diced	3
1/4 cup	extra virgin olive oil	50 mL
1	head romaine lettuce	1

1. In a large bowl, cover bulgur with warm water for 15 minutes or until softened. Squeeze out excess water. Add lemon juice, garlic, salt and pepper. Let stand until bulgur is tender, about 30 minutes.
2. Add mint, parsley, green onions and tomatoes to bulgur mixture. Toss with olive oil. Serve with small romaine lettuce leaves as scoops.

Taco Salad

Serves 8

My mom makes this great salad with minimal effort. You can make a huge batch and serve it on a platter for a crowd.

2 tbsp	olive oil	25 mL
1	onion, sliced	1
2	cloves garlic, minced	2
2 lbs	ground beef or ground turkey	1 kg
2 tsp	taco seasoning	10 mL
1/2 cup	water	125 mL
12 oz	corn chips	375 g
8 cups	salad greens	2 L
8 oz	Cheddar cheese, shredded	250 g
8 oz	Monterey Jack cheese, shredded	250 g
2	Roma (plum) tomatoes, diced	2
1/2 cup	sour cream	125 mL
1/2 cup	Guacamole (page 266) or store-bought	125 mL
1 cup	Ranch Dressing (page 61) or store-bought	250 mL

1. In a large skillet, heat oil over medium heat. Add onion and sauté until translucent, about 4 minutes. Add garlic and sauté for 2 minutes. Add ground meat and cook, breaking up with a spoon, until light brown, about 8 minutes. Add taco seasoning and water and cook, stirring, until liquid has evaporated, about 5 minutes. Set aside.
2. Divide corn chips, salad greens, Cheddar cheese, Monterey Jack cheese and tomatoes evenly onto 8 plates. Divide cooked meat evenly on top of prepared plates. Top with 1 tbsp (15 mL) each of the sour cream and guacamole. Drizzle with dressing.

Tarragon Tuna Salad

Serves 6

My mom always packed me a tuna salad sandwich when my elementary school had a field trip — even when we went to the tuna canning plant.

Tip

Serve this tuna salad on toasted bread with cheese or on a bed of greens with a vinaigrette.

2	cans (each 12 oz/340 g) solid white tuna, packed in water, drained	2
½ cup	Traditional Mayonnaise (page 106) or store-bought	125 mL
¼ cup	chopped fresh tarragon	50 mL
1	dill pickle, diced	1
2 tsp	freshly squeezed lemon juice	10 mL
1 tsp	sea salt	5 mL
1 tsp	ground white pepper	5 mL
½ tsp	Hungarian paprika	2 mL

1. In a bowl, using a fork, combine tuna, mayonnaise, tarragon, pickle, lemon juice, salt, white pepper and paprika. Mix just to combine.

Turkey Salad

Serves 4

I cook a huge turkey for the holidays so I can use the leftovers to make this salad for the days after.

Tip

Serve this turkey salad on a bagel or on a bed of greens with vinaigrette.

1 lb	cooked turkey, bones and skin removed, shredded	500 g
½ cup	Traditional Mayonnaise (page 106) or store-bought	125 mL
¼ cup	chopped fresh dill	50 mL
2 tbsp	chopped green olives	25 mL
2 tsp	Tarragon Pickle Relish (page 135) or store-bought	10 mL
1 tsp	freshly squeezed lime juice	5 mL
1 tsp	sea salt	5 mL
1 tsp	ground white pepper	5 mL
½ tsp	Hungarian paprika	2 mL

1. In a bowl, using a fork, combine turkey, mayonnaise, dill, olives, pickle relish, lime juice, salt, white pepper and paprika. Mix just to combine.

Waldorf Salad

The first Waldorf salad was created in 1893 by Oscar Tschirky, the maître d'hôtel of the Waldorf Astoria hotel in New York City. There have been many variations, but this is pretty close to the original.

3 tbsp	Traditional Mayonnaise (page 106) or store-bought	45 mL
1 tbsp	freshly squeezed lemon juice	15 mL
1 tsp	sea salt	5 mL
½ tsp	ground white pepper	2 mL
½ cup	walnuts, chopped and toasted	125 mL
½ cup	diced celery	125 mL
½ cup	red seedless grapes, sliced	125 mL
1	small cooking apple, chopped	1
4 cups	salad greens	1 L

1. In a bowl, whisk together mayonnaise and lemon juice. Add salt and white pepper. Fold in walnuts, celery, grapes and apple.
2. Divide greens evenly onto 4 plates. Top each plate evenly with walnut mixture.

Watergate Salad

This yummy salad has nothing to do with Nixon and Watergate. The origin of the name is unknown, but the salad made its debut in the 1970s after the development of pistachio pudding, a key ingredient in the salad.

1	can (20 oz/575 mL) crushed pineapple with juice	1
1	box (4-serving size) instant dry pistachio pudding	1
9 oz	nondairy whipped topping	280 g
1 cup	miniature marshmallows	250 mL
½ cup	pecans, chopped and toasted	125 mL

1. In large bowl, combine pineapple and pudding. Fold in whipped topping, marshmallows and pecans. Refrigerate, tightly covered, for 2 hours prior to serving or for up to 2 days.

Accompaniments

Toppings and spiced nuts are all the rage on salads. A crisp garnish enlivens any salad. The extra texture and flavor provides a nice contrast to the softer greens and vegetables. In the past few years I have seen an explosion of different "salad toppers" in the produce section. Here, I've created a few to mix and match for truly unique salads. Keep these on hand — you can also use them to sprinkle on soup.

Cheese Puffs

Serves 8

These simple puffs are great to top your salads or soups.

Tip
You can store these puffs in a dry container at room temperature just as you do bread. Don't refrigerate them or they will become soggy.

- **Preheat oven to 425°F (220°C)**
- **Baking sheets, lined with parchment paper**

1	package (18 oz/540 g) puff pastry, thawed	1
1	egg, beaten	1
1 cup	freshly grated Parmesan cheese, divided	250 mL

1. On a lightly floured surface, roll out thawed pastry into two 14- by 10-inch (35 by 25 cm) sheets. Brush top of both with beaten egg.
2. Sprinkle each sheet of pastry with $\frac{1}{2}$ cup (125 mL) of the cheese. Press cheese into dough. Starting at one short side, fold in half. Cut crosswise into $\frac{1}{4}$-inch (0.5 cm) strips. Working with one strip at a time, hold each end in your hands and twist in opposite directions. Place on prepared baking sheet, at least $\frac{1}{2}$ inch (1 cm) apart. Repeat with second sheet of puff pastry. Bake in preheated oven until golden brown and puffed up, 18 to 24 minutes.

Cheese Tuiles

Serves 6

Keep your eye on the baking tuiles as they can burn very quickly — in less than 30 seconds. I like to stand up the tuiles in a salad to create height.

Tip
Make the tuiles in the morning of the day they will be served. Store in a cool, dry place. Do not refrigerate them, or they will become soggy.

Variation
You can add 1 tsp (5 mL) dried herbs to the cheese mixture before baking. Choose herbs that complement the salad you'll be serving.

- **Preheat oven to 350°F (180°C)**
- **2 baking sheets, lined with parchment paper**

5 oz	Parmesan cheese, grated (about 1 1/4 cups/300 mL)	150 g

1. Place 6 equal mounds of cheese on each prepared baking sheet. Bake, one sheet at a time, in preheated oven until golden brown and melted, 5 to 6 minutes. Let cool completely on baking sheet prior to transferring to a cooling rack.

Fried Capers

Serves 6

These capers are crunchy and perfect to top a Caesar salad.

Tip
For best results, fry the capers in small batches so you don't overcook them.

1/2 cup	canola oil	125 mL
1/4 cup	capers, drained	50 mL

1. In a skillet, heat oil over medium heat. Add capers in small batches, frying until light brown and crunchy, about 2 minutes. Drain on paper towels.

Garlic Croutons

Makes 4 cups (1 L)

I always seem to have extra bread left over. Homemade croutons are the perfect way to use every crumb.

Tip
Store croutons in an airtight container in a cool, dry place. Do not refrigerate them, or they will become soggy.

- **Preheat oven to 350°F (180°C)**
- **Baking sheet, lined with parchment paper**

²⁄₃ cup	olive oil	150 mL
3	cloves garlic, minced	3
1 tsp	dried parsley	5 mL
½ tsp	dried onion flakes	2 mL
¼ tsp	sea salt	1 mL
¼ tsp	freshly ground black pepper	1 mL
4 cups	cubed day-old bread	1 L

1. In a large bowl, combine oil, garlic, parsley, onion flakes, salt and pepper. Add bread cubes and mix to coat evenly.
2. Spread on prepared baking sheet in a single layer. Bake in preheated oven, turning occasionally, until golden brown, 12 to 16 minutes.

Glazed Hot Pecans

Makes 1½ cups (375 mL)

These pecans add sweetness and crunch on a salad dressed with a light vinaigrette.

Tip
Store glazed pecans in an airtight container in a cool, dry place. Do not refrigerate them, or they will become soggy.

- **Preheat oven to 350°F (180°C)**
- **Baking sheet, lined with parchment paper**

1½ cups	pecan halves	375 mL
1	egg white, beaten	1
½ cup	granulated sugar	125 mL
¼ tsp	cayenne pepper	1 mL

1. In a bowl, combine pecan halves, egg white, sugar and cayenne.
2. Spread on prepared baking sheet in a single layer. Bake in preheated oven, turning occasionally, until caramelized, 20 to 22 minutes. Let cool completely before removing from baking sheet. They will dry and harden when cooling.

Fresh Herbed Croutons

Makes 4 cups (1 L)

When teaching in France, my rule was "fresh bread daily," so we could make croutons with any leftover day-old bread.

Tip
Store croutons in an airtight container in a cool, dry place. Do not refrigerate them, or they will become soggy.

- **Preheat oven to 350°F (180°C)**
- **Baking sheet, lined with parchment paper**

2/3 cup	herbed olive oil	150 mL
2 tsp	chopped fresh tarragon	10 mL
1 tsp	chopped fresh dill	5 mL
1/2 tsp	chopped fresh rosemary	2 mL
1/2 tsp	dried parsley	2 mL
1/2 tsp	dried onion flakes	2 mL
1/4 tsp	sea salt	1 mL
1/4 tsp	freshly ground black pepper	1 mL
4 cups	cubed day-old bread	1 L

1. In a large bowl, combine oil, tarragon, dill, rosemary, parsley, onion flakes, salt and pepper. Add bread cubes and mix to coat evenly.
2. Spread on prepared baking sheet in a single layer. Bake in preheated oven, turning occasionally, until golden brown, 12 to 16 minutes.

Peppered Walnuts

**Makes 2 cups
(500 mL)**

*Hot and spicy, these walnuts
are great on Asian salads.*

Tip
Store peppered walnuts in
an airtight container, in
a cool, dry place. Do not
refrigerate them, or they
will become soggy.

- **Preheat oven to 350°F (180°C)**
- **2 baking sheets, lined with parchment paper**

¾ cup	granulated sugar	175 mL
2 tbsp	unsalted butter	25 mL
2 cups	walnut halves	500 mL
1 tsp	sea salt	5 mL
1 tsp	freshly ground black pepper	5 mL
½ tsp	ground cumin	2 mL
¼ tsp	cayenne pepper	1 mL

1. In a small heavy-bottomed saucepan over high heat, cook sugar, stirring until it turns light caramel color, 4 to 5 minutes. Remove from heat and carefully add butter and stir until melted. Add nuts and stir to coat evenly.
2. Transfer nuts to one of the prepared baking sheets in a single layer. Bake in preheated oven, tossing every 5 minutes, until nuts are toasted, about 15 minutes.
3. Remove from oven and place in a large bowl. Add salt, black pepper, cumin and cayenne and quickly toss to coat evenly. Transfer nuts to other prepared baking sheet and separate nuts with a fork. Let cool completely before using.

Spicy Sunflower Seeds

**Makes 2 cups
(500 mL)**

When I was a kid, sunflower seeds were the rage. I never knew how good they were in salads until this recipe.

Tip

Store spicy sunflower seeds in an airtight container, in a cool, dry place. Do not refrigerate them, or they will become soggy.

- **Preheat oven to 350°F (180°C)**
- **Baking sheet, lined with parchment paper**

2 cups	sunflower seeds	500 mL
2 tbsp	granulated sugar	25 mL
3/4 tsp	sea salt	3 mL
1/2 tsp	ground cinnamon	2 mL
1/8 tsp	ground allspice	0.5 mL
1/8 tsp	curry powder	0.5 mL
1/8 tsp	cayenne pepper	0.5 mL
1 tbsp	water	15 mL
1 tbsp	canola oil	15 mL
2 tsp	vanilla extract	10 mL
1 tsp	lightly packed brown sugar	5 mL

1. Spread sunflower seeds on prepared baking sheet. Toast in preheated oven, stirring occasionally to make sure they brown evenly, for 6 minutes.
2. In a small bowl, stir together granulated sugar, salt, cinnamon, allspice, curry powder and cayenne. Set aside.
3. In a medium saucepan over medium heat, combine water, oil, vanilla and brown sugar. Bring to a boil, whisking constantly. Stir in toasted seeds and continue stirring until shiny and liquid has evaporated, 1 to 2 minutes.
4. Transfer seeds to a bowl. Sprinkle with spice mixture and toss to coat well. Spread coated nuts on same prepared baking sheet and return to preheated oven for another 4 minutes. Let cool on pan.

Roasted Corn

**Makes 2 cups
(500 mL)**

*I enjoy roasted corn kernels
shaved from the cob and
sprinkled on top of a spicy
salad with a peppery dressing.*

Tip

You can roast and use
2 cups (500 mL) frozen
corn kernels if fresh corn is
out of season.

2 tbsp	olive oil	25 mL
3	ears white corn, kernels removed (about 2 cups/500 mL) (see Tip, left)	3
½ tsp	sea salt	2 mL
¼ tsp	cayenne pepper	1 mL

1. In a skillet, heat oil over medium heat. Add corn, stirring until completely roasted, about 10 minutes. Sprinkle with salt and cayenne. Let cool. Transfer to a covered dish and refrigerate until ready to use or for up to 4 days.

Mayonnaise and Other Condiments

Mayonnaise and Aïolis

You can walk down the condiment aisle at the grocery store and see many brands and varieties, in jar after jar. I can't even pronounce many of the ingredients in these jars, let alone understand how they can last for months — or years — in the refrigerator. When you make your own condiments you know exactly what's in each, and how long it will last. Once you make mayonnaise, you will never purchase it again.

Traditional Mayonnaise

Makes 1 cup (250 mL)

If you've never tasted fresh homemade mayonnaise you are in for a treat. Fresh mayonnaise is so silky and nothing like its stepsister in the jar.

Tips

This recipe contains raw egg yolks. If you are concerned about the safety of using raw eggs, use pasteurized eggs in the shell or pasteurized liquid whole eggs, instead.

Mayonnaise keeps well, covered and refrigerated, for up to 5 days. If using pasteurized eggs, it will keep for up to 2 weeks.

If egg yolks are not processed for the full 2 minutes they will not emulsify correctly when the oil is incorporated.

Variation

Try flavored oils in place of the plain vegetable oil to enhance your dishes.

• **Food Processor**

2	egg yolks, at room temperature, or ¼ cup (50 mL) pasteurized eggs (liquid or in the shell) (see Tips, left)	2
2 tbsp	white wine vinegar	25 mL
1 tsp	dry mustard	5 mL
1 tsp	sea salt	5 mL
1 tsp	granulated sugar	5 mL
½ tsp	ground white pepper	2 mL
1 cup	vegetable oil	250 mL

1. In a food processor fitted with a metal blade, process egg yolks, vinegar, mustard, salt, sugar and pepper until smooth, for 2 minutes (see Tips, left). With the processor running, slowly drizzle oil through the small hole in the feed tube until it has been incorporated into the mayonnaise (see Tips, page 108).

2. When all the oil is drizzled into egg mixture, remove processor lid and, with a rubber spatula, scrape down the sides and bottom, which sometimes collect residue, as necessary to incorporate all of the mixture. Replace lid and process for about 15 seconds.

Cajun Mayonnaise

Makes 1 cup (250 mL)

Here's a hot and spicy mayonnaise to use in place of the Traditional Mayonnaise when you want to add zest.

Tip
Mayonnaise keeps well, covered and refrigerated, for up to 5 days. If using pasteurized eggs, it will keep for up to 2 weeks.

- **Blender**

½ cup	green onions, finely chopped	125 mL
2	egg yolks, at room temperature, or ¼ cup (50 mL) pasteurized eggs (liquid or in the shell) (see Tips, page 106)	2
1 tbsp	freshly squeezed lemon juice	15 mL
1 tsp	sea salt	5 mL
1	clove garlic, minced	1
⅛ tsp	hot pepper sauce	0.5 mL
1 cup	vegetable oil	250 mL

1. In a blender, combine green onions, egg yolks, lemon juice, salt, garlic and hot pepper sauce. Blend for 2 minutes (see Tips, page 106). With the motor running, slowly drizzle oil through the small hole in the feed tube until it has been incorporated into the mayonnaise (see Tips, page 108).

2. When all the oil is drizzled into egg mixture, remove blender lid and, with a rubber spatula, scrape down the sides and bottom, which sometimes collect residue, as necessary to incorporate all of the mixture. Replace lid and blend for about 30 seconds.

Fresh Dill Mayonnaise

Makes 1½ cups (375 mL)

I love using this spread on roasted chicken sandwiches.

Tips

Mayonnaise keeps well, covered and refrigerated, for up to 5 days. If using pasteurized eggs, it will keep for up to 1 week. I do not advise making a double batch of this mayonnaise unless you use it within a week, since the dill will turn dark after that.

If your food processor has a feed tube with the drip feature (a small hole in the bottom of the tube), fill the tube with oil and let it drizzle in, refilling the tube with oil as it drains until all of the oil is incorporated. Alternatively, pour a thin, steady stream of oil slowly into the feed tube. Adding the oil too quickly can cause the mayonnaise to separate.

Variation

Try the same amount of rosemary in place of the dill.

- **Food Processor**

3	egg yolks, at room temperature, or ⅓ cup (75 mL) pasteurized eggs (liquid or in the shell) (see Tips, page 106)	3
3 tbsp	sherry vinegar	45 mL
2 tsp	mustard seeds	10 mL
2 tsp	sea salt	10 mL
1½ tsp	granulated sugar	7 mL
1 tsp	ground white pepper	5 mL
1 cup	peanut oil	250 mL
2 tbsp	loosely packed fresh dill	25 mL

1. In a food processor fitted with a metal blade, process egg yolks, vinegar, mustard seeds, salt, sugar and pepper until smooth, for 2 minutes (see Tips, page 106). With the motor running, slowly drizzle oil through the small hole in the feed tube until it has been incorporated into the mayonnaise (see Tips, left).

2. When all the oil is drizzled into egg mixture, remove processor lid and, with a rubber spatula, scrape down the sides and bottom, which sometimes collect residue, as necessary to incorporate all of the mixture. Add fresh dill. Replace lid and process for about 15 seconds.

Chipotle Mayonnaise

A dollop of this tasty mayonnaise on the side of any meat dish will enhance the flavor.

Tips

If egg yolks are not processed for the full 2 minutes they will not emulsify correctly when the oil is incorporated.

Mayonnaise keeps well, covered and refrigerated, for up to 5 days. If using pasteurized eggs, it will keep for up to 2 weeks.

If you have any of the adobo sauce left from the chiles you can fold it into the mayonnaise to make a great dip for chips.

Variation

You can add $\frac{1}{8}$ tsp (0.5 mL) cayenne pepper for more heat.

● **Food processor**

2	egg yolks, at room temperature, or $\frac{1}{4}$ cup (50 mL) pasteurized eggs (liquid or in the shell) (see Tips, page 106)	2
2 tbsp	white wine vinegar	25 mL
1 tsp	dry mustard	5 mL
1 tsp	sea salt	5 mL
1 tsp	granulated sugar	5 mL
$\frac{1}{2}$ tsp	ground white pepper	2 mL
$\frac{1}{4}$ tsp	ground nutmeg	1 mL
$\frac{3}{4}$ cup	vegetable oil	175 mL
2	chipotle peppers in adobo sauce, drained and seeded	2

1. In a food processor fitted with a metal blade, process egg yolks, vinegar, mustard, salt, sugar, pepper and nutmeg until smooth, for 2 minutes (see Tips, left). With the motor running, slowly drizzle oil through the small hole in the feed tube until it has been incorporated into the mayonnaise (see Tips, page 108).
2. When all the oil is drizzled into egg mixture, remove processor lid and, with a rubber spatula, scrape down the sides and bottom, which sometimes collect residue, as necessary to incorporate all of the mixture. Add chipotle peppers. Replace lid and process for about 10 seconds.

No-Egg Mayonnaise

Makes 1⅓ cups (325 mL)

This is a perfect creamy mayonnaise when you can't have eggs.

Tip

Mayonnaise keeps well, covered and refrigerated, for up to 5 days.

- **Blender**

½ cup	soft tofu, drained	125 mL
2 tbsp	white wine vinegar	25 mL
½ tsp	dry mustard	2 mL
½ tsp	mustard seeds	2 mL
½ tsp	sea salt	2 mL
¾ cup	vegetable oil, divided	175 mL

1. In a blender, combine tofu, vinegar, mustard, mustard seeds, salt and ¼ cup (50 mL) of the vegetable oil. Blend for 2 minutes.
2. With the blender running, slowly drizzle remaining ½ cup (125 mL) of oil in a very thin stream through the hole in the lid until it has been incorporated into the mayonnaise (see Tips, page 108).

Avocado Mayonnaise

Makes 1 cup (250 mL)

Here's another no-egg mayonnaise that I also like to use as a spread.

- **Food processor**

1	ripe avocado, cut into quarters	1
2 tbsp	freshly squeezed lime juice	25 mL
2 tbsp	fresh cilantro	25 mL
¼ tsp	sea salt	1 mL
¼ tsp	freshly ground black pepper	1 mL
2 tbsp	extra virgin olive oil	25 mL

1. In a food processor fitted with a metal blade, process avocado, lime juice, cilantro, salt and pepper until smooth.
2. With the motor running, slowly drizzle oil through the small hole in the feed tube until it has been incorporated into mayonnaise. Use within a few hours.

Low-Fat No-Egg Mayonnaise

Makes 1 cup (250 mL)

Sometimes you need to make a low-fat and no-egg mayonnaise for dressings — you won't get much better than this.

Tip
Mayonnaise keeps well, covered and refrigerated, for up to 1 week.

Variation
Add 1 tsp (5 mL) Spicy Chile Sauce (page 124) to make a spicy mayonnaise.

1 cup	cold water	250 mL
1 tbsp	cornstarch	15 mL
2 tbsp	extra virgin olive oil	25 mL
2 tbsp	white wine vinegar	25 mL
2 tbsp	plain low-fat yogurt	25 mL
1 tsp	Dijon Mustard (page 120) or store-bought	5 mL
½ tsp	prepared horseradish	2 mL

1. In a small saucepan over medium heat, whisk together water and cornstarch. Whisk continuously until mixture comes to a boil and turns clear, about 3 minutes.
2. Pour mixture into a bowl and whisk in olive oil, vinegar, yogurt, mustard and horseradish until blended. Let cool before serving.

Tartar Sauce

Makes 1¼ cups (300 mL)

Kids love this sauce with fish sticks. Grown-ups love it with crab cakes.

Tip
Sauce keeps well, covered and refrigerated, for up to 2 weeks.

- **Food processor**

1 cup	Traditional Mayonnaise (page 106) or store-bought	250 mL
¼ cup	sour cream	50 mL
1	sweet pickle, cut into pieces	1
2 tbsp	capers, drained	25 mL
1 tbsp	white wine vinegar	15 mL
1 tbsp	Italian flat-leaf parsley	15 mL
5	fresh chives	5
2 tsp	fresh tarragon leaves	10 mL
	Salt and freshly ground black pepper	

1. In a food processor fitted with a metal blade, process mayonnaise, sour cream, pickle, capers, vinegar, parsley, chives and tarragon until smooth, about 30 seconds. Season with salt and pepper to taste.

Basic Aïoli

Makes 1 cup (250 mL)

Aïoli sauces are used most often with fish dishes to add richness, flavor and spice. This sauce has a similar texture to mayonnaise.

Tip
Aïoli keeps well, covered and refrigerated, for up to 3 days.

- **Food processor or blender**

6	cloves garlic	6
1	egg or ¼ cup (50 mL) pasteurized eggs (liquid or in the shell) (see Tips, page 106)	1
1 cup	extra virgin olive oil, divided	250 mL
1 tbsp	freshly squeezed lemon juice	15 mL
⅛ tsp	sea salt	0.5 mL
⅛ tsp	freshly ground white pepper	0.5 mL

1. In a food processor fitted with a metal blade with motor running, add garlic cloves through feed tube and process until minced. Add egg, ½ cup (125 mL) of the oil, lemon juice, salt and pepper.
2. With the motor running, slowly drizzle remaining oil through the small hole in the feed tube until it has been incorporated into aïoli, about 2 minutes. Use right away or refrigerate.

Basic Rémoulade Sauce

Makes ¾ cup (175 mL)

This sauce is great with crab or chicken cakes.

Tip
Sauce keeps well, covered and refrigerated, for up to 3 days.

½ cup	Traditional Mayonnaise (page 106) or store-bought	125 mL
2 tbsp	finely chopped green onions	25 mL
2 tbsp	finely chopped sweet pickles	25 mL
1 tbsp	chopped Italian flat-leaf parsley	15 mL
1 tbsp	extra virgin olive oil	15 mL
2 tsp	freshly squeezed lemon juice	10 mL
1 tsp	Dijon Mustard (page 120) or store-bought	5 mL
¼ tsp	garlic powder	1 mL
¼ tsp	Worcestershire Sauce (page 142) or store-bought	1 mL
¼ tsp	freshly ground black pepper	1 mL

1. In a bowl, whisk together mayonnaise, green onions, pickles, parsley, oil, lemon juice, mustard, garlic powder, Worcestershire sauce and black pepper. Cover and refrigerate immediately for at least 1 hour before serving.

Citrus Aïoli

Makes 1 cup (250 mL)

This aïoli is great spooned over freshly grilled fish.

Tip
Aïoli keeps well, covered and refrigerated, for up to 3 days.

● **Food processor**

6	cloves garlic	6
2	egg yolks, at room temperature, or 1/4 cup (50 mL) pasteurized eggs (liquid or in the shell) (see Tips, page 106)	2
1 cup	extra virgin olive oil, divided	250 mL
1 tbsp	freshly squeezed lemon juice	15 mL
1/2 tsp	grated lime zest	2 mL
1 tsp	freshly squeezed lime juice	5 mL
1/8 tsp	sea salt	0.5 mL
1/8 tsp	freshly ground white pepper	0.5 mL

1. In a food processor fitted with a metal blade with motor running, add garlic cloves through feed tube and process until minced. Add egg yolks, 1/2 cup (125 mL) of the oil, lemon juice, lime zest and juice, salt and white pepper.
2. With the motor running, slowly drizzle remaining oil through the small hole in the feed tube until it has been incorporated into aïoli, about 2 minutes. Use right away or refrigerate.

Latin Aïoli

Makes 1 cup (250 mL)

Try this aïoli with a spicy dish such as Jerk Chicken.

Tip
Aïoli keeps well, covered and refrigerated, for up to 3 days.

• **Food processor**

6	cloves garlic	6
1	egg or $\frac{1}{4}$ cup (50 mL) pasteurized eggs (liquid or in the shell) (see Tips, page 106)	1
1 cup	extra virgin olive oil, divided	250 mL
1 tbsp	freshly squeezed lemon juice	15 mL
1 tsp	cayenne pepper	5 mL
$\frac{1}{2}$ tsp	adobe seasoning	2 mL
$\frac{1}{8}$ tsp	sea salt	0.5 mL
$\frac{1}{8}$ tsp	ground white pepper	0.5 mL
3	drops hot pepper sauce	3
$\frac{1}{4}$ cup	chopped fresh cilantro	50 mL

1. In a food processor fitted with a metal blade with motor running, add garlic cloves through feed tube and process until minced. Add egg, $\frac{1}{2}$ cup (125 mL) of the oil, lemon juice, cayenne pepper, adobe seasoning, salt, white pepper and hot pepper sauce.
2. With the motor running, slowly drizzle remaining oil through the small hole in the feed tube until it has been incorporated into aïoli, about 2 minutes. Fold in cilantro. Use right away or refrigerate.

Ketchups and Mustards

Easy Ketchup

Makes 2 cups (500 mL)

Making your own ketchup may seem a bit over-the-top but it's worth it. It's easy to make, and the homemade version is so much more delicious than supermarket varieties, which are loaded with corn syrup.

Tip
Ketchup keeps well, tightly covered and refrigerated, for up to 1 week.

● **Blender or food processor**

1	can (28 oz/796 mL) crushed tomatoes	1
2 tbsp	extra virgin olive oil	25 mL
1	onion, chopped	1
1 tbsp	tomato paste	15 mL
2/3 cup	lightly packed brown sugar	150 mL
1/2 cup	cider vinegar	125 mL
1/2 tsp	sea salt	2 mL

1. In a blender, purée tomatoes until smooth.
2. In a heavy saucepan, heat oil over medium heat. Add onion and cook, stirring, until softened and translucent, about 8 minutes.
3. Add puréed tomatoes, tomato paste, brown sugar, vinegar and salt. Simmer, stirring occasionally, until very thick, about 1 hour. (Stir more frequently toward end of cooking to prevent scorching.)
4. Add ketchup to blender in 2 batches and purée until smooth. Let cool.

Country Ketchup

This ketchup is a little sweet, but the vinegar provides a perfect balance.

Tip
Ketchup keeps well, tightly covered and refrigerated, for up to 2 weeks.

● **Food mill**

4 lbs	Roma (plum) tomatoes, quartered	2 kg
1/2	onion, chopped	1/2
1/8 tsp	cayenne pepper	0.5 mL
1/2 cup	granulated sugar	125 mL
1/2 cup	white wine vinegar	125 mL
2 tsp	sea salt	10 mL
1/2 tsp	ground cinnamon	2 mL
1/2 tsp	dill seeds	2 mL
1/4 tsp	ground cloves	1 mL

1. In a Dutch oven over medium heat, bring tomatoes, onion and cayenne to a boil and cook, stirring occasionally, until tomatoes are soft, about 15 minutes. Transfer tomatoes to a food mill fitted with a fine plate and press to extract juice into a medium saucepan. Discard solids.
2. Stir in sugar. Place saucepan over medium–high heat and bring to a boil. Reduce heat to low and simmer, stirring occasionally, until thick enough to mound on a spoon, about 45 minutes.
3. In a small saucepan over medium heat, bring vinegar, salt, cinnamon, dill seeds and cloves to a boil. Let stand for 5 minutes. Stir in tomato sauce and cook until bubbling. Let cool.

Chunky Ketchup

I like to eat this ketchup on toasted bread that's topped with cheese — sort of a quick pizza for one.

Tip
Ketchup keeps well, tightly covered and refrigerated, for up to 3 days.

- **Preheat oven to 475°F (240°C)**
- **Baking sheet, lined with parchment paper**
- **Food processor**

12 oz	Roma (plum) tomatoes, cut in half lengthwise, seeded and juice removed	375 g
¼	large green bell pepper	¼
1	onion, sliced	1
2 tbsp	extra virgin olive oil	25 mL
1 tbsp	cider vinegar	15 mL
2 tsp	lightly packed brown sugar	10 mL
2 tsp	dried parsley	10 mL
1 tsp	dry mustard	5 mL
½ tsp	dried thyme leaves	2 mL
½ tsp	sea salt	2 mL
½ tsp	freshly ground black pepper	2 mL
⅛ tsp	garlic powder	0.5 mL
⅛ tsp	ground cinnamon	0.5 mL

1. On prepared baking sheet, place tomatoes, skin side up, green pepper and onion. Brush very lightly with olive oil. Roast in preheated oven until lightly browned, about 15 minutes. Let cool slightly.
2. In a food processor fitted with a metal blade, pulse tomatoes, pepper and onion until chunky, about 10 times. Place chunky vegetables in a bowl. Stir in vinegar, brown sugar, parsley, mustard, thyme, salt, pepper, garlic powder and cinnamon. Let cool.

Roasted Red Pepper Ketchup

**Makes 3 cups
(750 mL)**

*Here's a sweet ruby red
ketchup with the added flavor
of red peppers.*

Tips

Ketchup keeps well, tightly
covered and refrigerated, for
up to 1 week.

If you prefer smooth
ketchup, purée it in a
blender or food processor
until it's the desired texture.

1	can (14 oz/398 mL) diced tomatoes with juice	1
1	jar (7 oz/210 mL) roasted red peppers, drained	1
1	red onion, chopped	1
½ cup	dry red wine	125 mL
6 tbsp	lightly packed brown sugar	90 mL
3	cloves garlic, minced	3
2	large dried ancho chiles, seeded and coarsely chopped	2
1	bay leaf	1
2 tbsp	tomato paste	25 mL
2 tbsp	red wine vinegar	25 mL
1 tbsp	fennel seeds	15 mL
1 ½ tsp	ground cumin	7 mL

1 In large heavy saucepan over high heat, combine tomatoes
with juice, red peppers, onion, wine, brown sugar, garlic,
ancho chiles, bay leaf, tomato paste, vinegar, fennel seeds
and cumin and bring to a boil. Reduce heat and simmer,
stirring occasionally, until reduced to 3 cups (750 mL),
about 30 minutes. Let cool. Discard bay leaf.

No-Sugar Ketchup

Makes 2 cups (500 mL)

Use this ketchup when you want to cut calories — most store-bought ketchups are packed with sugars.

Tip
Ketchup keeps well, tightly covered and refrigerated, for up to 1 week.

3 cups	tomato juice	750 mL
1/4 cup	cider vinegar	50 mL
1/4 cup	sugar substitute, such as Splenda	50 mL
1 1/2 tsp	dried green pepper flakes	7 mL
1/2 tsp	dried onion flakes	2 mL
1/4 tsp	freshly ground black pepper	1 mL
1/8 tsp	dried rosemary	0.5 mL
1/8 tsp	dried thyme	0.5 mL
1/8 tsp	dried basil	0.5 mL
1/8 tsp	dried parsley	0.5 mL

1. In a large saucepan over medium heat, combine tomato juice, vinegar, sugar substitute, green pepper flakes, onion flakes, black pepper, rosemary, thyme, basil and parsley and bring to a boil. Reduce heat and simmer, stirring occasionally, until thickened, about 1 hour. Let cool.

Spiced Ketchup

Makes 1/2 cup (125 mL)

Here's a spicy ketchup for added punch.

Tip
Ketchup keeps well, tightly covered and refrigerated, for up to 1 week.

1/2 cup	Country Ketchup (page 116) or store-bought	125 mL
1/3 cup	freshly squeezed orange juice	75 mL
1	dried habanero chile	1
1 tbsp	light (fancy) molasses	15 mL
1/2 tsp	Worcestershire Sauce (page 142) or store-bought	2 mL
1/4 tsp	whole cloves	1 mL

1. In a small saucepan over medium-high heat, combine ketchup, orange juice, habanero, molasses, Worcestershire sauce and cloves. Reduce heat and simmer, stirring occasionally, for 5 minutes. Strain through a fine-mesh sieve into a bowl, discarding habanero and cloves. Let cool.

Honey Mustard Sauce

Makes 1 cup (250 mL)

I use this as a quick-to-make dipping sauce for scallops or shrimp.

Tip
Sauce keeps well, covered and refrigerated, for up to 2 weeks.

1 cup	liquid honey	250 mL
2 tbsp	prepared mustard	25 mL
1 tsp	hot pepper flakes	5 mL
1 tsp	sea salt	5 mL

1. In a small bowl, whisk together honey, mustard, hot pepper flakes and salt.

Dijon Mustard

Makes 1½ cups (375 mL)

Nothing tastes as good as homemade mustards. This is a perfect pantry mustard for you to try.

Tip
Mustard keeps well, covered and refrigerated, for up to 3 weeks.

2 cups	dry white wine	500 mL
1 cup	chopped onion	250 mL
2 tbsp	liquid honey	25 mL
2	cloves garlic, minced	2
½ cup	dry mustard	125 mL
1 tbsp	vegetable oil	15 mL
2 tsp	sea salt	10 mL
4	drops hot pepper sauce	4

1. In a medium saucepan over medium heat, combine wine, onion, honey and garlic and bring to a boil. Reduce heat and simmer for 5 minutes. Pour into a bowl and let cool.
2. Strain through a fine-mesh sieve back into the saucepan. Whisk in dry mustard until smooth. Whisk in oil, salt and hot pepper sauce. Cook over medium heat, stirring, until thickened, about 5 minutes. Let cool.

Fast and Easy Mustard

Makes 1²⁄₃ cups (400 mL)

Why purchase prepared mustard when you can make it yourself? It's quick and easy, and you'll know exactly what's in it.

Tip
Mustard keeps well, covered and refrigerated, for up to 2 weeks.

1 cup	dry mustard	250 mL
¹⁄₃ cup	cold water	75 mL
¹⁄₃ cup	red wine vinegar	75 mL

1. In a bowl, whisk together dry mustard, cold water and vinegar until smooth.
2. Refrigerate for at least 2 days for flavors to blend prior to use.

Honey Yellow Mustard

Makes ²⁄₃ cup (150 mL)

As this mustard ages, its initial heat will lessen.

Tip
Mustard keeps well, covered and refrigerated, for up to 2 weeks.

¹⁄₂ cup	dry mustard	125 mL
¹⁄₃ cup	white wine vinegar	75 mL
1 tsp	liquid honey	5 mL
¹⁄₂ tsp	sea salt	2 mL

1. In a bowl, whisk together dry mustard, vinegar, honey and sea salt.
2. Refrigerate for at least 2 days for flavors to blend prior to use.

Coarse Brown Mustard

Makes ²⁄₃ cup (150 mL)

Spread this mustard on ham slices or pork chops.

Tip
Mustard keeps well, covered and refrigerated, for up to 2 weeks.

¹⁄₂ cup	dry mustard	125 mL
¹⁄₃ cup	cider vinegar	75 mL
2 tbsp	brewed espresso	25 mL
2 tsp	mustard seeds	10 mL
¹⁄₂ tsp	salt	2 mL

1. In a bowl, whisk together dry mustard, vinegar, espresso, mustard seeds and salt.
2. Refrigerate for at least 2 days for flavors to blend prior to use.

Honey Stone-Ground Mustard

**Makes 1½ cups
(375 mL)**

*Sometimes you need a
mustard with texture.
This one has it.*

Tip
Mustard keeps well, covered
and refrigerated, for up to
3 weeks.

1 cup	dry mustard	250 mL
1 cup	dry white wine	250 mL
½ cup	chopped onion	125 mL
6 tbsp	water	90 mL
3 tbsp	white wine vinegar	45 mL
3	cloves garlic, minced	3
2 tsp	mustard seeds	10 mL
1 tsp	granulated sugar	5 mL
¾ tsp	sea salt	3 mL
1	bay leaf	1
½ tsp	whole allspice	2 mL
½ cup	liquid honey	125 mL

1. In a medium saucepan over medium heat, whisk together
   dry mustard, wine, onion, water, vinegar, garlic, mustard
   seeds, sugar, salt, bay leaf and allspice and bring to a boil.
   Reduce heat and boil, stirring, until reduced by half,
   about 12 minutes. Strain through a large mesh strainer,
   discarding bay leaf and allspice. Stir in honey. Let cool.

Creole Mustard

**Makes ¾ cup
(175 mL)**

*In New Orleans, I noticed
that all the city's restaurants
have a Creole mustard —
now you can make a quick
and easy version at home.*

Tip
Sauce keeps well, covered
and refrigerated, for up to
2 weeks.

½ cup	dry mustard	125 mL
⅓ cup	red wine vinegar	75 mL
2 tsp	mustard seeds	10 mL
½ tsp	sea salt	2 mL
¼ tsp	cayenne pepper	1 mL
5	drops hot pepper sauce	5

1. In a bowl, whisk together dry mustard, vinegar, mustard
   seeds, salt, cayenne and hot pepper sauce.
2. Refrigerate for at least 2 days for flavors to blend prior
   to use.

Chili Sauces

Smoked Chili Sauce

**Makes about
2 cups (500 mL)**

This sauce is so versatile, you can use it as a barbecue sauce or in many of the recipes mentioned in this book.

Tips
Sauce keeps well, covered and refrigerated, for up to 3 weeks.

Using two types of vinegars prevents a bitter aftertaste.

Variation
Omit the chipotle peppers for a basic chili sauce.

- **Food processor or blender**

1 cup	natural rice vinegar	250 mL
1 cup	cider vinegar	250 mL
2 tsp	ground cloves	10 mL
1 tsp	ground allspice	5 mL
1	onion, cut into quarters	1
10	cloves garlic	10
1 cup	lightly packed brown sugar	250 mL
1½ cups	Easy Ketchup (page 115) or store-bought	375 mL
1	can (7 oz/210 mL) chipotle peppers in adobo sauce, drained	1
2 tbsp	fresh cilantro leaves	25 mL
1 tbsp	Worcestershire Sauce (page 142) or store-bought	15 mL

1. In a deep saucepan over medium heat, combine rice vinegar, cider vinegar, cloves and allspice. Bring to a gentle boil. Set aside.

2. In a food processor fitted with a metal blade, process onion, garlic, brown sugar, ketchup, chipotle peppers, cilantro and Worcestershire sauce until finely chopped, about 30 seconds. Add to cider mixture and bring to a gentle boil, stirring occasionally, over medium heat. Reduce heat and boil gently, stirring often, until thickened, about 1 hour. Let cool.

Spicy Chili Sauce

**Makes 2 cups
(500 mL)**

*Here's a perfect condiment
for a hamburger or beef
sandwich.*

Tip
Sauce keeps well, covered
and refrigerated, for up to
1 week.

- **Food processor or blender**

1	can (7 oz/210 mL) chipotle peppers in adobo sauce with liquid	1
1	onion, cut into wedges	1
12	cloves garlic	12
1 cup	lightly packed brown sugar	250 mL
2 cups	white wine vinegar	500 mL
1 cup	Easy Ketchup or Country (pages 115 and 116) or store-bought	250 mL
1/4 cup	extra virgin olive oil	50 mL
1/4 cup	light (fancy) molasses	50 mL
1 tbsp	Worcestershire Sauce (page 142) or store-bought	15 mL
2 tsp	ground cloves	10 mL
2 tsp	ground coriander	10 mL
1 tsp	ground cinnamon	5 mL
1 tsp	ground allspice	5 mL
1 tsp	hot pepper sauce	5 mL
1/8 tsp	sea salt	0.5 mL

1. In a food processor fitted with a metal blade, process chipotle peppers in adobo sauce, onion and garlic until puréed, about 1 minute. Add brown sugar and purée until smooth. Set aside.
2. In a medium saucepan over medium heat, combine vinegar, ketchup, olive oil, molasses, Worcestershire sauce, cloves, coriander, cinnamon, allspice and hot pepper sauce. Cook, stirring occasionally, until reduced by half, 14 to 16 minutes. Stir in puréed pepper mixture. Reduce heat to low and cook, stirring occasionally, until thickened, for 1 hour. Season with salt. Let cool.

Bold Chili Sauce

**Makes 3 cups
(750 mL)**

*This bold and spicy sauce is
all you need on hot dogs or
steak burgers.*

Tip
Sauce keeps well, covered
and refrigerated, for up to
1 week.

- **Preheat oven to 400°F (200°C)**
- **Baking sheet, lined with parchment paper**
- **Food processor or blender**

16	dried guajillo chiles	16
2 tbsp	canola oil	25 mL
6	cloves garlic	6
1½ tbsp	extra virgin olive oil	22 mL
1½ tsp	granulated sugar	7 mL
1 tsp	dried oregano	5 mL
1 tsp	sea salt	5 mL
¼ tsp	freshly ground black pepper	1 mL
⅛ tsp	ground cumin	0.5 mL
3 cups	Beef Stock (page 147) or ready-to-use broth	750 mL

1. Place chiles on prepared baking sheet. Brush with canola oil. Roast in preheated oven until soft, about 15 minutes. Split the chiles and remove the seeds. Place in a bowl with enough hot water to cover and let soak for 10 minutes. Drain and transfer to a food processor fitted with a metal blade and process until smooth. Add garlic, olive oil, sugar, oregano, salt, pepper and cumin and process for 15 seconds.

2. Transfer mixture to a medium saucepan over medium heat. Add beef stock and simmer, stirring occasionally, until thickened, for 30 minutes. Let cool.

Steak Sauce

Makes 2 cups (500 mL)

Bottled steak sauce is full of sugar. Cut down on the sugar and create a sauce that will make your steaks burst with flavor.

Tip

Sauce keeps well, covered and refrigerated, for up to 1 week.

● **Blender or food processor**

1 cup	Country Ketchup (page 116) or store-bought	250 mL
1	onion, coarsely chopped	1
6	cloves garlic	6
1/4 cup	water	50 mL
1/4 cup	Worcestershire Sauce (page 142) or store-bought	50 mL
1/4 cup	freshly squeezed lemon juice	50 mL
1/4 cup	white wine vinegar	50 mL
1/4 cup	chopped shallots	50 mL
3 tbsp	lightly packed brown sugar	45 mL
2 tbsp	reduced-sodium soy sauce	25 mL
1 tsp	dry mustard	5 mL
1/2 tsp	dried onion powder	2 mL
1/4 tsp	ground cloves	1 mL
1/4 tsp	ground cinnamon	1 mL

1. In a blender, combine ketchup, onion, garlic, water, Worcestershire sauce, lemon juice, vinegar, shallots, brown sugar, soy sauce, mustard, onion powder, cloves and cinnamon. Blend until smooth. Transfer mixture to a medium saucepan over medium heat and bring to a boil. Reduce heat and simmer, stirring occasionally, until thickened, for 20 minutes. Let cool.

Chutneys

Cranberry Shallot Chutney

**Makes 3 cups
(750 mL)**

*Whether spread on turkey
sandwiches or served
as a condiment with
Thanksgiving dinner, this
chutney is perfection.*

Tips

Chutney keeps well,
covered and refrigerated,
for up to 1 week.

To toast nuts: Spread nuts in
a single layer on a baking
sheet. Bake in a preheated
350°F (180°C) oven until
fragrant, about 8 minutes.

3 cups	cranberries	750 mL
2	large baking apples (Granny Smith or Red Rome), peeled and chopped	2
1¼ cups	lightly packed brown sugar	300 mL
½ cup	golden raisins	125 mL
½ cup	minced shallots	125 mL
⅓ cup	red wine vinegar	75 mL
¼ cup	finely chopped candied ginger	50 mL
1 tsp	grated orange zest	5 mL
½ tsp	sea salt	2 mL
½ tsp	curry powder	2 mL
1 cup	pecans, chopped and toasted (see Tips, left)	250 mL

1. In a large saucepan over medium heat, combine cranberries, apples, brown sugar, raisins, shallots, vinegar, ginger, orange zest, salt and curry powder and bring to a gentle boil. Reduce heat and boil gently, stirring occasionally, until thickened, about 20 minutes. Stir in pecans. Let cool.

Apricot Anise Chutney

**Makes 2 cups
(500 mL)**

*Serve this refreshing chutney
with grilled poultry on a
summer day.*

Tip
Chutney keeps well,
covered and refrigerated,
for up to 2 weeks.

½ cup	unsweetened apple juice	125 mL
½ cup	chopped onion	125 mL
¼ cup	liquid honey	50 mL
¼ cup	white wine vinegar	50 mL
1 tbsp	ground aniseeds	15 mL
¼ tsp	freshly ground black pepper	1 mL
⅛ tsp	sea salt	0.5 mL
⅛ tsp	chili powder	0.5 mL
1 lb	dried apricots, chopped	500 g

1. In a large saucepan over medium heat, combine apple
   juice, onion, honey, vinegar, aniseeds, black pepper, salt
   and chili powder and bring to a gentle boil. Reduce heat
   and boil gently, stirring occasionally, until thickened,
   about 20 minutes. Reduce heat to low. Add apricots
   and simmer, stirring, until most of the liquid has been
   absorbed, about 10 minutes. Let cool.

Cabernet Sauvignon Vinaigrette (page 23)

Traditional Mayonnaise (page 106)

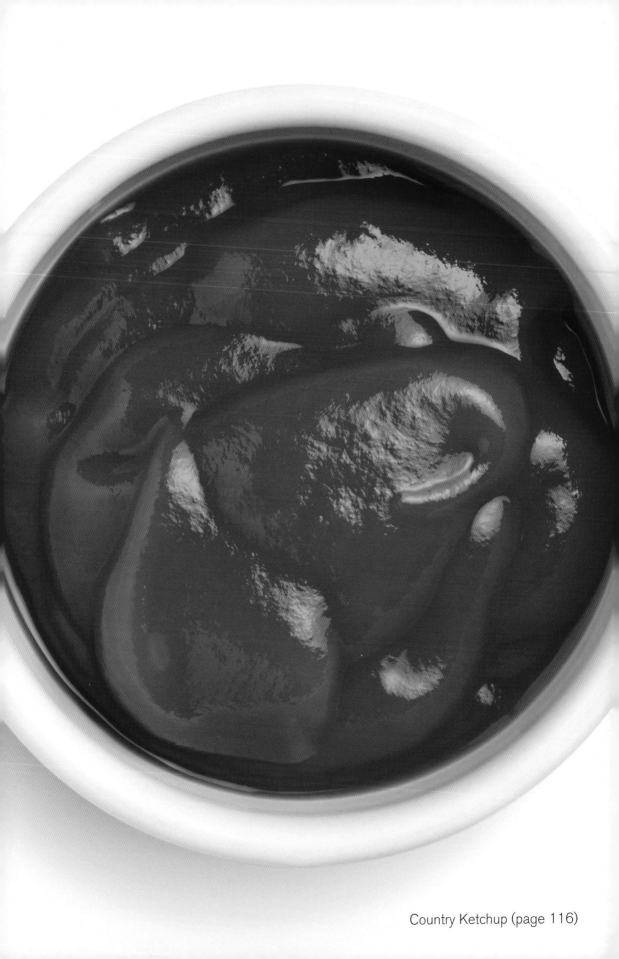

Country Ketchup (page 116)

Coarse Brown Mustard (page 121)

Mango Lime Chutney (page 130)

Tarragon Pickle Relish (page 135)

Basic Brown Sauce (page 151)

Hollandaise Sauce (page 169)

Vine-Ripened Tomato Orange Chutney

Makes 2 cups (500 mL)

This sweet and savory chutney is wonderful served with baked ham.

Tip
Chutney keeps well, covered and refrigerated, for up to 1 week.

- **Preheat oven to 400°F (200°C)**
- **Baking sheet, lined with parchment paper**

1 lb	vine-ripened tomatoes, cut in half	500 g
1/4 cup	extra virgin olive oil	50 mL
2 tbsp	balsamic vinegar	25 mL
4	green onions, chopped	4
2 tbsp	grated orange zest	25 mL
1/4 cup	freshly squeezed orange juice	50 mL
2 tbsp	freshly grated gingerroot	25 mL
2 tsp	grated lemon zest	10 mL
1 tbsp	freshly squeezed lemon juice	15 mL
1	jalapeño pepper, seeded and minced	1
1 tsp	coarsely cracked black peppercorns	5 mL
1/2 tsp	mustard seeds	2 mL
1/2 tsp	fennel seeds	2 mL
1/4 tsp	sea salt	1 mL

1. Place tomatoes, skin side down, in a single layer on prepared baking sheet. Brush with oil. Roast in preheated oven until skin has shriveled slightly, about 15 minutes. Let cool. Coarsely chop tomatoes.
2. In a bowl, combine vinegar, green onions, orange zest and juice, ginger, lemon zest and juice, jalapeño, black peppercorns, mustard seeds, fennel seeds and salt. Add tomatoes and stir to mix thoroughly. Let cool.

Mango Lime Chutney

Makes 3 cups (750 mL)

Mix chutney with Mexican rice or serve with roast chicken.

Tips

To tell if a mango is ripe, gently squeeze it in the palm of your hand; it is ready to use if it feels soft, like a tomato.

Chutney keeps well, covered and refrigerated, for up to 1 week.

Variation

Substitute lemon zest and juice for the lime.

1 cup	granulated sugar	250 mL
1/2 cup	white vinegar	125 mL
3 cups	chopped ripe mangos (see Tips, left)	750 mL
1	onion, chopped	1
1/2 cup	golden raisins	125 mL
2 tbsp	grated lime zest	25 mL
1/4 cup	freshly squeezed lime juice	50 mL
1	clove garlic, minced	1
1 tsp	mustard seeds	5 mL
1/4 tsp	cayenne pepper	1 mL

1. In a pot over medium heat, combine sugar and vinegar and bring to a boil. Add mangos, onion, raisins, lime zest and juice, garlic, mustard seeds and cayenne pepper. Reduce heat and simmer, stirring occasionally, until thickened, 30 to 45 minutes. Let cool.

Fast Red Pepper Chutney

Makes 2 cups (500 mL)

Make this chutney with sweet peppers and spices to create an all-purpose condiment

Tip

Chutney keeps well, covered and refrigerated, for up to 1 week.

- **Spice grinder or clean coffee grinder**

1/8 tsp	cumin seeds	0.5 mL
1/8 tsp	caraway seeds	0.5 mL
1/8 tsp	coriander seeds	0.5 mL
2	jars (each 7 oz/210 g) roasted red bell peppers, drained and finely chopped	2
1 tbsp	chopped fresh cilantro	15 mL
1 tbsp	red wine vinegar	15 mL
1/8 tsp	sea salt	0.5 mL
1/8 tsp	freshly ground black pepper	0.5 mL
1/8 tsp	cayenne pepper	0.5 mL

1. In a dry skillet over medium heat, toast cumin, caraway and coriander seeds, stirring, until fragrant, 1 to 2 minutes. In a spice grinder or clean coffee grinder, grind seeds until powdery, about 30 seconds.
2. In a bowl, combine spice mixture, red peppers, cilantro, vinegar, salt, black pepper and cayenne.

Pecan Peach Chutney

Makes 2 cups (500 mL)

Made with sweet peaches and pecans, this chutney has a nutty taste that's perfect for pork dishes.

Tips

If using frozen peaches, fully defrost them before cooking.

Chutney keeps well, covered and refrigerated, for up to 1 week.

Variation

Use macadamia nuts instead of pecans.

2 cups	fresh or frozen sliced, peeled peaches (about 12 oz/375 g) (see Tips, left)	500 mL
½ cup	lightly packed brown sugar	125 mL
½ cup	apple cider vinegar	125 mL
¼ cup	golden raisins	50 mL
1	clove garlic, minced	1
1 tsp	dried onion flakes	5 mL
½ tsp	ground ginger	2 mL
½ tsp	chili powder	2 mL
¼ tsp	mustard seeds	1 mL
⅛ tsp	curry powder	0.5 mL
1 cup	pecans, chopped and toasted (see Tips, page 127)	250 mL

1. In a large saucepan over medium heat, combine peaches, brown sugar, vinegar, raisins, garlic, onion flakes, ginger, chili powder, mustard seeds and curry powder and bring to a boil. Reduce heat and boil gently, stirring occasionally, until thickened, about 40 minutes. Stir in pecans. Let cool.

Classic Tomato Chutney

Makes 4 cups (1 L)

When you have a garden full of tomatoes, try this classic chutney.

Tip

Chutney keeps well, covered and refrigerated, for up to 2 weeks.

2 lbs	Roma (plum) tomatoes	1 kg
2½ cups	malt vinegar	625 mL
1 cup	golden raisins	250 mL
1 cup	chopped onions	250 mL
1 cup	granulated sugar	250 mL
1 tsp	sea salt	5 mL

1. In a large pot of boiling water, blanch tomatoes, in batches, for 30 seconds. Using a slotted spoon, immediately transfer to a bowl or sink full of cold water. Let cool. Peel off skins and remove cores. Cut in half, scoop out seeds and juice and coarsely chop.

2. In a medium saucepan over medium-high heat, combine tomatoes, vinegar, raisins, onions, sugar and salt and bring to a boil, stirring occasionally, until thickened. Reduce heat and simmer, stirring occasionally, until thickened, about 1 hour. Let cool.

Mediterranean Chutney

Try this chutney on lamb for a flavorful dish.

Tip
Chutney keeps well, covered and refrigerated, for up to 2 weeks.

2 lbs	Roma (plum) tomatoes	1 kg
3	cloves garlic, chopped	3
2	zucchini, cubed (about 1 lb/500 g)	2
1	large sweet onion, chopped (about 1 lb/500 g)	1
1	small eggplant, cubed (about 12 oz/375 g)	1
1	yellow bell pepper, chopped	1
1	red bell pepper, chopped	1
1 tbsp	sea salt	15 mL
1 tbsp	paprika	15 mL
1 tsp	dried rosemary	5 mL
½ tsp	dried thyme	2 mL
2	bay leaves	2
1¼ cups	malt vinegar, divided	300 mL
2 cups	granulated sugar	500 mL

1. In a large pot of boiling water, blanch tomatoes, in batches, for 30 seconds. Using a slotted spoon, immediately transfer to a bowl or sink full of cold water. Let cool. Peel off skins and remove cores. Cut in half, scoop out seeds and juice and chop coarsely.

2. In a large Dutch oven over medium heat, combine tomatoes, garlic, zucchini, onion, eggplant, yellow pepper and red pepper. Cover and bring to a boil. Reduce heat to low and boil gently until vegetables are softened, about 15 minutes.

3. Stir in salt, paprika, rosemary, thyme, bay leaves and ¾ cup (175 mL) of the malt vinegar and sugar. Simmer, uncovered, stirring occasionally, until thickened, about 30 minutes. Discard bay leaves. Stir in remaining vinegar and simmer, stirring occasionally, until slightly reduced, for 20 minutes. Let cool.

Apple Kashmir Chutney

Makes 4 cups (1 L)

Tart apples make the prefect chutney for pork dishes.

Tips

Granny Smith and Red Rome apples are good choices for this chutney.

Chutney keeps well, covered and refrigerated, for up to 2 weeks.

2 lbs	baking apples, peeled and quartered (see Tips, left)	500 mL
6	cloves garlic, minced	6
4 cups	malt vinegar, divided	1 L
3 cups	dates, pitted and chopped	750 mL
2 cups	lightly packed brown sugar	500 mL
2 tbsp	sea salt	25 mL
2 tsp	cayenne pepper	10 mL
1 tsp	ground ginger	5 mL

1. In a large Dutch oven over medium heat, combine apples, garlic and enough of the malt vinegar just to cover apples and bring to a boil. Reduce heat and boil gently, stirring occasionally, for 10 minutes. Add remaining vinegar, dates, brown sugar, salt, cayenne pepper and ginger. Reduce heat and simmer, stirring occasionally, until thickened, about 45 minutes. Let cool.

Peach and Chile Chutney

Makes 3 cups (750 mL)

This chutney is sweet and spicy and great on pork loin or a beef roast.

Tip

Chutney keeps well, covered and refrigerated, for up to 1 week.

3 cups	cider vinegar	750 mL
2¼ cups	golden raisins	550 mL
2 cups	lightly packed brown sugar	500 mL
1½ tsp	ground allspice	7 mL
1½ tsp	ground mace	7 mL
1½ lbs	peaches, peeled and cut into small chunks (about 6)	750 g
4	small hot red chiles, split, seeded and chopped	4
6	cloves garlic, minced	6
1½ tsp	sea salt	7 mL
¾ tsp	ground ginger	3 mL

1. In a large Dutch oven over medium heat, combine vinegar, raisins, brown sugar, allspice and mace and bring to a simmer. Simmer, stirring, until sugar is dissolved, about 5 minutes.
2. Stir in peaches, chiles, garlic, salt and ginger. Bring to a boil, stirring occasionally. Reduce heat and simmer, stirring occasionally, until thickened, 40 to 50 minutes. Let cool.

Pear Pecan Chutney

This sweet and nutty chutney is a delicious companion for the holiday turkey or goose.

Tip
Chutney keeps well, covered and refrigerated, for up to 1 week.

2 lbs	firm pears, peeled and chopped (about 8)	1 kg
2	baking apples, peeled, cored and chopped (see Tips, page 133)	2
1	onion, chopped	1
2 cups	cider vinegar	500 mL
2 cups	granulated sugar	500 mL
1 cup	golden raisins	250 mL
1 tbsp	grated orange zest	15 mL
2 tbsp	freshly squeezed orange juice	25 mL
1 cup	pecans, chopped and toasted (see Tips, page 127)	250 mL
2 tsp	ground cinnamon	10 mL

1. In a large Dutch oven over medium heat, combine pears, apples, onion and vinegar and bring to a boil. Stir in sugar, raisins and orange zest and juice. Bring to a boil. Reduce heat to low and simmer, stirring occasionally, until thickened, about 45 minutes. Stir in toasted pecans and cinnamon. Let cool.

Christmas Chutney

This sweet and colorful chutney also looks lovely next to the holiday ham.

Tip
Chutney keeps well, covered and refrigerated, for up to 1 week.

1 lb	baking apples, peeled and chopped (see Tips, page 133)	500 g
1½ lbs	mixed candied fruit	750 g
1¼ cups	lightly packed brown sugar	300 mL
¾ cup	cider vinegar	175 mL
1 tbsp	grated orange zest	15 mL
1 tbsp	ground cinnamon	15 mL
1 tsp	ground nutmeg	5 mL
½ tsp	ground cloves	2 mL
¼ tsp	ground mace	1 mL

1. In a Dutch oven over medium heat, combine apples, candied fruit, brown sugar, vinegar, orange zest, cinnamon, nutmeg, cloves and mace and bring to a gentle boil. Reduce heat and simmer, stirring occasionally, until thickened, about 45 minutes. Let cool.

Tarragon Pickle Relish

Makes 2 cups (500 mL)

Grilled hot dogs and sausages taste better with this homemade relish.

Tip
Relish keeps well, covered and refrigerated, for up to 1 week.

1½ cups	cider vinegar	375 mL
2 tbsp	granulated sugar	25 mL
1 tsp	mustard seeds	5 mL
1 tsp	coriander seeds	5 mL
8	large sour dill pickles, finely diced	8
2 tbsp	chopped fresh dill	25 mL
1	small red bell pepper, finely diced	1
1	small yellow bell pepper, finely diced	1
1	small onion, finely diced	1
1 tsp	dried tarragon	5 mL

1. In a medium saucepan over medium heat, combine vinegar, sugar, mustard seeds and coriander seeds and bring to a boil. Boil until reduced by half and syrupy, about 20 minutes.
2. Remove from heat. Stir in pickles, dill, red pepper, yellow pepper, onion and tarragon. Toss to coat. Let cool.

Onion Relish

This is the garnish to use for a gourmet hamburger.

Tip
Relish keeps well, covered and refrigerated, for up to 2 weeks.

3 tbsp	vegetable oil	45 mL
5	large sweet onions, finely chopped	5
1/3 cup	chopped celery	75 mL
1/2 cup	granulated sugar	125 mL
1/2 cup	cider vinegar	125 mL
1	jar (2 oz/60 mL) diced pimento, drained	1
1/4 cup	water	50 mL
1/2 tsp	celery seeds	2 mL
1/4 tsp	sea salt	1 mL
1/8 tsp	freshly ground black pepper	0.5 mL

1. In a large skillet, heat oil over medium heat. Add onions and celery and sauté until onions are translucent, about 10 minutes. Stir in sugar, vinegar, pimento, water, celery seeds, salt and pepper and bring to a boil. Reduce heat to low and simmer, stirring often, until the liquid has been absorbed, for 25 minutes. Let cool.

Cranberry Relish

Makes 4 cups (1 L)

This relish is made in a flash and is destined to be a holiday favorite.

Tip
Relish keeps well, covered and refrigerated, for up to 2 weeks.

2 cups	water	500 mL
2 cups	granulated sugar	500 mL
1 tsp	grated orange zest	5 mL
1/4 cup	freshly squeezed orange juice	50 mL
1 1/2 lbs	cranberries	750 g

1. In a medium saucepan over high heat, combine water, sugar and orange zest and juice and bring to a boil. Reduce heat to medium. Stir in cranberries and boil gently, stirring occasionally, until thickened, about 15 minutes. Let cool.

Fast Corn Relish

Try this relish on your favorite burger.

Tip
Relish keeps well, covered and refrigerated, for up to 1 week.

1	can (12 oz/375 mL) white sweet corn kernels, drained	1
¼ cup	Tarragon Pickle Relish (page 135)	50 mL
1 tbsp	granulated sugar	15 mL
1 tbsp	diced drained pimento	15 mL
1 tbsp	white wine vinegar	15 mL
1 tsp	sea salt	5 mL

1. In a bowl, combine corn kernels, pickle relish, sugar, pimento, vinegar and salt.
2. Cover and refrigerate for at least 2 hours for flavors to meld before serving cold.

Sweet Red Pepper Relish

Makes 3 cups (750 mL)

Top steak or burgers with this relish for a sweet taste that's much better than bottled ketchup.

Tip
Relish keeps well, covered and refrigerated, for up to 2 weeks.

- **Food processor**

4	red bell peppers, seeded and quartered	4
3	onions, chopped	3
1 tbsp	sea salt	15 mL
3 cups	granulated sugar	750 mL
2 cups	white wine vinegar	500 mL

1. In a food processor fitted with a metal blade, process peppers, onions and salt until smooth, about 30 seconds.
2. Transfer to a medium saucepan over low heat. Add sugar and vinegar and bring to a boil. Reduce heat and simmer, stirring occasionally, until thickened, about 30 minutes. Let cool.

Coney Island Chili Dog Sauce

**Makes about
3½ cups (875 mL)**

*Every time I teach in Indiana
I have to stop at Dog 'n'
Suds restaurant for a Coney
dog and root beer. Make
your own chili dog sauce and
always serve it hot.*

Tip
Sauce keeps well, covered
and refrigerated, for up
to 3 days. Reheat before
serving.

2 tbsp	vegetable oil	25 mL
1 lb	ground beef, preferably chuck	500 g
1	large onion, chopped	1
2	cloves garlic, minced	2
1	can (6 oz/175 mL) tomato paste	1
1 cup	water	250 mL
1 tbsp	granulated sugar	15 mL
1 tbsp	dry mustard	15 mL
1 tbsp	dried onion flakes	15 mL
2 tsp	chili powder	10 mL
1 tsp	Worcestershire Sauce (page 142) or store-bought	5 mL
1 tsp	sea salt	5 mL
½ tsp	celery seeds	2 mL
½ tsp	ground cumin	2 mL
½ tsp	freshly ground black pepper	2 mL

1. In a large skillet, heat oil over medium heat. Add beef
   and onion and cook, breaking up with a spoon, until
   browned, about 12 minutes. Add garlic, tomato paste,
   water, sugar, mustard, onion flakes, chili powder,
   Worcestershire sauce, salt, celery seeds, cumin and
   black pepper. Reduce heat to low and simmer, stirring
   occasionally, until thickened, for 15 minutes. Let cool
   prior to refrigerating unless you are using immediately.

Cucumber Relish

**Makes 2 cups
(500 mL)**

*Here's a summertime relish
for any spicy grilled meat.*

Tip
Relish keeps well, covered
and refrigerated, for up to
3 weeks.

1	cucumber, peeled, seeded and finely chopped	1
2	shallots, finely chopped	2
2	cloves garlic, minced	2
1 cup	plain yogurt	250 mL
2 tbsp	chopped fresh mint	25 mL
	Salt and freshly ground black pepper	

1. In a bowl, combine cucumber, shallots, garlic, yogurt and
   mint. Season with salt and pepper to taste. Serve cold.

Pineapple Relish

Makes 2½ cups (625 mL)

Try this relish on grilled sausages, fish or poultry for a tropical treat in your own backyard.

2 cups	finely chopped fresh pineapple	500 mL
1	small red onion, finely chopped	1
1	jalapeño pepper, seeded and minced	1
1 tbsp	freshly squeezed orange juice	15 mL
1 tbsp	extra virgin olive oil	15 mL
1 tbsp	liquid honey	15 mL
1	clove garlic, minced	1
	Sea salt and freshly ground black pepper	

1. In a large bowl, combine pineapple, red onion, jalapeño, orange juice, olive oil, honey and garlic. Refrigerate for at least 2 hours for flavors to develop or for up to 3 weeks.
2. When ready to serve, drain any liquid off. Season with salt and pepper to taste.

Corn Relish

Makes 2 cups (500 mL)

I like to top hamburgers with this relish but it's good with steaks, too.

Tip
You can use thawed frozen corn or the kernels from 2 cobs of cooked corn.

Variation
Replace the turnip with the same quantity of radishes or any similar root vegetable.

1 cup	corn kernels, drained (see Tip, left)	250 mL
1	turnip, finely diced	1
2	shallots, finely chopped	2
1	small red bell pepper, chopped	1
2 tbsp	chopped fresh chives	25 mL
1 tbsp	extra virgin olive oil	15 mL
2 tsp	freshly squeezed lemon juice	10 mL

1. In a large bowl, combine corn kernels, turnip, shallots, red pepper, chives, olive oil and lemon juice. Refrigerate for at least 30 minutes for flavors to develop or for up to 2 weeks.

Other Condiments

Tarragon Cheese Sauce

Makes 1 cup (250 mL)

This herb sauce is good for steamed vegetables such as cauliflower and broccoli.

1 tbsp	unsalted butter	15 mL
1 tbsp	all-purpose flour	15 mL
½ cup	Vegetable Stock (page 149) or ready-to-use broth	125 mL
½ cup	low-fat (1 or 2%) milk	125 mL
1 tbsp	tarragon-flavored vinegar	15 mL
1 tbsp	chopped fresh tarragon	15 mL
2 tsp	Dijon Mustard (page 120) or store-bought	10 mL
½ cup	finely shredded Cheddar cheese	125 mL
	Salt and freshly ground black pepper	

1. In a small saucepan, melt butter over low heat. Whisk in flour. Gradually whisk in stock and milk and cook, whisking constantly, until thickened, about 4 minutes. Remove from heat and whisk in vinegar, tarragon, mustard and cheese until melted. Season with salt and pepper to taste.

Easy Mustard Sauce

Makes ¾ cup (175 mL)

If you're looking for a creamy, easy mustard sauce for meats, this one fits the bill.

1 tbsp	unsalted butter	15 mL
1 tbsp	all-purpose flour	15 mL
½ cup	low-fat (1% or 2%) milk	125 mL
2 tbsp	Honey Mustard Sauce (page 120) or store-bought	25 mL
½ cup	finely shredded Cheddar cheese	125 mL
	Salt and freshly ground black pepper	

1. In a small saucepan, melt butter over low heat. Whisk in flour. Gradually whisk in milk and cook, whisking constantly, until thickened, about 4 minutes. Remove from heat and whisk in mustard and cheese until melted. Season with salt and pepper to taste.

Plum and Ginger Sauce

Makes 1 cup (250 mL)

Here's a thick sauce that's sweet and spicy. Use it on duck, chicken and Cornish hens.

Tip
Sauce keeps well, covered and refrigerated, for up to 3 weeks.

● **Blender**

1 tbsp	extra virgin olive oil	15 mL
1	red onion, chopped	1
1	clove garlic, minced	1
1	1-inch (2.5 cm) piece gingerroot, peeled and thinly sliced (about 2 tsp/10 mL)	1
3	plums, finely chopped	3
1/2 cup	dry red wine	125 mL
2 tbsp	lightly packed brown sugar	25 mL

1. In a skillet, heat oil over medium heat. Add red onion, garlic and ginger and sauté until soft, about 5 minutes. Add plums, wine and brown sugar and cook, stirring, until sugar has dissolved, about 3 minutes. Increase heat to high and bring to a boil. Cover, reduce heat to low and simmer until plums are soft, about 10 minutes.
2. Transfer to a blender and purée until smooth. Use hot or cold.

Thai Dipping Sauce

Makes 1/2 cup (125 mL)

This sauce turns plain chicken wings and shrimp into Thai delights.

3 tbsp	finely minced shallots	45 mL
3 tbsp	freshly squeezed lime juice	45 mL
2 tbsp	reduced-sodium soy sauce	25 mL
2 tbsp	Bold Chili Sauce (page 125) or store-bought	25 mL
1 tbsp	chopped fresh cilantro	15 mL
1 tbsp	lightly packed brown sugar	15 mL
1/2 tsp	Chinese 5-spice powder	2 mL
	Freshly grated black pepper	

1. In a bowl, combine shallots, lime juice, soy sauce, chili sauce, cilantro, brown sugar and 5-spice powder. Season with pepper to taste. Serve cold or hot. To reheat, place in the microwave for 30 seconds.

Worcestershire Sauce

Fresh homemade Worcestershire sauce is always better, and a little spicier and thicker, than what you find at the grocery store.

Tip

Tamarind paste is used in Mexican, Indian and Asian cooking. It is sour tangy. You can purchase it in a ready-made paste from Indian markets.

1 tbsp	olive oil	15 mL
1	onion, chopped	1
2	jalapeño peppers, seeded and chopped	2
4	cloves garlic, minced	4
1 tsp	whole black peppercorns	5 mL
1	can (1$\frac{2}{3}$ oz/48 g) anchovy fillets, drained	1
2$\frac{1}{2}$ cups	white wine vinegar	625 mL
1$\frac{1}{4}$ cups	water	300 mL
$\frac{2}{3}$ cup	pure cane syrup (see Sources, page 343)	150 mL
$\frac{2}{3}$ cup	dark (golden) corn syrup	150 mL
$\frac{1}{3}$ cup	blackstrap molasses	75 mL
2 tsp	sea salt	10 mL
$\frac{1}{2}$ tsp	whole cloves	2 mL
1	lemon, peeled and chopped	1
1 tbsp	tamarind paste (see Tip, left)	15 mL
2 tbsp	prepared horseradish	25 mL

1. In a large Dutch oven, heat oil over medium heat. Add onion, jalapeños and garlic and sauté until softened, about 4 minutes. Stir in peppercorns, anchovies, vinegar, water, cane syrup, corn syrup, molasses, salt, cloves, lemon, tamarind and horseradish. Bring to a boil. Reduce heat to low and simmer until mixture is thick enough to coat the back of a metal spoon, 90 minutes to 2 hours. Strain through a fine-mesh sieve, discarding solids.

Anchovy Cream Sauce

Makes 1 cup (250 mL)

Use this sauce on grilled tuna or try drizzling it over slices of mozzarella.

1½ tsp	unsalted butter	7 mL
1½ tsp	all-purpose flour	7 mL
1 cup	heavy or whipping (35%) cream, at room temperature	250 mL
2	anchovy fillets, finely chopped	2
1 tbsp	freshly squeezed lemon juice	15 mL
	Sea salt	
	Ground white pepper	

1. In a small saucepan, melt butter over medium heat. Whisk in flour. Gradually whisk in cream and cook, whisking constantly, until thickened, about 4 minutes. Remove from heat and whisk in anchovies and lemon juice. Season with salt and white pepper to taste.

Fresh Horseradish Cream

Makes 1 cup (250 mL)

All great prime-rib restaurants serve a horseradish cream alongside the main course. Here's one for you to dish up at home.

Tip

Use white pepper. Specks of black pepper will look like bits that have burned.

1 cup	heavy or whipping (35%) cream	250 mL
3 tbsp	grated fresh horseradish	45 mL
2 tsp	white wine vinegar	10 mL
½ tsp	granulated sugar	2 mL
	Sea salt	
	Ground white pepper (see Tip, left)	

1. In a bowl, lightly whip cream. Set aside.
2. In a small bowl, combine horseradish, vinegar and sugar. Fold into lightly whipped cream. Season with salt and white pepper to taste.

Simple Stocks
and Brown Sauces

Stocks are the base for brown sauces and are also a great way to get more goodness from leftover bones. They are easy to master and well worth the effort.

I enjoy the aroma from the kitchen when I'm making stock. Nothing from a can or carton tastes as good as fresh stock made from scratch — or the sauces and soups made from that stock. You control every aspect of the stock with what you put into it. Yes, it's time consuming at first, but once the ingredients are in the pot, you just have to leave it on simmer and let it reduce. If you freeze the finished stock in quantities that work for you, you'll have stock ready whenever you need it.

Fish Stock

Makes 4 to 6 cups (1 to 1.5 L)

Ask your fishmonger to sell you the fish pieces you need for stock.

Tips
You can purchase bouquet garni (also known as herb bouquet) in tight bundles (see Sources, page 343), or make your own: In a square of cheesecloth, tie 2 sprigs parsley, 2 sprigs thyme, 2 bay leaves, 5 whole peppercorns, 5 whole cloves and 2 sliced cloves garlic into a bouquet garni.

Stock keeps well, covered and refrigerated, for up to 2 days or freeze for up to 5 months.

2 lbs	fish skeletons (with heads from lean white fish such as flounder, halibut, etc.)	1 kg
2	onions, cut into wedges	2
3	stalks celery, cut into 2-inch (5 cm) pieces	3
10 cups	cold water (approx.)	2.5 L
1	lemon, thinly sliced	1
1 tsp	dried thyme	5 mL
½ tsp	whole black peppercorns	2 mL
1	bouquet garni (see Tips, left)	1
	Salt	

1. Rinse fish, cut out any gills and discard.
2. In a large stockpot, combine fish pieces, onions and celery. Add enough water to cover fish. Add lemon slices, thyme, peppercorns and bouquet garni. Bring to a full boil over high heat. Reduce heat and simmer for 30 minutes. If any foam rises to the surface, skim it off and discard.
3. Remove from heat and let stand for 20 minutes. Strain through a large fine-mesh sieve or chinois. Discard any solids. Add salt to taste.

Beef Stock

*Make sure you ask your
butcher for meaty beef bones
for stock. They are normally
kept in the back or discarded.*

Tip

Stock keeps well, covered
and refrigerated, for up to
2 days or freeze for up to
5 months.

Variation

Reduced Beef Stock: After
straining it, return some or
all of the stock to a clean
pot and bring to a boil over
high heat. Reduce heat and
boil gently until the stock
is reduced by half. Do not
add salt to taste until after
the stock has been reduced.
Be sure to label the stock as
"reduced" since it will have
a very concentrated flavor.

- **Preheat oven to 450°F (230°C)**
- **Roasting pan, lined with a Silpat or foil**

4 lbs	beef bones	2 kg
3	onions, quartered	3
4	large carrots, cut into 2-inch (5 cm) pieces	4
5	stalks celery, cut into 2-inch (5 cm) pieces	5
4	Roma (plum) tomatoes, cut in half and seeded	4
4 to 6 cups	cold water	1 to 1.5 L
1	bunch Italian flat-leaf parsley	1
2	bay leaves	2
2 tsp	dried thyme	10 mL
1 tsp	whole black peppercorns	5 mL
1/4 tsp	whole cloves	1 mL
	Salt	

1. Rinse bones in cold water and place in a single layer in prepared roasting pan. Roast in preheated oven, turning halfway through cooking, for 30 minutes.
2. Arrange onions, carrots, celery and tomatoes on top of bones. Roast for 30 minutes.
3. Transfer roasted bones and vegetables to a large stockpot. Scrape brown bits from Silpat into pot. Cover bones and vegetables with cold water. Add parsley, bay leaves, thyme, peppercorns and cloves. Bring to a boil over high heat. Reduce heat and simmer for 3 hours. Skim any foam off the top and discard.
4. Remove from heat and let stand for 20 minutes. Strain through a large sieve or chinois. Discard any solids. Add salt to taste.

Chicken Stock

**Makes about
10 cups (2.5 L)**

*You can use chicken or
turkey (see Variation, below)
for this stock. I like to
make this the day after
Thanksgiving dinner.*

Tip
Stock keeps well, covered
and refrigerated, for up to
2 days or freeze for up to
5 months.

Variation
Turkey Stock: Follow
the recipe, but use
1 turkey carcass instead
of 2 chicken ones.

2	chicken carcasses	2
2	onions, quartered	2
3	large carrots, cut into 2-inch (5 cm) pieces	3
3	stalks celery, cut into 2-inch (5 cm) pieces	3
3	cloves garlic, crushed	3
2	bay leaves	2
8	sprigs Italian flat-leaf parsley	8
1 tsp	whole black peppercorns	5 mL
½ tsp	dried thyme	2 mL
½ tsp	dried rosemary	2 mL
3 quarts	cold water	3 L
	Salt (approx.)	

1. In a large stockpot, combine chicken carcasses, onions, carrots, celery, garlic, bay leaves, parsley, peppercorns, thyme and rosemary. Add enough cold water to cover. Bring to a boil over high heat. Reduce heat and simmer for 3 hours. Skim any foam off the top and discard.
2. Remove from heat and let stand for 20 minutes. Strain through a large sieve or chinois. Discard any solids. Add salt to taste.

Vegetable Stock

*You can use an array of
vegetables for this stock.
Check out your refrigerator
and use what you have.*

Tip
Stock keeps well, covered
and refrigerated, for up to
2 days or freeze for up to
5 months.

2 tbsp	vegetable oil	25 mL
2	onions, quartered	2
1	bunch green onions, chopped	1
2	large leeks, cleaned and chopped	2
4	stalks celery, cut into 2-inch (5 cm) pieces	4
8 cups	cold water	2 L
1 lb	carrots, cut into 2-inch (5 cm) pieces	500 g
1	medium jicama, peeled and sliced	1
4	cloves garlic, smashed	4
1 tsp	dried parsley	5 mL
1 tsp	dried thyme	5 mL
1 tsp	whole peppercorns	5 mL
2	bay leaves	2
	Salt	

1. In a large stockpot, heat oil over medium–high heat. Add
   onions, green onions, leeks and celery and sauté until
   vegetables are translucent, about 5 minutes. Add water,
   carrots, jicama, garlic, parsley, thyme, peppercorns and
   bay leaves. Increase heat to high and bring to a boil.
   Reduce heat and simmer for 1 hour.
2. Remove from heat and let stand for 20 minutes. Strain
   through a large sieve or chinois. Discard any solids. Add
   salt to taste.

Fresh Herb Stock

*Instead of using a vegetable
stock, try this herb stock with
your recipes.*

Tip
Stock keeps well, covered
and refrigerated, for up to
2 days or freeze for up to
5 months.

12 cups	cold water	3 L
1	onion, quartered	1
1	bunch Italian flat-leaf parsley, leaves only	1
½ cup	fresh sage sprigs	125 mL
½ cup	fresh thyme	125 mL
½ cup	fresh tarragon	125 mL
½ cup	fresh rosemary	125 mL
12	cloves garlic, smashed	12
5	bay leaves	5
2 tbsp	tomato paste	25 mL
1 tsp	sea salt	5 mL
1 tsp	whole black peppercorns	5 mL
¼ tsp	whole cloves	1 mL
	Salt	

1. In a large stockpot, combine water, onion, parsley, sage, thyme, tarragon, rosemary, garlic, bay leaves, tomato paste, salt, peppercorns and cloves. Bring to a boil over high heat. Reduce heat and simmer for 45 minutes.
2. Remove from heat and let stand for 20 minutes. Strain through a large sieve or chinois. Discard any solids. Add salt to taste.

Brown Sauces

Basic Brown Sauce

*It is easy to master a basic
brown sauce. Learn how, and
you'll be amazed at what you
can do with it.*

Tip
Sauce keeps well, covered
and refrigerated, for up to
3 days or freeze for up to
2 months.

● **Food mill or strainer**

⅓ cup	unsalted butter	75 mL
1	stalk celery, cut into 2-inch (5 cm) pieces	1
1	onion, chopped	1
3	carrots, cut into 2-inch (5 cm) pieces	3
¼ cup	all-purpose flour	50 mL
1 cup	dry red wine	250 mL
4 cups	Beef Stock (page 147) or ready-to-use broth	1 L
¼ tsp	dried thyme	1 mL
1	bay leaf	1
3	cloves garlic, minced	3
⅛ tsp	sea salt	0.5 mL
⅛ tsp	freshly ground black pepper	0.5 mL

1. In a stockpot, melt butter over medium heat. Add celery, onion and carrots and cook, stirring slowly, about 5 minutes. Sprinkle in flour and toss vegetables to coat. Cook, stirring, until flour is light brown in color, about 5 minutes. Gradually whisk in wine, then beef stock, thyme, bay leaf and garlic. Cover, reduce heat to low and simmer, stirring occasionally, for 1 hour. Remove lid and continue to simmer, stirring occasionally, until thickened, about 30 minutes.
2. Transfer sauce to a food mill fitted with a fine plate or strainer and strain, discarding solids. Season with salt and pepper. Use immediately or let cool completely.

Bigarade Sauce

**Makes about
2 cups (500 mL)**

*This brown and orange sauce
is perfect for duck.*

Tip
Sauce keeps well, covered
and refrigerated, for up to
3 days or freeze for up to
2 months.

¼ cup	unsalted butter	50 mL
2 tbsp	finely chopped shallots	25 mL
½ cup	port wine	125 mL
2 tbsp	grated orange zest	25 mL
⅓ cup	freshly squeezed orange juice	75 mL
¼ cup	orange-flavored liqueur	50 mL
1 cup	Reduced Beef Stock (see Variation, page 147) or ready-to-use broth	250 mL
2	large oranges, divided into segments	2

1. In a saucepan, melt butter over medium heat. Add shallots and sauté until browned, about 5 minutes. Add wine, orange zest and juice, liqueur and stock. Cook, stirring occasionally, until thickened, about 8 minutes. Stir in orange segments. Serve over prepared duck.

Bordelaise Sauce

**Makes 2 cups
(500 mL)**

*Here's a beautiful sauce for
beef tenderloin.*

Tip
Sauce keeps well, covered
and refrigerated, for up to
3 days or freeze for up to
2 months.

½ cup	unsalted butter	125 mL
¼ cup	shallots, finely chopped	50 mL
2 cups	Reduced Beef Stock (see Variation, page 147) or ready-to-use broth	500 mL
½ cup	dry red wine	125 mL
1 tsp	freshly cracked black peppercorns	5 mL
¼ tsp	chopped fresh thyme	1 mL

1. In a saucepan, melt butter over medium-high heat. Add shallots and sauté until browned, about 5 minutes. Add stock, red wine, peppercorns and thyme and cook until thickened, about 8 minutes.

Easy Classic Mushroom Sauce

Makes 1 cup (250 mL)

Use this sauce as a topping for Salisbury steak or ground beef.

Tip

Sauce keeps well, covered and refrigerated, for up to 4 days. Warm it in a saucepan over medium heat prior to use.

¼ cup	unsalted butter	50 mL
12 oz	button mushrooms, thinly sliced	375 g
1 tbsp	freshly squeezed lemon juice	15 mL
¼ cup	all-purpose flour	50 mL
2 cups	Beef Stock (page 147) or ready-to-use broth	500 mL

1. In a saucepan, melt butter over medium heat. Add mushrooms and lemon juice and cook, stirring occasionally, until mushrooms are soft, about 5 minutes. Using a slotted spoon, transfer mushrooms to a bowl.
2. In same saucepan, add flour to mushroom liquid and cook, stirring, until browned, about 3 minutes. Gradually whisk in beef stock and cook, stirring, until thickened, about 15 minutes. Add reserved mushrooms. Serve hot.

Cognac Cherry Sauce

Makes 2 cups (500 mL)

Serve this sauce with beef or pork dishes.

Tip

Sauce keeps well, covered and refrigerated, for up to 4 days. Warm in a saucepan over medium heat prior to use.

- **Food processor**

¾ cup	cognac	175 mL
¾ cup	dried cherries	175 mL
2 cups	Beef Stock (page 147) or ready-to-use broth	500 mL
¾ cup	heavy or whipping (35%) cream, at room temperature	175 mL
1 tsp	sea salt	5 mL
1 tsp	freshly cracked black peppercorns	5 mL
2 tbsp	unsalted butter	25 mL

1. In a medium saucepan over low heat, warm cognac. Turn off heat. Add cherries and let soak for 1 hour to absorb most of the liquid.
2. In a food processor fitted with a metal blade, process cherries and any liquid until smooth, about 30 seconds.
3. In same saucepan, bring stock to a boil over high heat. Boil until reduced by half, about 10 minutes. Add cherries, cream, salt and peppercorns. Reduce heat and simmer, stirring occasionally, for 3 minutes. Remove from heat and whisk in butter until melted. Serve hot.

Creole Sauce

Makes 3 cups (750 mL)

This rich sauce is perfect for chicken or crayfish.

Tips

Sauce keeps well, covered and refrigerated, for up to 4 days. Warm it in a saucepan over medium heat prior to use.

Save the juice drained from the tomatoes to enrich another stock or sauce.

2 tbsp	vegetable oil	25 mL
¼ cup	diced onion	50 mL
¼ cup	diced celery	50 mL
¼ cup	diced green bell pepper	50 mL
2	cloves garlic, minced	2
1	can (28 oz/796 mL) tomato sauce	1
1	can (28 oz/796 mL) diced tomatoes, drained (see Tips, left)	1
1	bay leaf	1
½ tsp	chopped fresh thyme	2 mL
¼ tsp	sea salt	1 mL
¼ tsp	garlic powder	1 mL
¼ tsp	dried oregano	1 mL
¼ tsp	dried basil	1 mL
⅛ tsp	cayenne pepper	0.5 mL

1. In a skillet, heat oil over medium heat. Add onion, celery, green pepper and garlic. Sauté until onions are translucent, about 3 minutes. Add tomato sauce, diced tomatoes, bay leaf, thyme, salt, garlic powder, oregano, basil and cayenne and bring to a simmer. Reduce heat and simmer until thickened, for 15 minutes. Discard bay leaf. Serve hot.

Herb Mustard Sauce

Makes 2 cups (500 mL)

This sauces is great as a condiment for steak.

Tip
Sauce keeps well, covered and refrigerated for up to 4 days. Warm it in a saucepan over medium heat prior to use.

1 tbsp	unsalted butter	15 mL
1 tsp	vegetable oil	5 mL
¼ cup	chopped onion	50 mL
1 cup	dry white wine	250 mL
2 cups	Basic Brown Sauce (page 151)	500 mL
¼ cup	Honey Stone-Ground Mustard (page 122) or store-bought	50 mL
½ tsp	chopped fresh tarragon	2 mL
½ tsp	chopped fresh dill	2 mL
½ tsp	chopped fresh rosemary	2 mL
½ tsp	chopped fresh basil	2 mL
¼ tsp	granulated sugar	1 mL
3 tbsp	chopped Italian flat-leaf parsley	45 mL

1. In a medium saucepan, melt butter and oil over medium heat. Add onion and sauté until tender and lightly browned, about 4 minutes.
2. Increase heat to high. Add wine and boil until reduced to ¼ cup (50 mL), about 10 minutes.
3. Reduce heat to medium. Stir in brown sauce and simmer, stirring occasionally, for 10 minutes. Whisk in mustard, tarragon, dill, rosemary, basil, sugar and parsley. Serve hot.

Fast Norwegian Brown Sauce

Makes ½ cup
(125 mL)

*Use this sauce in any meat
or game dish when you are in
a hurry.*

Tips

For the concentrated beef
bouillon, crumble bouillon
cubes or use concentrated
beef paste that's available
in Asian markets and
well-stocked supermarkets.

Sauce keeps well, covered
and refrigerated, for up
to 4 days. Warm it in a
saucepan over medium heat
prior to use.

1 tbsp	concentrated beef bouillon (see Tips, left)	15 mL
¼ cup	hot water	50 mL
¼ cup	unsalted butter	50 mL
2 tbsp	all-purpose flour	25 mL
1 tsp	reduced-sodium soy sauce	5 mL
¼ tsp	freshly ground black pepper	1 mL

1. In a small bowl, combine beef bouillon and hot water to dilute. Stir to dissolve.
2. In a medium saucepan, melt butter over medium heat. Add flour and cook, stirring until flour browns, about 5 minutes. Gradually whisk in dissolved bouillon. Add soy sauce and pepper. Reduce heat and simmer, stirring occasionally, until reduced, about 2 minutes. Serve hot.

Agrodolce Sauce

Makes 1 cup (250 mL)

*I think this sour-sweet
Italian sauce is best used for
wild game such as venison,
bison or elk, but some people
love it on wild Alaskan
salmon. The name comes
from the Italian agro (sour)
and dolce (sweet).*

Tip

Sauce keeps well, covered
and refrigerated, for up
to 4 days. Warm it in a
saucepan over medium heat
prior to use.

1 cup	white wine vinegar	250 mL
½ cup	currants	125 mL
1 tbsp	lightly packed brown sugar	15 mL
1 tbsp	grated orange zest	15 mL
1 tbsp	grated lemon zest	15 mL
1 tbsp	capers, drained	15 mL
2 oz	bittersweet chocolate, chopped	60 g
1 tbsp	unsalted butter	15 mL

1. In a medium saucepan over medium–high heat, combine vinegar, currants, brown sugar, orange zest, lemon zest and capers and bring to a simmer. Reduce heat and simmer, stirring occasionally, until slightly reduced, about 20 minutes. Stir in chocolate and butter until melted and smooth. Serve hot.

Anchovy Sauce

When you want a salty contrast, use this rich sauce on vegetables, pasta or fish.

Tip
Sauce keeps well, covered and refrigerated, for up to 4 days. Warm it in a saucepan over medium heat prior to use.

4	anchovy fillets	4
1 tbsp	all-purpose flour	15 mL
1 tbsp	unsalted butter	15 mL
1 cup	Beef Stock (page 147) or ready-to-use broth	250 mL
1 tsp	capers, drained	5 mL
½ tsp	sea salt	2 mL
½ tsp	freshly ground black pepper	2 mL

1. Rinse anchovies and pat dry. Dredge in flour. Set aside.
2. In a skillet, melt butter over medium heat. Add anchovies and fry, turning halfway through cooking, for 5 minutes. Add stock and simmer for 15 minutes. Add capers and stir. Season with salt and pepper. Serve hot.

Brown Cream Sauce

Makes 2 cups (500 mL)

Here's a creamy sauce to enhance any cut or type of meat.

Tips
To make browned flour: Place desired amount of flour in a nonstick pan over medium heat and cook, stirring, until flour is a caramel color.

Sauce keeps well, covered and refrigerated, for up to 4 days. Warm it in a saucepan over medium heat prior to use.

3 tbsp	all-purpose flour	45 mL
1 tbsp	browned flour (see Tips, left)	15 mL
1½ cups	whole milk, divided	375 mL
½ cup	heavy or whipping (35%) cream	125 mL
	Sea salt	
	Ground white pepper	

1. In a small bowl, combine all-purpose and browned flours. Add enough of the milk (about ½ cup/125 mL) to make a slurry or thin paste (see Tips, left). Set aside.
2. In a medium saucepan over medium heat, combine remaining milk and cream and scald. Whisk in flour paste and cook, stirring, until thickened, about 3 minutes. Season with salt and white pepper to taste.

Champagne Sauce

Makes 1 cup (250 mL)

This rich-tasting sauce is perfect for beef or game, and it's a good way to use up leftover Champagne.

Tip

Sauce keeps well, covered and refrigerated, for up to 4 days. Warm it in a saucepan over medium heat prior to use.

1 cup	flat champagne	250 mL
½ cup	Basic Brown Sauce (page 151)	125 mL
1 tsp	granulated sugar	5 mL
3	cloves garlic, minced	3

1. In a saucepan over medium heat, combine champagne, brown sauce, sugar and garlic and bring to a boil. Reduce heat, stirring occasionally, about 5 minutes. Strain through a fine-mesh sieve, discarding garlic. Serve hot.

Madeira Sauce

Makes 1 cup (250 mL)

I like to serve chicken breasts in this sauce for a full-flavored meal.

Tip

Sauce keeps well, covered and refrigerated, for up to 4 days. Warm it in a saucepan over medium heat prior to use.

1 cup	Basic Brown Sauce (page 151)	250 mL
1 tbsp	real bacon bits	15 mL
1 tbsp	diced celery	15 mL
½ tsp	Hungarian paprika	2 mL
¼ cup	Madeira wine	50 mL

1. In a saucepan over medium-heat, combine brown sauce, bacon and celery and bring to a boil. Reduce heat to medium. Add paprika and simmer, stirring occasionally, until slightly thickened, for 20 minutes. Add Madeira wine. Serve hot.

Olive Brown Sauce

**Makes 2 cups
(500 mL)**

*Serve this sauce with duck
or any hearty meat.*

Tip
Sauce keeps well, covered
and refrigerated, for up
to 4 days. Warm it in a
saucepan over medium heat,
prior to use.

2 tbsp	unsalted butter	25 mL
2 tbsp	all-purpose flour	25 mL
2 cups	Beef Stock (page 147) or ready-to-use broth	500 mL
1 tbsp	walnut oil	15 mL
1 tbsp	Easy or Country Ketchup (pages 115 and 116) or store-bought	15 mL
1 tbsp	Worcestershire Sauce (page 142) or store-bought	15 mL
1 tsp	dried onion flakes	5 mL
½ cup	olives, pitted and chopped	125 mL

1. In a saucepan over medium heat, brown butter, about 5 minutes. Add flour and cook, stirring, until browned, about 5 minutes. Gradually whisk in stock, walnut oil, ketchup and Worcestershire sauce until smooth. Add onion flakes and bring to a simmer. Reduce heat and simmer, stirring occasionally, until slightly thickened, for 5 minutes. Stir in olives. Serve hot.

Port Wine Sauce

**Makes 1½ cups
(375 mL)**

*This spicy and sweet sauce is
lovely with roast lamb or beef.*

Tip
Sauce keeps well, covered
and refrigerated, for up
to 4 days. Warm it in a
saucepan over medium heat,
prior to use.

½ cup	Beef Stock (page 147) or ready-to-use broth	125 mL
½ tsp	cayenne pepper	2 mL
¼ tsp	ground allspice	1 mL
¼ tsp	ground cinnamon	1 mL
⅛ tsp	ground mace	0.5 mL
½ cup	port wine	125 mL
½ cup	currant jelly	125 mL
1 tsp	freshly squeezed lemon juice	5 mL

1. In a saucepan over high heat, combine beef stock, cayenne, allspice, cinnamon and mace and bring to a boil. Reduce heat and simmer for 5 minutes. Add port, jelly and lemon juice, stirring until the jelly dissolves. Serve hot.

Sauce Finiste

*This tomato-based sauce
can be served with any type
of meat.*

Tips

Save the juice drained from
the tomatoes to enrich
another stock or sauce.

Sauce keeps well, covered
and refrigerated, for up
to 4 days. Warm it in a
saucepan over medium heat,
prior to use.

6 tbsp	unsalted butter	90 mL
1	can (19 to 20 oz/540 to 567 mL) stewed tomatoes, drained (see Tips, left)	
1 tbsp	Worcestershire Sauce (page 142) or store-bought	15 mL
2 tsp	freshly squeezed lemon juice	10 mL
1 tsp	Honey Stone-Ground Mustard (page 122) or store-bought	5 mL
½ tsp	cayenne pepper	2 mL

1. In a saucepan over medium heat, brown butter, about 5 minutes. Add tomatoes, Worcestershire sauce, lemon juice, mustard and cayenne and bring to a simmer. Reduce heat and simmer, stirring occasionally, for 3 minutes. Serve hot.

Espagnole Sauce

This classic brown sauce is one of the "mother sauces" developed by the French, which form the base of all sauces. For more on the mother sauces, see page 164.

Tips

You can purchase bouquet garni (herb bouquet) in tight bundles (see Sources page 343) or make your own (see Tips, page 146).

Sauce keeps well, covered and refrigerated, for up to 4 days. Warm it in a saucepan over medium heat, prior to use.

3 tbsp	unsalted butter	45 mL
¼ cup	real bacon bits	50 mL
½	onion, diced	½
1	large carrot, diced	1
¼ cup	all-purpose flour	50 mL
4 cups	Beef Stock (page 147) or ready-to-use broth	1 L
2 tbsp	tomato paste	25 mL
1	bouquet garni (see Tips, left)	1
¼ tsp	sea salt	1 mL
¼ tsp	freshly ground black pepper	1 mL

1. In a medium saucepan, melt butter over medium heat. Add bacon bits and sauté to soften. Add onion and carrot and sauté until softened, about 4 minutes. Add flour and cook, stirring, until mixture is dark brown, about 5 minutes. Let cool.
2. In a large saucepan, bring beef stock to a boil over high heat. Stir in cooled vegetables, tomato paste and bouquet garni. Simmer, stirring occasionally, until reduced by half, 30 to 40 minutes. Strain through a fine-mesh sieve, discarding solids. Season with salt and pepper.

Marchand de Vin Sauce

**Makes 2 cups
(500 mL)**

*In New Orleans you'll find
many spicy dishes that have
Creole and French influences.
This is a rich sauce for Eggs
Hussarde, a dish served for
brunch at Brennan's in the
French Quarter. You can use
it as a topping for an omelet
or egg dish.*

Tip

Sauce keeps well, covered
and refrigerated, for up
to 4 days. Warm it in a
saucepan over medium heat,
prior to use.

3 tbsp	unsalted butter	45 mL
4 oz	Parma ham, diced	125 g
1/2 cup	chopped green onions	125 mL
1/2 cup	mushrooms, sliced	125 mL
6	cloves garlic, minced	6
2 tbsp	all-purpose flour	25 mL
1 1/2 cups	Beef Stock (page 147) or ready-to-use broth	375 mL
3/4 cup	dry red wine	175 mL
1/8 tsp	cayenne pepper	0.5 mL
1/8 tsp	sea salt	0.5 mL
1/8 tsp	freshly ground black pepper	0.5 mL

1. In a medium saucepan, melt butter over medium heat.
   Add ham, green onions, mushrooms and garlic and sauté
   until onions are translucent, about 5 minutes. Add flour
   and cook, stirring, until lightly browned, 5 to 7 minutes.
   Gradually whisk in beef stock and wine and bring to
   a boil. Add cayenne, salt and pepper. Reduce heat and
   simmer, stirring occasionally, until sauce is thick enough
   to coat the back of a metal spoon, about 15 minutes.
   Serve hot.

White Sauces and Warm Butter Sauces

White Sauces

"Mother sauces" (also called "grand sauces") are the base of all French sauces classified in the 19th century by Chef Antonin Carême. All are based on different ingredients and methods of making. The four original mother sauces are:

- *Allemande sauce: A classic velouté sauce that is thickened with egg yolks and heavy cream*
- *Béchamel sauce: A basic white sauce made with milk that is thickened with white roux (flour/butter mixture)*
- *Espagnole sauce: A basic brown stock that is thickened with brown roux (browned flour/butter mixture)*
- *Velouté sauce: A clear stock that is thickened with white roux (flour/butter mixture)*

In the 20th century, Chef Auguste Escoffier added two more mother sauces:

- *Tomato sauce: A vegetable-based sauce*
- *Emulsified sauces: Hollandaise and mayonnaise*

Velouté Sauce

Makes 3 cups (750 mL)

Also known as white sauce, this mother sauce is made with a light stock.

Tip
Use white pepper; black pepper resembles burnt specks in this sauce.

4 cups	Chicken Stock (page 148) or ready-to-use broth	1 L
¼ cup	unsalted butter	50 mL
¼ cup	all-purpose flour	50 mL
⅛ tsp	sea salt	0.5 mL
⅛ tsp	ground white pepper	0.5 mL

1. In large saucepan, bring stock to a boil over medium heat.
2. In a medium saucepan, melt butter over medium heat. Add flour. Increase heat to high. Cook, whisking constantly, until you have a pale roux or flour is slightly browned, 2 to 3 minutes. Gradually add roux to boiling stock, whisking until smooth. Reduce heat and simmer, stirring occasionally, until thickened, for 30 minutes. Strain sauce through a fine-mesh strainer or a chinois. Season with salt and white pepper.

Béchamel Sauce

Makes 2½ cups (625 mL)

Another mother sauce, this Italian white sauce is a favorite with pasta.

¼ cup	unsalted butter	50 mL
⅓ cup	all-purpose flour	75 mL
2¼ cups	whole milk, at room temperature	550 mL
¼ cup	freshly grated Parmesan cheese	50 mL
⅛ tsp	sea salt	0.5 mL

1. In a medium saucepan, melt butter over medium–high heat. Add flour and cook, stirring rapidly, until thickened and light brown, about 2 minutes. Gradually whisk in milk and cook, whisking constantly, until thickened, about 5 minutes. Remove from heat and stir in cheese and salt.

Spicy New Orleans Béchamel Sauce

Makes 1½ cups (375 mL)

This sauce gets its inspiration from the traditional Béchamel Sauce with the addition of hot pepper sauce.

Tip
White sauces tend to break down and do not store well. Use them as fresh as possible.

¼ cup	unsalted butter	50 mL
3 tbsp	all-purpose flour	45 mL
1½ cups	whole milk, at room temperature	375 mL
1	bay leaf	1
1½ tsp	hot pepper sauce	7 mL
1 tsp	sea salt	5 mL

1. In a medium saucepan, melt butter over low heat. Add flour and cook, stirring rapidly, until thickened and light brown, about 2 minutes. Gradually whisk in milk. Add bay leaf and cook, whisking constantly, until thickened, about 5 minutes. Remove from heat and stir in hot pepper sauce and salt. Discard bay leaf.

Mornay Sauce

Makes 1 cup (250 mL)

This thick cooked cheese sauce — for vegetables such as broccoli and cauliflower — is thought to be named after the French nobleman Duke de Mornay.

1½ tsp	butter	7 mL
1½ tsp	all-purpose flour	7 mL
1 cup	whole milk, at room temperature	250 mL
1 tsp	Honey Mustard Sauce (page 120) or store-bought	5 mL
½ cup	shredded Cheddar cheese	125 mL
	Sea salt	
	Ground white pepper	

1. In a small saucepan, melt butter over medium heat. Add flour and cook, stirring rapidly, until thickened and light brown. Gradually whisk in milk and cook, whisking constantly, until thickened, about 4 minutes. Remove from heat and whisk in mustard sauce and cheese until melted. Season with salt and white pepper to taste.

Warm Butter Sauces

When making butter sauces I like to use the more expensive European-style butter, which has a higher butterfat content than regular butter. I prefer this butter because the higher fat lets me create a sauce with less added water and with a true "butter" taste and mouth feel. You can find it in specialty food stores.

Beurre Blanc Sauce

Makes 2 cups (500 mL)

This classic butter sauce can be used on fish, eggs or vegetables.

⅔ cup	dry white wine	150 mL
⅓ cup	white wine vinegar	75 mL
¼ cup	minced shallots	50 mL
¼ cup	whole milk, at room temperature	50 mL
1 lb	unsalted butter, at room temperature, cut into cubes	500 g
	Sea salt and ground white pepper	

1. In a medium saucepan over medium heat, combine white wine, vinegar and shallots and bring to a simmer. Simmer until nearly all of the liquid has evaporated, about 5 minutes. Whisk in milk. Increase heat to high. Whisk in butter, a few cubes at a time, until melted. Season with salt and white pepper to taste.

Beurre Noisette

Makes ½ cup (125 mL)

Also known as brown butter or hazelnut butter because of its nutty taste, this butter is nice to drizzle over steamed vegetables.

Tip
Butter keeps well, covered and refrigerated, for up to 2 weeks.

½ cup	unsalted butter	125 mL

1. In a medium saucepan over low heat, melt butter, swirling pan a few times, until milk solids separate and start to turn light brown, about 15 minutes. Butter can be used hot, or let cool and use as a spread when it firms up.

Beurre Noir

Also known as black butter, it is similar to Beurre Noisette (page 167), but it's cooked longer and has an acid, such as lemon juice, added.

Tip
Butter keeps well, covered and refrigerated, for up to 2 weeks.

| ½ cup | unsalted butter | 125 mL |
| 1 tsp | freshly squeezed lemon juice | 5 mL |

1. In a medium saucepan over low heat, melt butter, swirling pan a few times, until milk solids separate and start to turn a dark brown, about 20 minutes. Whisk in lemon juice. Butter can be used hot, or let cool and use as a spread when it firms up.

Beurre Fondue

Makes 1½ cups
(375 mL)

Here is a rich sauce that's delicious on fish or shellfish.

Tip
Butter keeps well, covered and refrigerated, for up to 2 weeks.

1 cup	heavy or whipping (35%) cream	250 mL
1 cup	unsalted butter, at room temperature, cut into cubes	250 mL
½ tsp	freshly squeezed lemon juice	2 mL
¼ tsp	sea salt	1 mL
¼ tsp	ground white pepper	1 mL

1. In small saucepan over medium heat, bring cream to a boil. Reduce heat and boil gently, stirring occasionally, until reduced by half, about 10 minutes.
2. Gradually whisk in butter, a few cubes at a time, until melted. Whisk in lemon juice, salt and white pepper. Serve warm.

Grenobloise Sauce

Mainly used for salmon or trout dishes, this sauce is named after Grenoble, France.

Tip
Butter keeps well, covered and refrigerated, for up to 2 weeks.

½ cup	unsalted butter	125 mL
1 tsp	freshly squeezed lemon juice	5 mL
½ tsp	capers, drained	2 mL

1. In a medium saucepan over low heat, melt butter, swirling pan a few times, until milk solids separate and start to turn light brown, about 15 minutes. Whisk in lemon juice and capers. Sauce can be used hot, or let cool and use as a spread when it firms up.

Hollandaise Sauce

An emulsified sauce, hollandaise is a staple on eggs Benedict.

Tip
To keep the sauce warm prior to use, place the sauce in a bowl, then set the bowl in a pan of warm water. Whisk the sauce for 30 seconds or until smooth, before serving.

2 tbsp	apple cider vinegar	25 mL
¼ tsp	whole black peppercorns	1 mL
¼ cup	cold water	50 mL
6	egg yolks, beaten	6
1 lb	unsalted butter, melted	500 g
1 tbsp	freshly squeezed lemon juice	15 mL
⅛ tsp	freshly ground black pepper	0.5 mL

1. In a small saucepan over medium heat, cook vinegar and peppercorns until most of the liquid has evaporated. Add water and strain through a fine-mesh sieve. Discard peppercorns.
2. Transfer to a large stainless-steel bowl and whisk in egg yolks. Set bowl on top of a saucepan of simmering water (do not let bowl touch water). Cook, whisking constantly, until thickened, about 8 minutes. Gradually whisk in melted butter in a thin, steady stream until blended. Whisk in lemon juice and pepper.

Mousseline Sauce

*This is a flavorful sauce
that's light and airy. Use it
on grilled chicken, steamed
asparagus or artichoke hearts.*

2	egg yolks	2
1 tbsp	freshly squeezed lemon juice	15 mL
¼ cup	unsalted butter, softened, cut into 5 pieces	50 mL
½ cup	heavy or whipping (35%) cream, lightly whipped	125 mL
	Salt	
	Ground white pepper	

1. In a heatproof bowl set over a saucepan of lightly simmering water (do not let bowl touch water), whisk together egg yolks and lemon juice. Cook, whisking constantly, until pale and thickened, about 5 minutes.
2. Whisk in butter, one piece at a time, until the last piece is fully blended in. Remove from heat and whisk vigorously for 1 minute. Fold in cream. Season with salt and white pepper to taste. Serve warm.

Pasta Sauces

Pairing Sauces with Pasta

Old-school wisdom on selecting pasta (and choosing which one to make from scratch) is based on how a sauce will adhere to the pasta. Long noodles, such as spaghetti, linguine and fettuccine, are the most versatile since red or white sauces made with butter will cling to the long strands. Sauces made with olive oil cling better to the thinnest spaghettini. A meat sauce needs smaller, cupped or textured pasta shapes, such as rigatoni, fusilli, conchiglie or rotelle, to trap the sauce and meat.

Now that we have the thinnest time available to get dinner on the table, we are much more flexible. Whatever pasta you have on hand, in the shapes and sizes that appeal to you or your family, is good. Choose the enhanced pastas made with a variety of flours that provide the extra nutrition you think your family needs. Experiment with fresh or imported pastas as your budget allows. Homemade or fresh pasta will always taste better than dried and, in general, cooks more quickly than dried. If you do have a choice, here are some good sauce-and-pasta pairings.

Sauce	Suggested Pastas	
Vegetable Sauces		
Cabernet Marinara Sauce	capellini	rotelle
Chunky Tomato Mushroom Sauce	cavatappi	rotini
Fast and Easy Marinara Sauce	spaghetti	rotini
15-Minute Pasta Sauce	spaghetti	rotini
Fra Diavolo Sauce	spaghettini	fettuccine
Fresh Herb Sauce	spaghettini	orecchiette
Garden Fresh Pesto Sauce	spaghetti	linguine
Pepper Mushroom Sauce	campanelle	penne
Pesto and Tomato Sauce	fusilli	fettuccine
Red Wine Marinara Sauce	spaghettini	capellini
Roasted Garlic and Pepper Sauce	linguine	rotelle
Roasted Garlic Sauce	penne	rotini
Roasted Red Pepper Sauce	orecchiette	farfalle
Sauce à la Newman	rigatoni	bucatini
Slow-Cooker Garlic and Onion Tomato Sauce	bucatini	rigatoni
Slow-Cooker Lentil Sauce	orecchiette	pappardelle
Spinach and Sun-Dried Tomato Pasta Sauce	fusilli	penne

Sauce	Suggested Pastas		
Vegetable Sauces			
Sweet-and-Sour Sauce	penne	ziti	
Tomato Basil Sauce	penne	ziti	
Wild Mushroom Sauce	ravioli	conchiglie	
Fish, Poultry and Meat Sauces			
Bolognese Sauce	conchiglie	fettuccine	
Chicken and Bean Pasta Sauce	pappardelle	orecchiette	
Chicken and Dried Plum Sauce	penne	fusilli	
Chicken Mushroom Pasta Sauce	cavatappi	rotini	
Creamy Chicken Sauce	pappardelle	fusilli	
Creamy Chicken Tomato Sauce	penne	farfalle	
Creamy Mushroom Sauce	penne	rotini	
Easy Meat Sauce	penne	rigatoni	
Grandma's Rich Meat Sauce	cavatappi	ravioli	
Italian Sausage and Pepper Sauce	bowties	penne	
Mushroom and Sausage Sauce	conchiglie	pappardelle	
Quick Pasta Meat Sauce	conchiglie	penne	
Spaghetti Anchovy Puttanesca	spaghettini	fettuccine	
Tomato Bacon Pomodoro Sauce	campanelle	penne	
Turkey Pasta Sauce	conchiglie	fusilli	rotelle
Cream Sauces			
Alexander Sauce	fettuccine	linguine	
Alfredo Sauce	linguine	fettuccine	
Blue Cheese Pasta Sauce	fusilli	farfalle	
Clam Sauce	linguine	fettuccine	
Cream Peach Sauce	spaghetti	fettuccine	
Creamy Mushroom Sauce	fettuccine	spaghetti	
Creamy Tomato Sauce	penne	rigatoni	
Figgy Cream Sauce	spaghetti	fettuccine	
Four-Cheese Sauce	spaghetti	penne	
Gorgonzola and Mascarpone Sauce	penne	fettuccine	
Mascarpone Cream Sauce	penne	bucatini	
Parsley Cream Sauce	penne	rotelle	
Pasta Carbonara	rigatoni	orecchiette	
Spinach and Cream Sauce	penne	campanelle	
Vodka Sauce	farfalle	penne	
Walnut Cream Sauce	ravioli	cavatappi	

Vegetable Sauces

Serve pasta sauces hot, right out of the pot with your choice of pasta (see Pairing Sauces with Pasta, page 172). Most sauces will keep for about 1 week in the refrigerator. I like to make double and triple batches, then freeze small portions in airtight containers for up to 3 months. Sauces taste even better a few days after preparation, since the flavors have had time to "marry."

Authentic Homemade Pizza Sauce

Makes 1½ cups (375 mL), enough for 2 medium pizzas

After looking at the price of prepared pizza sauce and all of the strange ingredients, I decided I could make a flavorful sauce for a lot less money. Now you can, too. Spread this sauce thinly on your pizza dough.

Tip

I like to make this sauce ahead, then freeze it for up to 3 months. To use, I just defrost it the day before I'm going to make pizza.

2 tbsp	extra virgin olive oil	25 mL
1	onion, finely chopped	1
1	can (16 oz/500 mL) plum tomatoes with juice, chopped	1
2 tbsp	tomato paste	25 mL
1 tbsp	white wine vinegar	15 mL
1 tbsp	granulated sugar	15 mL

1. In a large saucepan, heat oil over medium heat. Add onion and sauté until translucent, about 5 minutes.
2. Stir in tomatoes with juice, tomato paste, vinegar and sugar and bring to a boil. Reduce heat and simmer, stirring occasionally, until thickened, for 45 minutes. Transfer to a blender and purée until smooth.

Fast and Easy Marinara Sauce

**Makes 2 cups
(500 mL)**

*Use this sauce on fried
cheese or pasta for a truly
Italian dish.*

¼ cup	extra virgin olive oil	50 mL
6	cloves garlic, minced	6
1	can (28 oz/796 mL) diced tomatoes with juice	1
½ cup	loosely packed fresh basil leaves, chopped	125 mL
½ tsp	dried oregano	2 mL
½ tsp	sea salt	2 mL
½ tsp	freshly ground black pepper	2 mL

1. In a skillet, heat oil over medium heat. Add garlic and sauté until lightly browned, about 2 minutes. Add tomatoes with juice, basil, oregano, salt and pepper. Bring to a boil. Reduce heat and simmer, stirring occasionally, until sauce thickens, 25 to 30 minutes.

Red Wine Marinara Sauce

**Makes 2 cups
(500 mL)**

*To add zest, red wine is
added to the basic marinara
sauce, which makes this
a delicious way to use
leftover wine.*

¼ cup	extra virgin olive oil	50 mL
6	cloves garlic, minced	6
1	can (28 oz/796 mL) diced tomatoes with juice	1
1 cup	dry red wine	250 mL
1 tsp	dried basil	5 mL
½ tsp	dried oregano	2 mL
1 tsp	granulated sugar	5 mL
¼ tsp	sea salt	1 mL
¼ tsp	freshly ground black pepper	1 mL

1. In a skillet, heat oil over medium heat. Add garlic and sauté until lightly browned, about 2 minutes. Add tomatoes with juice and red wine and bring to a boil. Add basil and oregano. Reduce heat and simmer, stirring occasionally, for 20 minutes. Stir in sugar, salt and pepper.

Pepper Mushroom Sauce

Red and green peppers make this a colorful as well as flavorful sauce.

2 tbsp	extra virgin olive oil	25 mL
2 tbsp	vegetable oil	25 mL
1	red bell pepper, diced	1
1	green bell pepper, diced	1
1	onion, diced	1
8 oz	mushrooms, sliced	250 g
4	cloves garlic, minced	4
2	cans (each 28 oz/796 mL) diced tomatoes with juice	2
1	can (6 oz/175 mL) tomato paste	1
½ tsp	dried tarragon	2 mL
½ tsp	dried oregano	2 mL
1 tbsp	granulated sugar	15 mL
1 tsp	sea salt	5 mL

1. In a large skillet, heat olive and vegetable oils over medium heat. Add red and green peppers and onion and sauté until softened, about 5 minutes. Add mushrooms and garlic and sauté for 3 minutes. Add tomatoes with juice and tomato paste and bring to a boil. Add tarragon and oregano. Reduce heat and simmer, stirring occasionally, for 20 minutes. Stir in sugar and salt.

Sweet-and-Sour Sauce

**Makes 2 cups
(500 mL)**

*This sauce is a perfect
balance of sweet and sour
for meatballs.*

Variation
Serve this sauce with penne
or ziti pasta and 2 lbs (1 kg)
meatballs.

1 tbsp	all-purpose flour	15 mL
¼ cup	dry red wine	50 mL
1	can (14 oz/398 mL) diced tomatoes with juice	1
⅔ cup	unsweetened apple or pear juice	150 mL
2 tbsp	red wine vinegar	25 mL
2 tbsp	lightly packed brown sugar	25 mL
1 tbsp	sun-dried tomatoes, finely chopped	15 mL

1. In a bowl, combine flour and wine and stir until a smooth paste. Set aside.
2. In a skillet over medium heat, combine tomatoes with juice, apple juice, vinegar, brown sugar and sun-dried tomatoes and heat, stirring occasionally, until bubbling. Stir in paste and cook, stirring often, until thickened, about 15 minutes. Serve hot.

Sauce à la Newman

Makes 4 cups (1 L)

*The late, great Paul
Newman created a line of
pasta sauces. Here is my
version of Newman's Own
Bombolina Sauce.*

¼ cup	vegetable oil	50 mL
1	onion, diced	1
4	cloves garlic, minced	4
2	cans (each 28 oz/796 mL) crushed whole tomatoes	2
1 tsp	dried basil	5 mL
½ tsp	dried tarragon	2 mL
½ tsp	dried oregano	2 mL
¼ tsp	cayenne pepper	1 mL
1 tbsp	granulated sugar	15 mL
1 tsp	sea salt	5 mL

1. In a large skillet, heat oil over medium heat. Add onion and sauté until softened, about 5 minutes. Add garlic and sauté for 3 minutes. Add tomatoes and bring to a boil. Add basil, tarragon, oregano and cayenne. Reduce heat and simmer, stirring occasionally, for 20 minutes. Stir in sugar and salt.

Fra Diavolo Sauce

Italian for "brother devil," this sauce is fiery hot.

¼ cup	extra virgin olive oil	50 mL
1	onion, diced	1
4	cloves garlic, minced	4
2	cans (each 28 oz/796 mL) diced tomatoes with juice	2
1	can (6 oz/175 mL) tomato paste	1
¼ cup	chopped Italian flat-leaf parsley	50 mL
1 tbsp	granulated sugar	15 mL
1 tsp	sea salt	5 mL
1 tsp	dried basil	5 mL
½ tsp	dried tarragon	2 mL
½ tsp	dried oregano	2 mL
½ tsp	hot pepper flakes	2 mL
¼ tsp	cayenne pepper	1 mL

1. In a large skillet, heat oil over medium heat. Add onion and sauté until softened, about 5 minutes. Add garlic and sauté for 3 minutes. Add tomatoes with juice and tomato paste and bring to a boil. Reduce heat and simmer, stirring occasionally, for 20 minutes. Stir in parsley, sugar, salt, basil, tarragon, oregano, hot pepper flakes and cayenne. Simmer, stirring occasionally, for 20 minutes.

Roasted Garlic and Pepper Sauce

Makes 4 cups (1 L)

Sweet roasted garlic and peppers make this a favorite.

Tip
Dried red or green bell peppers are small diced peppers that yield a concentrated fresh taste and flavor. They are available in bulk-food and spice stores. If you can't find them use a double amount of diced fresh bell peppers, instead.

2	cans (each 28 oz/796 mL) diced tomatoes with juice	2
2	cans (each 6 oz/175 mL) tomato paste	2
1	whole head garlic, roasted (see Tip, below)	1
1/4 cup	olive oil	50 mL
1/4 cup	hot water	50 mL
1 tbsp	dried red and green bell peppers (see Tip, left)	15 mL
1 tbsp	granulated sugar	15 mL
1 tsp	sea salt	5 mL
1/2 tsp	dried oregano	2 mL
1/2 tsp	freshly ground black pepper	2 mL
1/4 cup	freshly grated Romano cheese	50 mL

1. In a large saucepan over medium heat, combine tomatoes with juice, tomato paste, garlic, olive oil, hot water, dried peppers, sugar, salt, oregano and black pepper and bring to a boil. Reduce heat and simmer, stirring occasionally, for 30 minutes. Stir in Romano cheese.

Roasted Garlic Sauce

Makes 2 cups (500 mL)

I like to top stuffed pasta, such as ravioli or conchiglie, with this rich sauce.

Tip
To roast garlic: Preheat oven to 400°F (200°C). Cut about 1/4 inch (0.5 cm) off the top of the bulb and drizzle with 1 tsp (5 mL) olive oil. Wrap in foil and roast until golden brown and very soft, 30 to 35 minutes. Let cool, turn upside down and press cloves out of bulb.

1	can (28 oz/796 mL) diced tomatoes with juice	1
1	can (6 oz/175 mL) tomato paste	1
6	cloves garlic, roasted (see Tip, left)	6
1/4 cup	hot water	50 mL
2 tbsp	olive oil	25 mL
1 tsp	freshly squeezed lemon juice	5 mL
1/2 tsp	dried oregano	2 mL
1/4 tsp	dried rosemary	1 mL
1/4 tsp	dried sage	1 mL
1/4 tsp	sea salt	1 mL

1. In a large saucepan over medium heat, combine tomatoes with juice, tomato paste, garlic, hot water, olive oil, lemon juice, oregano, rosemary, sage and salt and bring to a boil. Reduce heat and simmer, stirring occasionally, for 30 minutes.

Pesto and Tomato Sauce

**Makes 2 cups
(500 mL)**

*Try dipping Italian bread
sticks into this flavorful
sauce, as well as eating it
with pasta.*

- **Food processor**

2 cups	lightly packed fresh basil leaves	500 mL
6	cloves garlic	6
1/4 cup	extra virgin olive oil	50 mL
1/4 cup	pine nuts, toasted	50 mL
1/4 cup	freshly grated Parmesan cheese	50 mL
1	can (28 oz/796 mL) diced tomatoes with juice	1
1 tbsp	granulated sugar	15 mL
1 tbsp	dried onion flakes	15 mL
1 tsp	dried oregano	5 mL

1. In a food processor fitted with a metal blade, process basil leaves, garlic and oil until smooth, about 2 minutes. With motor running, add pine nuts and Parmesan cheese through feed tube and process until combined.
2. Transfer mixture to a medium saucepan. Add tomatoes with juice, sugar, onion flakes and oregano and bring to boil over medium heat. Reduce heat and simmer, stirring occasionally, until slightly thickened, for 45 minutes.

Garden Fresh Pesto Sauce

If you're lucky enough to have fresh basil growing in your garden, this recipe is the perfect way to use it. Serve over pasta with cut-up pieces of chicken.

Tip

Basil and parsley need to be washed well to remove all sand and dirt. Be sure to dry them well. If the basil and parsley are not dried completely, the pesto will have a watered-down taste. I like to use an herb spinner to get out the excess water.

Variation

For a nutty taste, add ½ cup (125 mL) toasted pine nuts when you pulse the pesto for the last time.

- **Food processor**

6 oz	Parmesan cheese, cut into chunks	175 g
2 cups	tightly packed fresh basil leaves (see Tip, left)	500 mL
¾ cup	extra virgin olive oil, divided	175 mL
8	sprigs Italian flat leaf parsley (see Tip, left)	8
4	cloves garlic	4
Pinch	salt	Pinch
Pinch	freshly ground black pepper	Pinch

1. In a food processor fitted with a metal blade with motor running, add Parmesan through feed tube and process until grated. Transfer to a bowl. Set aside.
2. In same work bowl fitted with a metal blade, process basil leaves, ½ cup (125 mL) of the oil, parsley and garlic until finely chopped, about 30 seconds. Season with salt and pepper.
3. Add remaining oil and the Parmesan and pulse until well blended, 2 to 3 seconds.
4. If not using immediately, scrape pesto into a jar or plastic container. Top with ¼ cup (50 mL) olive oil, cover and refrigerate for up to 1 week or freeze for up to 1 year. Place in the refrigerator for 1 day to defrost.

Cabernet Marinara Sauce

**Makes 2 cups
(500 mL)**

This sauce is a staple in my freezer at all times. It's so good, I could eat it without pasta. I hate to waste good wine, so when I have a bit left, I use it to make sauces.

¼ cup	extra virgin olive oil	50 mL
6	cloves garlic, minced	6
1	can (28 oz/796 mL) diced tomatoes with juice	1
1	can (6 oz/175 mL) tomato paste	1
1 cup	Cabernet Sauvignon wine	250 mL
¼ cup	loosely packed fresh basil, chiffonade	50 mL
½ tsp	dried oregano	2 mL
1 tsp	granulated sugar	5 mL
¼ tsp	sea salt	1 mL
¼ tsp	freshly ground black pepper	1 mL

1. In a skillet, heat oil over medium heat. Add garlic and sauté until lightly browned, about 2 minutes. Add tomatoes with juice, tomato paste and wine and bring to a boil. Add basil and oregano. Reduce heat and simmer, stirring occasionally, for 20 minutes. Stir in sugar, salt and pepper.

Fresh Herb Sauce

When I purchase fresh herbs for cooking I always seem to have some to spare. Try this sauce with your herbs, adjusting the flavor by adding more or less to suit your taste.

¼ cup	olive oil	50 mL
1	onion, diced	1
1	can (28 oz/796 mL) diced tomatoes with juice	1
2	cans (each 6 oz/175 mL) tomato paste	2
1 cup	hot water	250 mL
¼ cup	loosely packed fresh basil chiffonade	50 mL
2 tbsp	chopped fresh thyme	25 mL
1 tbsp	chopped fresh rosemary	15 mL
1 tsp	granulated sugar	5 mL
1 tsp	dried oregano	5 mL
1 tsp	freshly squeezed lemon juice	5 mL
½ tsp	sea salt	2 mL
½ tsp	freshly ground black pepper	2 mL

1. In a large skillet, heat oil over medium heat. Add onion and sauté until softened, about 5 minutes. Add tomatoes with juice, tomato paste and hot water and bring to a boil. Reduce heat and simmer, stirring occasionally, for 20 minutes. Stir in basil, thyme, rosemary, sugar, oregano, lemon juice, salt and pepper and simmer, stirring often, for 20 minutes.

Tomato Basil Sauce

**Makes 3 cups
(750 mL)**

*This sauce is so simple and
it's always so good.*

¼ cup	extra virgin olive oil	50 mL
1	onion, diced	1
4	cloves garlic, minced	4
2	cans (each 28 oz/796 mL) diced tomatoes with juice	2
1	can (6 oz/175 mL) tomato paste	1
¼ cup	loosely packed fresh basil chiffonade	50 mL
1 tbsp	granulated sugar	15 mL
1 tsp	sea salt	5 mL
½ tsp	dried oregano	2 mL
½ tsp	hot pepper flakes	2 mL

1. In a large skillet, heat oil over medium heat. Add onion and sauté until softened, about 5 minutes. Add garlic and sauté for 3 minutes. Add tomatoes with juice and tomato paste and bring to a boil. Reduce heat and simmer, stirring occasionally, for 20 minutes. Stir in basil, sugar, salt, oregano and hot pepper flakes and simmer, stirring often, for 20 minutes.

15–Minute Pasta Sauce

**Makes 3 cups
(750 mL)**

*Sometimes you just need a
really fast sauce and this is it.*

2 tbsp	extra virgin olive oil	25 mL
1	onion, finely chopped	1
2	cloves garlic, minced	2
1	can (28 oz/796 mL) diced tomatoes with juice	1
¼ tsp	freshly ground black pepper	1 mL

1. In a large skillet, heat oil over medium heat. Add onion and garlic and sauté until lightly browned, about 5 minutes. Add tomatoes with juice and pepper. Reduce heat and simmer, stirring occasionally, for 10 minutes.

Roasted Red Pepper Sauce

**Makes 2 cups
(500 mL)**

*This sauce is also known
as* acquasale, *which means
sweet pepper sauce.*

- **Food processor**

3 tbsp	extra virgin olive oil	45 mL
1	medium red onion, thinly sliced	1
1	clove garlic, minced	1
1½ cups	chopped roasted red bell peppers (about 4)	375 mL
2	Roma (plum) tomatoes, seeded and diced	2
½ cup	heavy or whipping (35%) cream	125 mL
¼ tsp	sea salt	1 mL
¼ cup	Italian bread crumbs (optional)	50 mL

1. In a skillet, heat oil over medium heat. Add red onion and sauté until softened, about 5 minutes. Stir in garlic and red peppers. Cover, reduce heat and sweat vegetables, until very soft, for 20 to 25 minutes. Add tomatoes, cream and salt. Cook, stirring, for 3 minutes. Let cool to room temperature.

2. In a food processor fitted with a metal blade, pulse sauce until finely chopped, about 20 times. Transfer to a saucepan over low heat and reheat until simmering, about 2 minutes. If sauce is too thin for you, add bread crumbs.

Chunky Tomato Mushroom Sauce

Makes 4 cups (1 L)

I enjoy a chunky sauce and this one fits the bill.

Tip

Use kitchen shears to cut the whole tomatoes while they're still in the can.

¼ cup	extra virgin olive oil	50 mL
1	onion, diced	1
4	cloves garlic, minced	4
2	cans (each 28 oz/796 mL) whole tomatoes with juice, chopped	2
1	can (6 oz/175 mL) tomato paste	1
12 oz	mushrooms, cut into large pieces	375 g
½ tsp	dried tarragon	2 mL
½ tsp	dried oregano	2 mL
1 tbsp	granulated sugar	15 mL
1 tsp	sea salt	5 mL
	Freshly ground black pepper	

1. In a large skillet, heat oil over medium heat. Add onion and sauté until softened, about 5 minutes. Add garlic and sauté for 3 minutes. Add tomatoes with juice, tomato paste and mushrooms and bring to a boil. Add tarragon and oregano. Reduce heat and simmer, stirring occasionally, for 20 minutes. Stir in sugar, salt, and pepper to taste.

Wild Mushroom Sauce

**Makes 2 cups
(500 mL)**

*This sauce is excellent on
ready-made cheese ravioli.*

1	onion, chopped	1
1 oz	dried sliced mushrooms	30 g
½ tsp	dried tarragon	2 mL
¼ tsp	dried dill	1 mL
¼ tsp	dried thyme	1 mL
1 tbsp	cornstarch	15 mL
2 cups	whole milk	500 mL
¼ cup	cooking sherry	50 mL
	Salt and freshly ground black pepper	

1. In a medium saucepan, bring 1 cup (250 mL) water to a boil over medium heat. Add onion, mushrooms, tarragon, dill and thyme. Reduce heat, cover and simmer until soft, about 4 minutes. Whisk cornstarch into milk, stir into sauce with sherry and bring to a simmer over medium heat, stirring constantly. Reduce heat and simmer, stirring, until thickened, about 5 minutes. Season with salt and pepper to taste.

Slow-Cooker Garlic and Onion Tomato Sauce

**Makes about 10 cups
(2.5 L)**

*It makes me feel good all day
to know the slow cooker is
working on dinner while I'm
out and about.*

- **Large (approx. 5 quart) slow cooker**

3	cans (each 28 oz/796 mL) whole tomatoes with juice	3
3	onions, chopped	3
12	cloves garlic, minced	12
¼ cup	extra virgin olive oil	50 mL
1 tbsp	freshly ground black pepper	15 mL
1 tbsp	sea salt	15 mL
1½ tsp	dried thyme	7 mL
1½ tsp	dried basil	7 mL

1. In a slow cooker, combine tomatoes with juice, onions, garlic, olive oil, pepper, salt, thyme and basil. Cover and cook on Low for 8 to 10 hours. Mash to break up tomatoes or pulse with an immersion blender for a smoother sauce.

Spinach and Sun-Dried Tomato Pasta Sauce

Makes 2 cups (500 mL)

Using sun-dried tomatoes in this sauce adds an extra punch of flavor.

Tip

If you have oil-packed tomatoes, drain and pat them dry with paper towels to eliminate excess oil, then use them as you would the sun-dried variety.

6 oz	sun-dried tomatoes (see Tip, left)	175 g
1/2 cup	hot water	125 mL
2 tsp	olive oil	10 mL
1	onion, chopped	1
4	cloves garlic, minced	4
1 lb	mushrooms, sliced	500 g
1/2 tsp	freshly ground black pepper	2 mL
1	jar (14 oz/398 mL) artichoke hearts, drained and chopped	1
1/4 cup	kalamata olives, chopped	50 mL
1/4 cup	pine nuts, toasted	50 mL
8 oz	fresh spinach, stems removed	250 g

1. In a small bowl, soak sun-dried tomatoes in hot water for 30 minutes. Drain. Slice into thin strips.
2. In a skillet, heat oil over medium heat. Add onion and garlic and sauté until lightly browned, 3 to 4 minutes. Add mushrooms and pepper and sauté until tender, about 3 minutes. Add soaked sun-dried tomatoes, artichoke hearts, olives and pine nuts and sauté until hot. Add spinach and heat, stirring, until wilted and bright green, about 3 minutes.

Slow-Cooker Lentil Sauce

Makes about 12 cups (3 L)

Lentils and cumin add texture and favor to this sauce. Serve a hearty salad on the side.

Tip

To toast cumin seeds: Place seeds in a single layer in a dry skillet over medium heat and cook, stirring continuously, until light brown and fragrant, about 4 minutes.

● **Large (approx. 5 quart) slow cooker**

3	cans (each 28 oz/796 mL) crushed tomatoes	3
¾ cup	lentils, rinsed	175 mL
6	onions, chopped	6
15	cloves garlic, minced	15
1 tbsp	granulated sugar	15 mL
1½ tsp	toasted cumin seeds (see Tip, left)	7 mL
3	small green chile peppers, seeded and minced	3

1. In a slow cooker, combine tomatoes, lentils, onions, garlic, sugar, cumin seeds and chile peppers. Cover and cook on Low, until lentils are tender, 8 to 10 hours.

Bolognese Sauce

Makes 4 cups (1 L)

This Italian favorite always seems special.

3 tbsp	extra virgin olive oil	45 mL
3 tbsp	unsalted butter	45 mL
1	large carrot, diced	1
1	onion, diced	1
2	stalks celery, diced	1
12 oz	ground beef	375 g
12 oz	ground veal	375 g
1 cup	whole milk	250 mL
1 cup	dry white wine	250 mL
1	can (28 oz/796 mL) crushed tomatoes	1
½ tsp	sea salt	2 mL
⅛ tsp	ground allspice	0.5 mL

1. In a large skillet, heat oil and butter over medium heat. Add carrot, onion and celery and sauté until softened, about 4 minutes. Add beef and veal and cook, breaking up with a spoon, until no longer pink, about 12 minutes.
2. Increase heat to high. Add milk and bring to a boil. Reduce heat to low and simmer, stirring, until milk has evaporated, about 20 minutes. Add wine and cook, stirring, until evaporated, about 15 minutes. Stir in tomatoes, salt and allspice and simmer, stirring occasionally, until thickened, for 30 minutes.

Creamy Chicken Sauce

**Makes 2 cups
(500 mL)**

*Here's a perfect use for
leftover chicken and ham.*

½ cup	dry white wine	125 mL
12 oz	chicken breast, cut into strips	375 g
6 oz	cooked ham, cut into strips	175 g
¾ cup	heavy or whipping (35%) cream	175 mL
1	egg, lightly beaten, at room temperature	1
¼ tsp	freshly grated nutmeg	1 mL
¼ tsp	sea salt	1 mL
¼ tsp	freshly ground black pepper	1 mL

1. In a large skillet, bring wine to a boil over medium heat. Add chicken and ham.
2. Reduce heat to low. Gradually stir in cream and egg and simmer, stirring, until thickened, about 8 minutes. Season with nutmeg, salt and pepper.

Creamy Chicken Tomato Sauce

**Makes 3 cups
(750 mL)**

*Sometimes you need a change
from the typical beef/pork
sauces. Make this creamy
chicken variation.*

¼ cup	extra virgin olive oil	50 mL
2 tbsp	unsalted butter	25 mL
1	onion, sliced	1
2	cloves garlic, minced	2
4 oz	prosciutto, cut into thin strips	125 g
4 oz	boneless chicken breast, cut into thin strips	125 g
1 cup	port wine	250 mL
2	cans (each 28 oz/796 mL) whole tomatoes, chopped and drained	2
1 tbsp	chopped Italian flat-leaf parsley	15 mL
1 tsp	chopped fresh rosemary	5 mL
1 tsp	chopped fresh sage	5 mL
1 tsp	chopped fresh basil	5 mL
½ tsp	sea salt	2 mL

1. In a large saucepan, heat oil and butter over medium heat. Add onion and garlic and sauté for 3 minutes. Add prosciutto and chicken and cook, stirring, for 3 minutes. Add port and boil, stirring, until it has evaporated. Add tomatoes. Cover, reduce heat to low and simmer, stirring occasionally, for 30 minutes. Stir in parsley, rosemary, sage, basil and salt. Cook, stirring often, for 10 minutes.

Mushroom and Sausage Sauce

**Makes 2 cups
(500 mL)**

*This chunky sauce is perfect
for a winter supper.*

Tip
If the sauce seems too
dry, add a little water and
simmer to the consistency
you like.

½ cup	extra virgin olive oil	125 mL
2	onions, chopped	2
3	cloves garlic, minced	3
8 oz	Italian sausage, casings removed (see Tips, page 193)	250 g
1¼ lbs	fresh mushrooms, sliced	625 g
1 cup	minced Italian flat-leaf parsley	250 mL
1 tsp	sea salt	5 mL

1. In a large skillet, heat oil over medium heat. Add onions and garlic and sauté until softened, about 6 minutes. Add sausage and cook, breaking up with a spoon, until no longer pink, about 10 minutes. Stir in mushrooms and cook, stirring occasionally, for 10 minutes. Stir in parsley and salt. Reduce heat and simmer, stirring, for 10 minutes.

Italian Sausage and Pepper Sauce

Makes 4 cups (1 L)

I like to make this sauce with some of the specialty sausages sold in Italian meat markets.

Tips

You can use either spicy or mild sausage for this sauce.

Removing the meat from the casing is easy. While the sausage is cold, snip one end of the casing, then squeeze out the meat. Sometimes you can purchase Italian sausage meat without the casings (called ground Italian sausage).

Reserve the juice drained from the tomatoes to enrich a sauce, stock or soup.

¼ cup	olive oil	50 mL
1	red bell pepper, chopped	1
1	green bell pepper, chopped	1
6	cloves garlic, minced	6
1 lb	Italian pork sausage, casings removed (see Tips, left)	500 g
2	cans (each 28 oz/796 mL) diced tomatoes, drained (see Tips, left)	2
1 tsp	freshly squeezed lemon juice	5 mL
1 tsp	granulated sugar	5 mL
1 tsp	dried oregano	5 mL
½ tsp	Hungarian paprika	2 mL
½ tsp	sea salt	2 mL
½ tsp	hot pepper flakes	2 mL

1. In a large skillet, heat oil over medium heat. Add red and green peppers and garlic and sauté until softened, about 3 minutes. Add sausage and cook, breaking up with a spoon, until no longer pink, 8 to 10 minutes. Drain off any fat from pan. Add tomatoes, lemon juice, sugar, oregano, paprika, salt and hot pepper flakes and bring to a boil. Reduce heat and simmer, stirring occasionally, until slightly thickened, for 45 minutes.

Chicken and Bean Pasta Sauce

**Makes 3 cups
(750 mL)**

*The jalapeño pepper gives
this sauce a little kick.*

3 tbsp	extra virgin olive oil	45 mL
1	onion, chopped	1
1	small jalapeño pepper, seeded and diced	1
1	green bell pepper, diced	1
6 oz	skinless boneless chicken breasts, cut into thin strips	175 g
1	can (12 oz/375 mL) pinto beans, rinsed and drained	1
5	Roma (plum) tomatoes, seeded and diced	5
2 tsp	freshly squeezed lime juice	10 mL

1. In a skillet, heat oil over medium heat. Add onion and sauté until softened, about 4 minutes. Add jalapeño and cook for 1 minute. Add bell pepper, chicken, pinto beans, tomatoes and lime juice and bring to a boil. Reduce heat and simmer, stirring, for 20 minutes.

Chicken and Dried Plum Sauce

**Makes 2 cups
(500 mL)**

*Sweet plums make this a
flavorful sauce.*

1¼ cups	chopped dried plums (about 8 oz/250 g)	300 mL
2 cups	hot water	500 mL
⅓ cup	unsalted butter	75 mL
12 oz	skinless boneless chicken breasts, cut into thin strips	375 g
1 cup	dry red wine	250 mL
1 cup	Chicken Stock (page 148) or ready-to-use broth	250 mL
⅛ tsp	freshly grated nutmeg	0.5 mL
⅛ tsp	sea salt	0.5 mL
⅛ tsp	freshly ground black pepper	0.5 mL

1. In a bowl, soak plums in hot water for 10 minutes. Drain.
2. In a medium saucepan, melt butter over medium heat. Stir in chicken and plums. Add wine and bring to a boil. Boil, stirring occasionally, until wine has evaporated, about 5 minutes. Add stock, nutmeg, salt and pepper and return to a boil. Reduce heat and simmer, stirring, until thickened, about 5 minutes.

Quick Pasta Meat Sauce

Makes 4 cups (1 L)

In a hurry? Try this fast sauce.

1 tbsp	extra virgin olive oil	15 mL
1	onion, chopped	1
6	cloves garlic, minced	6
1½ lbs	ground beef	750 g
1	can (28 oz/796 mL) diced tomatoes with juice	1
½ cup	dry red wine	125 mL
¼ cup	lightly packed fresh basil, chiffonade	50 mL
½ tsp	hot pepper flakes	2 mL

1. In a large skillet, heat oil over medium heat. Add onion and garlic and sauté until softened, for 3 minutes. Add ground beef and cook, breaking up with a spoon, until no longer pink, about 12 minutes. Drain off any fat from pan. Stir in tomatoes, wine, basil and hot pepper flakes and bring to a boil. Reduce heat and simmer, stirring occasionally, until thickened, about 20 minutes.

Chicken Mushroom Pasta Sauce

Makes 4 cups (1 L)

A rich sauce — perfect for a one-dish meal.

3 tbsp	extra virgin olive oil	45 mL
1	onion, chopped	1
8 oz	mushrooms, sliced	250 g
1	green bell pepper, diced	1
1 lb	skinless boneless chicken breasts, cut into thin strips	500 g
1 cup	heavy or whipping (35%) cream	250 mL
5	Roma (plum) tomatoes, seeded and diced	5
1 tsp	freshly ground black pepper	5 mL
1 tsp	sea salt	5mL

1. In a skillet, heat oil over medium heat. Add onion and sauté until softened, about 4 minutes. Add mushrooms and sauté for 1 minute. Stir in bell pepper, chicken, cream, tomatoes, black pepper and salt and bring to a boil. Reduce heat and simmer, stirring occasionally, until thickened, for 20 minutes.

Easy Meat Sauce

Makes 4 cups (1 L)

Sometimes simplicity is best.

1 lb	ground beef	500 g
1	clove garlic, minced	1
1 tbsp	dried onion flakes	15 mL
½ tsp	hot pepper flakes	2 mL
¼ tsp	dried oregano	1 mL
1	can (29 oz/822 g) tomato purée or 28 oz (796 mL) crushed tomatoes	1
1 cup	water	250 mL

1. In a large skillet over high heat, brown beef and garlic, breaking up with a spoon, until beef is no longer pink, about 10 minutes. Stir in onion flakes, hot pepper flakes, oregano, tomato purée and water. Cover, reduce heat and simmer, stirring occasionally, until thickened, about 30 minutes.

Turkey Pasta Sauce

Makes 3 cups (750 mL)

Try this sauce the next time you're looking for a change from the usual beef pasta sauces.

Tip
If the sauce begins to look dry during the 1-hour simmering, add a bit of water.

2 tbsp	vegetable oil	25 mL
1	onion, chopped	1
2	cloves garlic, minced	2
1 lb	ground turkey	500 g
6	Roma (plum) tomatoes, seeded and chopped	6
1	can (6 oz/175 mL) tomato paste	1
1 tbsp	dried oregano	15mL
1½ tsp	dried basil	7 mL
1 cup	dry red wine	250 mL
1 tsp	freshly ground black pepper	5 mL

1. In a large skillet, heat oil over medium heat. Add onion and sauté until translucent, about 3 minutes. Add garlic and turkey and sauté, breaking up with a spoon, until lightly browned, about 10 minutes. Stir in tomatoes, tomato paste, oregano, basil, wine and pepper and bring to a boil. Reduce heat and simmer, stirring occasionally, until thickened, for 1 hour.

Grandma's Rich Meat Sauce

**Makes 3 cups
(750 mL)**

*My grandmother used to
make everything homemade.
Here is her version of a fast
and easy sauce.*

1 lb	ground beef	500 g
1	clove garlic, minced	1
1 tsp	dried onion flakes	5 mL
½ tsp	onion powder	2 mL
½ tsp	celery salt	2 mL
¼ tsp	freshly ground white pepper	1 mL
¼ tsp	dried oregano	1 mL
1	can (29 oz/822 g) tomato purée or 28 oz (796 mL) crushed tomatoes	1
1 cup	dry white wine	250 mL

1. In a large skillet over medium heat, brown beef and garlic, breaking up beef with a spoon, until beef is no longer pink, about 10 minutes. Stir in onion flakes, onion powder, celery salt, white pepper, oregano, tomato purée and wine and bring to a boil. Cover, reduce heat and simmer, stirring occasionally, until thickened, about 30 minutes.

Tomato Bacon Pomodoro Sauce

**Makes 2 cups
(500 mL)**

*Pomodoro means red tomato
in Italian. Luckily, this great
red tomato sauce lets you
enjoy the taste without a trip
to Italy.*

1 tbsp	olive oil	15 mL
8 oz	bacon, diced	250 g
½ cup	diced onion	125 mL
1	clove garlic, minced	1
1¾ cups	canned crushed tomatoes	425 mL
⅓ cup	tomato paste	75 mL
⅔ cup	Chicken Stock (page 148) or ready-to-use broth	150 mL
½ tsp	dried parsley	2 mL
¼ tsp	dried basil	1 mL
¼ tsp	dried oregano	1 mL
	Sea salt	
	Freshly ground black pepper	

1. In a large saucepan, heat oil over medium heat. Add bacon and sauté until browned, about 7 minutes. Add onion and garlic and sauté until softened, about 5 minutes. Stir in tomatoes, tomato paste, stock, parsley, basil, oregano and salt and pepper to taste. Simmer, stirring occasionally, for 15 minutes.

Spaghetti Anchovy Puttanesca

**Makes 2 cups
(500 mL)**

*Most sauces are made with
the harvest from the garden.
This off-season favorite
from Naples is made with
the bounty of a good Italian
market.*

Tip
I don't add salt to this pasta
sauce because the anchovies
are salty enough.

2 tbsp	extra virgin olive oil	25 mL
3	cloves garlic, minced	3
2 tbsp	chopped Italian flat-leaf parsley	25 mL
½ tsp	hot pepper flakes	2 mL
1	can (28 oz/796 mL) diced tomatoes with juice	1
½ cup	whole black olives, coarsely chopped	125 mL
1 tbsp	capers, drained	15 mL
3	anchovy fillets	3
¼ cup	freshly grated Parmesan cheese	50 mL

1. In a skillet, heat oil over medium heat. Add garlic,
   parsley and hot pepper flakes and sauté, about 2 minutes.
   Add tomatoes with juice and bring to a boil. Reduce
   heat and simmer, stirring occasionally, until liquid has
   almost evaporated, about 30 minutes. Stir in olives,
   capers and anchovies and heat through. Garnish with
   Parmesan cheese.

Cream Sauces

Alexander Sauce

**Makes 3 cups
(750 mL)**

*Many restaurants in
the Deep South have a
seafood-based sauce called
Alexander. Some use
crayfish, others use shrimp.*

¾ cup	unsalted butter, divided	175 mL
1	onion, chopped	1
1½ tbsp	all-purpose flour	22 mL
½ cup	clam juice	125 mL
2 cups	heavy or whipping (35%) cream	500 mL
½ tsp	sea salt	2 mL
½ tsp	cayenne pepper	2 mL
¼ tsp	freshly ground white pepper	1 mL
8 oz	cooked small salad shrimp	250 g
5 oz	lump crabmeat	150 g

1. In a large saucepan, melt butter over medium heat. Add onion and sauté until softened, about 4 minutes. Sprinkle in flour and cook, stirring constantly, for 2 minutes. Gradually whisk in clam juice and cream and cook, whisking constantly, until thickened, about 3 minutes. Season with salt, cayenne and white pepper. Stir in shrimp and crabmeat and simmer, stirring, until seafood is hot, about 2 minutes.

Creamy Mushroom Sauce

Makes 2 cups (500 mL)

Top a beef dish or Salisbury steak with this sauce.

½ cup	Vegetable Stock (page 149) or ready-to-use broth	125 mL
1 cup	heavy or whipping (35%) cream	250 mL
1½ tbsp	unsalted butter	22 mL
6 oz	portobello mushrooms, stemmed and chopped	175 g
4 oz	button mushrooms, stemmed and sliced	125 g
1 tsp	chopped fresh oregano	5 mL
1 tsp	chopped fresh chives	5 mL
1 tsp	chopped Italian flat-leaf parsley	5 mL
	Sea salt	
	Ground white pepper	

1. In a medium saucepan over low heat, combine stock and cream and bring to a boil. Reduce heat and simmer until thickened, about 4 minutes. Remove from heat.
2. In a skillet, melt butter over medium heat. Add portobello and button mushrooms and sauté until softened, about 5 minutes. Stir into cream sauce with oregano, chives and parsley. Season with salt and white pepper to taste. Serve warm.

Vodka Sauce

This is my all-time favorite pasta sauce. I have heard that vodka is also a secret ingredient in the pasta sauces of other chefs.

¼ cup	unsalted butter	50 mL
2 tbsp	extra virgin olive oil	25 mL
1 tbsp	minced onion	15 mL
1	clove garlic, minced	1
¼ cup	vodka	50 mL
1½ cups	heavy or whipping (35%) cream, at room temperature	375 mL
½ cup	Chicken Stock (page 148) or ready-to-use broth	125 mL
2	Roma (plum) tomatoes, chopped	2
2 tsp	finely chopped fresh sage	10 mL
1 tsp	kosher salt	5 mL
1	egg yolk	1
⅓ cup	freshly grated Parmesan cheese	75 mL
1 tbsp	chopped Italian flat-leaf parsley	15 mL

1. In a skillet, heat butter and oil over medium heat. Add onion and garlic and sauté until softened, about 3 minutes. Add vodka and bring to a boil. Boil until almost evaporated, about 4 minutes. Whisk in cream, stock, tomatoes, sage and salt. Reduce heat and simmer, stirring often, until sauce is thick enough to coat the back of a spoon, about 8 minutes. Remove from heat.

2. In a small bowl, combine egg yolk and a few spoonfuls of sauce. Stir into sauce and return to low heat. Cook, stirring, until slightly thickened, for 2 minutes. Stir in cheese. Garnish with parsley.

Four-Cheese Sauce

Makes 4 cups (1 L)

This sauce is so rich that a small amount goes a long way.

3 tbsp	extra virgin olive oil	45 mL
½ cup	chopped onion	125 mL
4	cloves garlic, minced	4
1	can (29 oz/822 mL) tomato purée or 28 oz (796 mL) crushed tomatoes	1
1	can (14½ oz/411 mL) diced tomatoes with juice	1
1 cup	white wine	250 mL
½ cup	heavy or whipping (35%) cream, at room temperature	125 mL
6 oz	Asiago cheese, grated	175 g
6 oz	provolone cheese, grated	175 g
4 oz	Romano cheese, grated	125 g
2 oz	blue cheese, crumbled	60 g
1 tbsp	granulated sugar	15 mL
½ tsp	sea salt	2 mL

1. In a skillet, heat oil over medium heat. Add onion and garlic and sauté until lightly browned and onion is softened, about 4 minutes. Add tomato purée and diced tomatoes and bring to a boil. Reduce heat and simmer for 2 minutes. Stir in wine and cream and simmer, stirring, until slightly thickened, for 5 minutes.
2. Transfer mixture to a large saucepan over medium heat. Stir in Asiago, provolone, Romano and blue cheeses and cook until bubbling. Season with sugar and salt.

Pasta Carbonara

This is a very rich pasta dish — just add some bread and you'll have a complete meal.

1 lb	pasta, such as rigatoni or orecchiette	500 g
8 oz	Italian sausage, casings removed (see Tips, page 193)	250 g
8 oz	prosciutto, thinly sliced	250 g
1 cup	chopped Italian flat-leaf parsley	250 mL
3 tbsp	unsalted butter, melted	45 mL
4	eggs, beaten	4
1 cup	grated Romano cheese	250 mL
1 tsp	freshly ground black pepper	5 mL

1. In a large pot of boiling salted water, cook pasta according to package directions until tender but firm. Drain well.
2. Meanwhile, in a skillet over medium heat, brown sausage, breaking up with a spoon, until no longer pink, about 5 minutes. Add prosciutto and parsley and cook, stirring, until parsley is wilted, about 3 minutes.
3. In a large bowl, combine hot sausage mixture, hot pasta, butter, eggs, Romano cheese and pepper.

Gorgonzola and Mascarpone Sauce

I made this for an Italian Christmas party once. It was a hit there, and it will be at your home, too.

½ cup	heavy or whipping (35%) cream	125 mL
¼ cup	unsalted butter, softened	50 mL
5 oz	Gorgonzola cheese, crumbled	150 g
3 oz	mascarpone cheese	90 g
1 tbsp	vodka	15 mL
1 tsp	sea salt	5 mL
1 tsp	freshly ground white pepper	5 mL

1. In a medium saucepan over medium heat, combine cream and butter and heat until bubbling, about 3 minutes. Whisk in Gorgonzola and mascarpone until melted and smooth. Add vodka, salt and white pepper.

Figgy Cream Sauce

Makes 2 cups (500 mL)

The figs add a sweet taste to this rich sauce.

¼ cup	unsalted butter	50 mL
8	fresh figs, peeled and chopped	8
½ cup	dry white wine	125 mL
2	anchovy fillets, chopped	2
½ cup	heavy or whipping (35%) cream, at room temperature	125 mL
1 tsp	sea salt	5 mL
1 tsp	freshly ground black pepper	5 mL

1. In a large skillet, melt butter over medium heat. Add figs and sauté until soft enough to be smashed with the back of a wooden spoon, about 4 minutes. Add wine and cook until evaporated, about 5 minutes. Add anchovies and cook for 2 minutes. Whisk in cream and heat, stirring, until simmering, about 3 minutes. Season with salt and pepper.

Cream Peach Sauce

Makes 2 cups (500 mL)

Here's a fresh-fruit twist on pasta sauce.

Variations

You can use any fresh stone fruits, such as nectarines or plums, in place of the peaches.

• **Food processor**

3	ripe peaches, peeled and halved	3
1 tbsp	unsalted butter	15 mL
1½ tbsp	all-purpose flour	22 mL
1 cup	heavy or whipping (35%) cream, at room temperature	250 mL
¼ cup	freshly grated Romano cheese	50 mL
1 tsp	sea salt	5 mL
1 tsp	freshly ground black pepper	5 mL
⅛ tsp	freshly grated nutmeg	0.5 mL

1. In a food processor fitted with metal blade, process peaches until smooth, about 2 minutes. Set aside.
2. In a skillet, melt butter over high heat. Sprinkle in flour and cook, whisking, until lightly browned, about 3 minutes. Remove from heat and whisk in peach purée. Whisk in cream, Romano cheese, salt, pepper and nutmeg. Reduce heat to low, and cook, stirring gently, until thickened, about 8 minutes.

Parsley Cream Sauce

*The color of this light green
sauce is perfect for spring.*

2 tbsp	unsalted butter	25 mL
1	onion, finely chopped	1
1¼ cups	chopped Italian flat-leaf parsley	300 mL
½ cup	dry white wine	125 mL
⅓ cup	heavy or whipping (35%) cream, at room temperature	75 mL
½ cup	freshly grated Romano cheese	125 mL
½ tsp	sea salt	2 mL
½ tsp	freshly ground black pepper	2 mL

1. In a skillet, melt butter over medium-low heat. Add onion and sauté until softened, about 4 minutes. Stir in parsley, wine and cream and heat until bubbling. Whisk in Romano cheese. Season with salt and pepper.

Mascarpone Cream Sauce

*Here's a no-cook sauce that's
so creamy even a little serving
is satisfying.*

6 oz	mascarpone cheese, at room temperature	175 g
¼ cup	heavy or whipping (35%) cream	50 mL
1	egg yolk (see Tip, page 37)	1
1 lb	hot cooked pasta, such as penne	500 g
¼ cup	freshly grated Parmesan cheese	50 mL
¼ tsp	sea salt	1 mL
¼ tsp	freshly ground black pepper	1 mL
⅛ tsp	freshly grated nutmeg	0.5 mL

1. In a bowl, beat together mascarpone cheese, cream and egg yolk. Toss with very hot pasta. Stir in Parmesan cheese, salt, pepper and nutmeg.

Creamy Tomato Sauce

Makes 2½ cups (625 mL)

This simple creamy tomato sauce is best eaten as soon as it's made.

1	can (8 oz/227 mL) tomato sauce	1
1 cup	heavy or whipping (35%) cream, at room temperature (see Tips, below)	250 mL
½ cup	freshly grated Parmesan cheese	125 mL
2	cloves garlic, minced	2
½ tsp	sea salt	2 mL
½ tsp	freshly ground black pepper	2 mL

1. In a small saucepan, bring tomato sauce to a gentle boil over medium heat. Stir in cream, Parmesan, garlic, salt, and pepper and heat thoroughly, stirring often, about 4 minutes.

Alfredo Sauce

Makes 1 cup (250 mL)

Here's a standard sauce that you can build on to make it your own.

Tips

Make sure your cream is at room temperature when added to heated ingredients or it may curdle.

If you need to warm up this sauce, it's best to do it in a saucepan over low heat, stirring constantly. Microwaving it will create hot spots and burn the sauce.

Variation

Customize this sauce by adding cooked chicken, cooked shrimp or blanched vegetables such as broccoli.

2 tbsp	unsalted butter	25 mL
1 tbsp	all-purpose flour	15 mL
1 cup	whole milk	250 mL
⅓ cup	heavy or whipping (35%) cream, at room temperature (see Tips, left)	75 mL
¼ cup	freshly grated Parmesan cheese	50 mL
½ tsp	sea salt	2 mL
½ tsp	freshly ground black pepper	2 mL

1. In a medium saucepan, melt butter over medium heat. Sprinkle in flour and cook, stirring, until pale brown, about 3 minutes. Gradually whisk in milk in a thin steady stream and cook, whisking, until thickened, about 2 minutes. Whisk in cream, Parmesan, salt and pepper.

Blue Cheese Pasta Sauce

Makes 3½ cups (875 mL)

This sauce has a bit of a bite thanks to the blue cheese.

Variation

If blue cheese is too strong for your taste, you can substitute the same amount of feta or Gorgonzola.

1 cup	heavy or whipping (35%) cream	250 mL
½ cup	unsalted butter, softened	125 mL
1 cup	freshly grated Parmesan cheese	250 mL
6 oz	blue cheese, crumbled	175 g
½ tsp	freshly ground black pepper	2 mL

1. In a medium saucepan, bring cream and butter to a gentle boil over medium heat. Stir in Parmesan and blue cheeses until melted. Stir in pepper.

Walnut Cream Sauce

Makes 1½ cups (375 mL)

Nuts make a perfect addition to pasta sauces.

Tip

To toast walnuts: Spread nuts in a single layer on a baking sheet. Bake in a preheated 400°F (200°C) oven until fragrant, about 5 minutes.

3 tbsp	unsalted butter	45 mL
¼ cup	all-purpose flour	50 mL
1¼ cups	whole milk	300 mL
½ cup	walnuts, chopped and toasted (see Tip, left)	125 mL
½ tsp	sea salt	2 mL
½ tsp	ground white pepper	2 mL

1. In a medium saucepan, melt butter over medium heat. Sprinkle in flour. Reduce heat to low and cook, whisking constantly, until flour is lightly browned, about 3 minutes. Gradually whisk in milk in a thin steady stream and cook, whisking, until smooth and thickened, about 3 minutes. Stir in walnuts, salt and white pepper.

Spinach and Cream Sauce

Makes 2 cups (500 mL)

Even people who say they don't like spinach will like this sauce.

3 tbsp	extra virgin olive oil	45 mL
1	clove garlic, minced	1
1	package (10 oz/300 g) frozen spinach, thawed, squeezed dry and chopped	1
1/2 cup	heavy or whipping (35%) cream, at room temperature (see Tips, page 206)	125 mL
1/3 cup	whole milk	75 mL
1/2 tsp	sea salt	2 mL
1/2 tsp	freshly ground black pepper	2 mL

1. In a skillet, heat oil over medium heat. Add garlic and sauté until lightly browned, about 2 minutes. Stir in spinach and cook, stirring, for 2 minutes. Stir in cream and milk and heat until bubbling. Season with salt and pepper.

Clam Sauce

Makes 5 cups (1.25 L)

If you have canned clams in your pantry, and you want a new recipe for them — try this one.

1	can (12 oz/375 mL) clams, drained and chopped, reserving juice	1
2 cups	heavy or whipping (35%) cream	500 mL
2 cups	whole milk	500 mL
1 tsp	sea salt	5 mL
1/4 tsp	ground thyme	1 mL
3 tbsp	unsalted butter	45 mL
1/2 cup	chopped onion	125 mL
3	stalks celery, chopped	3
2	cloves garlic, minced	2
3 tbsp	all-purpose flour	45 mL

1. In a medium saucepan, combine clam juice, cream, milk, salt and thyme and bring almost to a boil over medium heat. Reduce heat to low and keep hot.
2. In another medium saucepan, melt butter over medium heat. Add onion, celery and garlic and sauté until softened. Sprinkle in flour and cook, whisking constantly, until thickened, about 4 minutes. Gradually whisk in hot clam juice mixture and cook, whisking, until thickened, about 4 minutes. Stir in chopped clams and cook until heated through .

Marinades, Barbecue Sauces and Rubs

continued on next page

Internal Temperatures for Cooked Meats

Meat	Rare	Medium-Rare	Medium	Medium-Well
Beef	125°F (52°C)	135°F (57°C)	145°F (63°C)	155°F (68°C)
Lamb chop or roast	125°F (52°C)	135°F (57°C)	145°F (63°C)	155°F (68°C)
Lamb shoulder or shank	*	*	*	155°F (68°C)
Pork loin or tenderloin	*	*	*	155°F (68°C)
Pork shoulder	*	*	165°F (74°C)	170°F (77°C)
Chicken	*	*	*	165°F (74°C)
Cornish hens	*	*	*	165°F (74°C)
Turkey	*	*	*	165°F (74°C)

The temperature will continue to rise 5° to 10°F (3° to 6°C), depending on the size of the meat or poultry, so it is best to remove the item from the oven or barbecue when the internal temperature is slightly lower than the desired temperature.

★ *To ensure food safety, not recommended*

Marinades

Years ago, marinades were used to enhance the flavor and textures of low-quality meats. Today most marinades are used just to add flavors. After marinating your meat, dispose of the used marinade carefully; it is contaminated, as is anything that came into contact with it.

An easy and efficient container for marinating is a large resealable freezer bag. The meat will be immersed in the marinade, and the bag will fit into odd spaces in your refrigerator. It's also easy to turn the bag a few times, if necessary, to keep the meat covered with the marinade. The times in the Meat Marinade Chart (page 213) are the minimum times to marinate. Personally, I like to marinate meats for a minimum of 4 hours — overnight is even better. Shrimp and fish are exceptions, needing less than an hour due to their size, and, if you leave them too long, the acid in the marinade will start to chemically cook them.

Grill, roast or broil the marinated meat to your preference. Although food-safety guidelines recommend cooking most meat to at least 140°F (60°C) to kill bacteria, the personal preference of many people — to ensure optimum flavor and juiciness of beef, lamb and fish — is cooking to medium-rare or medium. A trusted source for your meat is especially important if you enjoy rare meat or raw fish. See Meat Marinade Chart (page 213) for the best uses for each marinade and the marinating times.

Meat Marinade Chart

Adjust the marinating times to suit your taste — it's very subjective. If you would like an intense flavor, marinate for a longer period. Never go past a full day, though, or the marinade will break down the meat and you'll be left with just pieces to cook.

Meat	Marinades	Marinating Time
Poultry		
Cornish hens	Chile Lime Marinade	1 to 2 hours
	Italian Herb Marinade	1 to 2 hours
	Moroccan Marinade	1 to 2 hours
Whole chickens	Basic Chicken Marinade	2 to 4 hours
	Citrus Marinade	2 to 4 hours
	Firehouse Marinade	2 to 4 hours
	Orange Nutmeg Marinade	2 to 4 hours
	Tomato Garlic Marinade	2 to 4 hours
	12-Clove Garlic Lime Marinade	1 to 3 hours
Chicken breasts	Asian Marinade	45 minutes to 2 hours
	Greek Marinade	1 to 3 hours
	Provençal Marinade	1 to 4 hours
	12-Clove Garlic Lime Marinade	30 minutes to 2 hours
Chicken pieces	Chipotle Chile Marinade	1 to 2 hours
	Citrus Marinade	1 to 4 hours
	Lemon Marinade	1 to 4 hours
	Orange Nutmeg Marinade	1 to 4 hours
	Peanut Marinade	20 to 30 minutes
Chicken wings	Caribbean Jerk Marinade	45 minutes to 2 hours
	Citrus Marinade	1 to 4 hours
	Firehouse Marinade	45 minutes to 2 hours
	Honey Sesame Marinade	2 to 5 hours
	Peanut Marinade	20 to 30 minutes
	Teriyaki Marinade	45 minutes to 2 hours
Turkey breasts	Chipotle Chile Marinade	45 minutes to 2 hours
	Italian Herb Marinade	45 minutes to 2 hours
	Orange Mint Marinade	45 minutes to 2 hours
	Simple Basic Marinade	45 minutes to 2 hours
	Soy Sesame Marinade	45 minutes to 2 hours

Meat	Marinades	Marinating Time
Beef		
Roast	Beef Satay Marinade	1 to 2 hours
	Cuban Spice Marinade	1 to 2 hours
	Espresso Marinade	1 to 2 hours
	Teriyaki Marinade	1 to 2 hours
Ribs	Chipotle Chile Marinade	45 to 90 minutes
	Dark Beer Marinade	45 to 90 minutes
	Firehouse Marinade	45 to 90 minutes
	Soy Sesame Marinade	1 hour to 90 minutes
Steaks	Fresh Garlic Marinade	45 to 90 minutes
	Spicy South-of-the-Border Marinade	45 to 90 minutes
Lamb		
Shanks/Legs	Greek Marinade	1 to 2 hours
	Italian Herb Marinade	1 to 2 hours
	Moroccan Marinade	1 to 2 hours
	Tandoori Marinade	1 to 2 hours
	Tequila Lime Marinade	1 to 2 hours
	Turkish Lime Yogurt Marinade	30 minutes to 1 hour
Pork		
Chops	Caribbean Jerk Marinade	45 to 90 minutes
	Cuban Spice Marinade	30 minutes to 1 hour
	Provençal Marinade	45 to 90 minutes
	Tequila Lime Marinade	30 minutes to 2 hours
	12-Clove Garlic Marinade	30 minutes to 2 hours
Shoulder	Chile Lime Marinade	1 to 2 hours
	Spicy South-of-the-Border Marinade	45 to 90 minutes
	Soy Sesame Marinade	1 to 2 hours
	Tandoori Marinade	45 to 90 minutes

Meat	Marinades	Marinating Time
Pork		
Loin	Cuban Spice Marinade	1 to 2 hours
	Provençal Marinade	1 to 2 hours
	Tequila Lime Marinade	30 minutes to 2 hours
	12-Clove Garlic Marinade	30 minutes to 2 hours
Ribs	Caribbean Jerk Marinade	45 to 90 minutes
	Chile Lime Marinade	45 to 90 minutes
	Soy Sesame Marinade	1 to 2 hours
	Spicy South-of-the-Border Marinade	45 to 90 minutes
Fish and Seafood		
Salmon	Citrus Marinade	20 to 30 minutes
	Cool Cucumber Parsley Marinade	45 to 90 minutes
	Honey Sesame Marinade	45 to 90 minutes
	Orange Mint Marinade	20 to 30 minutes
	Teriyaki Marinade	20 to 30 minutes
Shrimp	Firehouse Marinade	10 to 20 minutes
	Greek Marinade	10 to 20 minutes
	Soy Sesame Marinade	10 to 20 minutes
	Tequila Lime Marinade	10 to 20 minutes
	12-Clove Garlic Marinade	10 to 20 minutes
Scallops	Asian Marinade	10 to 20 minutes
	Chile Lime Marinade	10 to 20 minutes
	Citrus Marinade	10 to 20 minutes
	Cool Cucumber Parsley Marinade	10 to 20 minutes
	Lemon Marinade	10 to 20 minutes

Asian Marinade

Gingerroot adds a tang to this marinade.

¼ cup	extra virgin olive	50 mL
¼ cup	natural rice vinegar	50 mL
¼ cup	dry red wine	50 mL
4	cloves garlic, minced	4
2 tbsp	freshly squeezed orange juice	25 mL
1 tbsp	granulated sugar	15 mL
1 tbsp	grated gingerroot	15 mL
⅛ tsp	kosher salt	0.5 mL
⅛ tsp	freshly ground black pepper	0.5 mL

1. In a bowl, whisk together oil, vinegar, red wine, garlic, orange juice, sugar, ginger, salt and pepper.

Basic Chicken Marinade

Makes 2½ cups (625 mL)

This is my standard simple marinade I use with chicken.

1 cup	tomato sauce	250 mL
½ cup	plum jam	125 mL
¼ cup	firmly packed brown sugar	50 mL
¼ cup	malt vinegar	50 mL
¼ cup	Worcestershire Sauce (page 142) or store-bought	50 mL
2	cloves garlic, smashed	2

1. In a bowl, whisk together tomato sauce, plum jam, brown sugar, vinegar, Worcestershire sauce and garlic.

Beef Satay Marinade

Makes ¾ cup (175 mL)

When I worked for the Walt Disney Company, we made a great beef satay during our barbecue festival. Here it is for you to enjoy.

3 tbsp	extra virgin olive oil	45 mL
3 tbsp	chopped fresh cilantro	45 mL
2 tbsp	freshly squeezed lemon juice	25 mL
2 tbsp	tamari	25 mL
2 tbsp	minced gingerroot	25 mL
4	cloves garlic, minced	4
1 tbsp	granulated sugar	15 mL
1½ tsp	ground cumin	7 mL
2	small red chile peppers, chopped	2

1. In a bowl, whisk together oil, cilantro, lemon juice, tamari, ginger, garlic, sugar, cumin and chile peppers.

Caribbean Jerk Marinade

Makes 1½ cups (375 mL)

Toss shrimp into this marinade for a dynamite dish.

½ cup	thawed frozen orange juice concentrate	125 mL
¼ cup	extra virgin olive oil	50 mL
¼ cup	freshly squeezed lemon juice	50 mL
¼ cup	chopped fresh cilantro	50 mL
¼ cup	minced onion	50 mL
2 tbsp	tequila	25 mL
1 tbsp	orange-flavored liqueur	15 mL
3	cloves garlic, minced	3
1 tsp	sea salt	5 mL
½ tsp	ground cumin	2 mL
½ tsp	curry powder	2 mL
¼ tsp	ground turmeric	1 mL
¼ tsp	hot pepper flakes	1 mL
¼ tsp	freshly ground black pepper	1 mL

1. In a bowl, whisk together orange juice concentrate, oil, lemon juice, cilantro, onion, tequila, orange liqueur, garlic, salt, cumin, curry powder, turmeric, hot pepper flakes and black pepper.

Chile Lime Marinade

Makes 1 cup (250 mL)

The chiles and lime make this marinade spicy and cool all at once.

½ cup	white wine vinegar	125 mL
¼ cup	soybean oil	50 mL
1 tbsp	freshly squeezed lime juice	15 mL
2 tsp	Dijon Mustard (page 120) or store-bought	10 mL
2 tsp	minced garlic	10 mL
2 tsp	dried onion flakes	10 mL
1 tsp	hot pepper flakes	5 mL
1 tsp	freshly ground black pepper	5 mL
1	small red chile pepper, minced	1

1. In a bowl, whisk together vinegar, oil, lime juice, mustard, garlic, onion flakes, hot pepper flakes, black pepper and chile pepper.

Chipotle Chile Marinade

Makes 1½ cups (375 mL)

Here's a smoky, spicy marinade that's perfect for ribs.

¾ cup	red wine vinegar	175 mL
½ cup	extra virgin olive oil	125 mL
1	chipotle pepper in adobo sauce, seeded and minced	1
2 tsp	Dijon Mustard (page 120) or store-bought	10 mL
2 tsp	minced dried garlic	10 mL
1 tsp	sea salt	5 mL
1 tsp	freshly ground black pepper	5 mL
½ tsp	hot pepper flakes	2 mL

1. In a bowl, whisk together vinegar, oil, chipotle, mustard, garlic, salt, black pepper and hot pepper flakes.

Citrus Marinade

Makes 1 cup (250 mL)

This light marinade adds a sweet, sharp hit of citrus.

½ cup	sherry wine vinegar	125 mL
¼ cup	extra virgin olive oil	50 mL
½ tsp	grated lemon zest	2 mL
1 tbsp	freshly squeezed lemon juice	15 mL
1½ tsp	freshly squeezed lime juice	7 mL
1 tsp	dried mint	5 mL
1 tsp	dried cilantro	5 mL

1. In a bowl, whisk together vinegar, oil, lemon zest and juice, lime juice, mint and cilantro.

Cool Cucumber Parsley Marinade

Makes 2 cups (500 mL)

Here's a light and fresh Italian marinade.

½ cup	canola oil	125 mL
1	cucumber, finely chopped	1
¼ cup	sherry vinegar	50 mL
¼ cup	Chianti wine	50 mL
¼ cup	chopped Italian flat-leaf parsley	50 mL
2 tsp	dried Italian seasoning	10 mL

1. In a bowl, whisk together oil, cucumber, vinegar, wine, parsley and Italian seasoning.

Cuban Spice Marinade

**Makes 1¾ cups
(425 mL)**

*Subtle spices warm up this
island marinade for poultry
or beef.*

1 cup	extra virgin olive oil	250 mL
	Grated zest and juice of 1 orange	
5	cloves garlic, minced	5
2 tbsp	minced onion	25 mL
½ tsp	ground cumin	2 mL
½ tsp	dried oregano	2 mL
1	bay leaf, crushed	1
¼ tsp	sea salt	1 mL

1. In a bowl, whisk together oil, orange zest and juice, garlic, onion, cumin, oregano, bay leaf and salt.

Dark Beer Marinade

**Makes 1¾ cups
(425 mL)**

*The dark stout ale lends
much more flavor than a
light beer.*

1 cup	dark stout beer, at room temperature	250 mL
½ cup	canola oil	125 mL
2	cloves garlic, minced	2
2 tbsp	soy sauce	25 mL
1 tbsp	minced onion	15 mL
1 tbsp	minced shallot	15 mL
1 tbsp	chopped fresh tarragon	15 mL
1 tbsp	chopped Italian flat-leaf parsley	15 mL
1 tsp	Dijon Mustard (page 120) or store-bought	5 mL
⅛ tsp	freshly ground black pepper	0.5 mL
⅛ tsp	sea salt	0.5 mL

1. In a bowl, whisk together beer, oil, garlic, soy sauce, onion, shallot, tarragon, parsley, mustard, pepper and salt.

Espresso Marinade

Makes 1 cup (250 mL)

I like using this marinade on cuts of beef to add another level of flavor.

½ cup	extra virgin olive oil	125 mL
¼ cup	strong espresso, at room temperature (about 3 shots)	50 mL
4	cloves garlic, minced	4
1 tbsp	soy sauce	15 mL
1 tbsp	minced onion	15 mL
1 tsp	chopped fresh tarragon	5 mL
1 tsp	chopped fresh sage	5 mL
⅛ tsp	freshly ground black pepper	0.5 mL
⅛ tsp	sea salt	0.5 mL

1. In a bowl, whisk together oil, espresso, garlic, soy sauce, onion, tarragon, sage, pepper and salt.

Firehouse Marinade

Makes 1¼ cups (300 mL)

I named this for the hot, hot, hot flavor of the jalapeño peppers.

½ cup	red wine vinegar	125 mL
¼ cup	freshly squeezed lemon juice	50 mL
¼ cup	extra virgin olive oil	50 mL
3	jalapeño peppers, seeded and minced	3
2 tsp	Dijon Mustard (page 120) or store-bought	10 mL
2 tsp	minced dried garlic	10 mL
2 tsp	dried onion flakes	10 mL
1 tsp	hot pepper flakes	5 mL

1. In a bowl, whisk together vinegar, lemon juice, oil, jalapeños, mustard, garlic, onion flakes and hot pepper flakes.

Fresh Garlic Marinade

Makes 1½ cups (375 mL)

Especially for garlic lovers, this marinade has four cloves of fresh garlic.

1 cup	extra virgin olive oil	250 mL
1 tbsp	grated lime zest	15 mL
¼ cup	freshly squeezed lime juice	50 mL
4	cloves garlic, minced	4
2 tsp	kosher salt	10 mL
1½ tsp	freshly ground black pepper	7 mL

1. In a bowl, whisk together oil, lime zest and juice, garlic, salt and pepper.

Greek Marinade

Makes 1 cup (250 mL)

Olives make this a perfect Mediterranean marinade.

½ cup	red wine vinegar	125 mL
¼ cup	soybean oil	50 mL
¼ cup	kalamata olives, finely chopped	50 mL
1 tsp	Dijon Mustard (page 120) or store-bought	5 mL
1 tsp	chopped fresh thyme	5 mL
1 tsp	chopped fresh oregano	5 mL
1 tsp	capers, drained	5 mL

1. In a bowl, whisk together vinegar, oil, olives, mustard, thyme, oregano and capers.

Honey Sesame Marinade

Makes 1¼ cups (300 mL)

This marinade is sweet and nutty and will enhance any meat.

½ cup	apple cider vinegar	125 mL
⅓ cup	sesame oil	75 mL
¼ cup	liquid honey	50 mL
1 tsp	Dijon Mustard (page 120) or store-bought	5 mL
1 tsp	sesame seeds	5 mL
½ tsp	dried sage	2 mL
½ tsp	freshly ground black pepper	2 mL

1. In a bowl, whisk together vinegar, oil, honey, mustard, sesame seeds, sage and pepper.

Italian Herb Marinade

Makes 1 cup (250 mL)

Here's a fast and flavorful marinade.

½ cup	red wine vinegar	125 mL
¼ cup	soybean oil	50 mL
1 tbsp	freshly squeezed lime juice	15 mL
2 tsp	Dijon Mustard (page 120) or store-bought	10 mL
2 tsp	minced garlic	10 mL
2 tsp	dried onion flakes	10 mL
1 tsp	dried Italian seasoning	5 mL
1 tsp	sea salt	5 mL
1 tsp	freshly ground black pepper	5 mL

1. In a bowl, whisk together vinegar, oil, lime juice, mustard, garlic, onion flakes, Italian seasoning, salt and pepper.

Lemon Marinade

Makes 1 cup (250 mL)

Pucker up with this zesty marinade.

½ cup	sherry vinegar	125 mL
¼ cup	extra virgin olive oil	50 mL
1 tbsp	grated lemon zest	15 mL
1 tbsp	freshly squeezed lemon juice	15 mL
2 tsp	capers, drained	10 mL
1 tsp	dried mint	5 mL

1. In a bowl, whisk together vinegar, oil, lemon zest and juice, capers and mint.

Orange Mint Marinade

Makes 1 cup (250 mL)

The fresh flavors in this marinade lend a bright citrus taste.

½ cup	apple cider vinegar	125 mL
¼ cup	extra virgin olive oil	50 mL
¼ cup	orange marmalade	50 mL
1 tbsp	grated orange zest	15 mL
1 tbsp	freshly squeezed orange juice	15 mL
1 tsp	dried mint	5 mL

1. In a bowl, whisk together vinegar, oil, orange marmalade, orange zest and juice and mint.

Orange Nutmeg Marinade

Makes 1 cup (250 mL)

Grating fresh nutmeg for this marinade makes all the difference.

Tip
You can use a nutmeg or Microplane grater to grate the nutmeg.

½ cup	apple cider vinegar	125 mL
¼ cup	extra virgin olive oil	50 mL
¼ cup	thawed frozen orange juice concentrate	50 mL
1 tbsp	grated orange zest	15 mL
1 tsp	freshly grated nutmeg (see Tip, left)	5 mL

1. In a bowl, whisk together vinegar, oil, orange juice concentrate, orange zest and nutmeg.

Peanut Marinade

Makes 1 cup (250 mL)

The nutty taste of peanuts enhances this marinade.

⅓ cup	peanut oil	75 mL
⅓ cup	Smooth Peanut Butter (page 298) or store-bought	75 mL
3 tbsp	freshly squeezed lemon juice	45 mL
2 tbsp	granulated sugar	25 mL
1 tbsp	sesame oil	15 mL
1 tbsp	hoisin sauce	15 mL
1 tbsp	soy sauce	15 mL
1 tsp	dry mustard	5 mL
¼ tsp	ground white pepper	1 mL
¼ tsp	Chinese 5-spice powder	1 mL
⅛ tsp	ground ginger	0.5 mL

1. In a bowl, whisk together peanut oil, peanut butter, lemon juice, sugar, sesame oil, hoisin sauce, soy sauce, dry mustard, white pepper, 5-spice powder and ground ginger.

Provençal Marinade

Makes 1⅓ cups (325 mL)

Capture the flavors of the south of France with this lively marinade.

1 cup	extra virgin olive oil	250 mL
1 tbsp	grated lime zest	15 mL
½ cup	freshly squeezed lime juice	125 mL
1½ tsp	freshly ground black pepper	7 mL
1 tsp	herbes de Provence	5 mL
1 tsp	kosher salt	5 mL

1. In a bowl, whisk together oil, lime zest and juice, pepper, herbes de Provence and salt.

Garden Fresh Pesto Sauce (page 181)

Spaghetti Anchovy Puttanesca (page 198)

All-American BBQ Sauce (page 231)

Guacamole (page 266)

South-of-the-Border Salsa (page 277)

Milk Chocolate Sauce (page 322)

Rich Caramel Sauce (page 325)

Crème Anglaise (page 328)

Moroccan Marinade

Makes 1¾ cups (425 mL)

This marinade adds a powerful flavor to lamb.

½ cup	extra virgin olive oil	125 mL
½ cup	diced onion	125 mL
½ cup	freshly squeezed lemon juice	125 mL
5	cloves garlic, minced	5
1 tbsp	ground cumin	15 mL
3	bay leaves, crushed	3
2 tsp	Hungarian paprika	10 mL
½ tsp	ground turmeric	2 mL

1. In a bowl, whisk together oil, onion, lemon juice, garlic, cumin, bay leaves, paprika and turmeric.

Simple Basic Marinade

Makes ¾ cup (175 mL)

Sometimes you need a simple marinade to enhance less expensive cuts of meat. This one does the trick.

½ cup	white wine vinegar	125 mL
¼ cup	extra virgin olive oil	50 mL
2 tsp	Dijon Mustard (page 120) or store-bought	10 mL
1 tsp	dried basil	5 mL
1 tsp	dried rosemary	5 mL

1. In a bowl, whisk together vinegar, oil, mustard, basil, and rosemary.

Soy Sesame Marinade

Makes 1¼ cup (300 mL)

Add a little Asian flavor to your meats with this marinade.

½ cup	apple cider vinegar	125 mL
⅓ cup	sesame oil	75 mL
¼ cup	reduced-sodium soy sauce	50 mL
1 tbsp	lightly packed brown sugar	15 mL
1 tsp	Honey Yellow Mustard (page 121) or store-bought	5 mL
1 tsp	sesame seeds	5 mL
½ tsp	freshly ground black pepper	2 mL

1. In a bowl, whisk together vinegar, oil, soy sauce, brown sugar, mustard, sesame seeds and pepper.

Spicy South-of-the-Border Marinade

Makes 1¼ cups (300 mL)

I like to use this marinade when making fajitas.

¾ cup	red wine vinegar	175 mL
½ cup	extra virgin olive oil	125 mL
1	jalapeño pepper, seeded and minced	1
2 tsp	prepared mustard	10 mL
2 tsp	minced dried garlic	10 mL
1 tsp	sea salt	5 mL
1 tsp	freshly ground black pepper	5 mL
1 tsp	cayenne pepper	5 mL
½ tsp	hot pepper flakes	2 mL

1. In a bowl, whisk together vinegar, oil, jalapeno, mustard, garlic, salt, black pepper, cayenne and hot pepper flakes.

Tandoori Marinade

Makes 1½ cups (375 mL)

Yogurt cheese makes this spicy marinade perfect for lamb or poultry dishes. It's well worth the time it takes to make it.

● **Colander, lined with cheesecloth**

2 cups	plain yogurt	500 mL
¼ cup	freshly squeezed lime juice	50 mL
1½ tbsp	minced gingerroot	22 mL
3	cloves garlic, minced	3
2	jalapeño peppers, seeded and minced	2
2	bay leaves, crushed	2
2 tsp	Hungarian paprika	10 mL
2 tsp	ground cumin	10 mL
2 tsp	ground coriander	10 mL
1 tsp	turmeric	5 mL
1 tsp	sea salt	5 mL
½ tsp	freshly ground black pepper	2 mL
⅛ tsp	ground cardamom	0.5 mL

1. In prepared colander, drain yogurt for 2 hours until thickened to make yogurt cheese. Discard liquid.
2. In a bowl, whisk together drained yogurt, lime juice, ginger, garlic, jalapeños, bay leaves, paprika, cumin, coriander, turmeric, salt, black pepper and cardamom.

Tequila Lime Marinade

Makes 2 cups (500 mL)

The tequila adds a Mexican punch to this marinade.

½ cup	freshly squeezed orange juice	125 mL
⅓ cup	reduced-sodium soy sauce	75 mL
⅓ cup	tequila	75 mL
⅓ cup	freshly squeezed lime juice	75 mL
¼ cup	water	50 mL
1 tbsp	lightly packed brown sugar	15 mL
1 tbsp	liquid honey	15 mL
1½ tsp	sea salt	7 mL
1 tsp	onion powder	5 mL
½ tsp	garlic powder	2 mL
¼ tsp	freshly ground black pepper	1 mL

1. In a bowl, whisk together orange juice, soy sauce, tequila, lime juice, water, brown sugar, honey, salt, onion powder, garlic powder and pepper.

Teriyaki Marinade

Makes 2½ cups (625 mL)

The rum gives an added bite to this marinade — don't omit it!

1 cup	reduced-sodium soy sauce	250 mL
1 cup	teriyaki sauce	250 mL
⅓ cup	dark rum	75 mL
2 tbsp	minced gingerroot	25 mL
4	cloves garlic, minced	4

1. In a bowl, whisk together soy sauce, teriyaki sauce, rum, ginger and garlic.

Tomato Garlic Marinade

Makes 1¼ cups (300 mL)

Along with their flavor, the tomatoes add color and texture to this marinade.

4	Roma (plum) tomatoes, seeded and diced	4
¼ cup	firmly packed brown sugar	50 mL
¼ cup	malt vinegar	50 mL
¼ cup	Worcestershire Sauce (page 142) or store-bought	50 mL
2	cloves garlic, smashed	2

1. In a bowl, combine tomatoes, brown sugar, vinegar, Worcestershire sauce and garlic.

Turkish Lime Yogurt Marinade

Makes 1½ cups (375 mL)

Fresh lime juice makes the difference in this marinade.

• **Colander, lined with cheesecloth**

2 cups	plain yogurt	500 mL
¼ cup	freshly squeezed lime juice	50 mL
1½ tbsp	minced gingerroot	22 mL
3	cloves garlic, minced	3
2	bay leaves, crushed	2
2 tsp	ground cumin	10 mL
2 tsp	ground coriander	10 mL
1 tsp	turmeric	5 mL
1 tsp	sea salt	5 mL
½ tsp	freshly ground black pepper	2 mL

1. In prepared colander, drain yogurt for 2 hours until thick to make yogurt cheese. Discard liquid.
2. In a bowl, whisk together drained yogurt, lime juice, ginger, garlic, bay leaves, cumin, coriander, turmeric, salt and pepper.

12-Clove Garlic Lime Marinade

Makes 2½ cups (625 mL)

Here's a marinade with a citrus bite and the surprise of sage. With 12 cloves of garlic, it works fast for bold flavor.

• **Food processor**

12	cloves garlic	12
2 cups	extra virgin olive oil	500 mL
2 tsp	kosher salt	10 mL
1½ tsp	freshly ground black pepper	7 mL
2 tbsp	grated lime zest	25 mL
½ cup	freshly squeezed lime juice	125 mL
½ cup	fresh sage leaves	125 mL

1. In a food processor fitted with a metal blade, process garlic for 10 seconds. With motor running, add oil, salt and pepper through feed tube and process for 30 seconds. Add lime zest and juice and sage and pulse 10 times.

Barbecue Sauces

Barbecue Sauce Chart

Barbecue sauce is not a marinade so should not be put on meat before cooking. When it's brushed on before grilling, the sugars in the sauce burn before the meat is done and make the finished food look unappetizing. Serve the sauce hot or cold at the table, or brush the meat with it in the last few minutes of grilling. Store sauce in an airtight container, and refrigerate up to 2 weeks. Do not store any leftover sauce that has come into contact with any meat that has not been fully cooked.

Meat	Barbecue Sauces
Poultry	
Cornish hens	Double Chile BBQ Sauce
	Honey Orange BBQ Sauce
	Island BBQ Sauce
	Mexican Chile BBQ Sauce
Whole chickens	Pepper Spice BBQ Sauce
	Pucker Up BBQ Sauce
	Tamarind BBQ Sauce
Chicken breasts	Indian Yogurt BBQ Sauce
	Strawberry BBQ Sauce
	Sweet-and-Smoky BBQ Sauce
	Tamarind BBQ Sauce
Chicken pieces	Double Chile BBQ Sauce
	Pucker Up BBQ Sauce
	Sweet-and-Sour BBQ Sauce
	Whiskey BBQ Sauce
Chicken wings	Blackberry BBQ Sauce
	Hot Hot Hot BBQ Sauce
	Island BBQ Sauce
	Pepper Spice BBQ Sauce
Turkey breasts	All-American BBQ Sauce
	Honey Orange BBQ Sauce
	Sun-Dried Tomato BBQ Sauce
	Sweet-and-Smoky BBQ Sauce

Meat	Barbecue Sauces
Beef	
Roast	All-American BBQ Sauce
	Orange Pepper BBQ Sauce
	Sun-Dried Tomato BBQ Sauce
Ribs	Kansas City BBQ Sauce
	Memphis BBQ Sauce
	Mexican Chile BBQ Sauce
	Orange Pepper BBQ Sauce
Steaks	Orange Pepper BBQ Sauce
	Pepper Spice BBQ Sauce
Lamb	
Shanks/Legs	Honey Orange BBQ Sauce
	Indian Yogurt BBQ Sauce
	Tamarind BBQ Sauce
Pork	
Chops	All-American BBQ Sauce
	Creole Spicy BBQ Sauce
	Mexican Chile BBQ Sauce
Ribs	Honey Orange BBQ Sauce
	Island BBQ Sauce
	Memphis BBQ Sauce
	Mexican Chile BBQ Sauce
	Whiskey BBQ Sauce
Shoulder	All-American BBQ Sauce
	Creole Spicy BBQ Sauce
	Mexican Chile BBQ Sauce
Fish and Seafood	
Salmon	Island BBQ Sauce
	Sweet-and-Sour BBQ Sauce
	Tamarind BBQ Sauce
Shrimp	Blackberry BBQ Sauce
	Creole Spicy BBQ Sauce
	Honey Balsamic Mustard BBQ Sauce
	Island BBQ Sauce

Meat	Barbecue Sauces
Scallops	Honey Balsamic Mustard BBQ Sauce
	Pepper Spice BBQ Sauce
	Strawberry BBQ Sauce

All-American BBQ Sauce

**Makes 2 cups
(500 mL)**

This is a basic sauce that can be used on any cut and type of meat.

1 tbsp	extra virgin olive oil	15 mL
1	large onion, finely chopped	1
1/2 cup	Easy Ketchup (page 115) or store-bought	125 mL
1/3 cup	lightly packed brown sugar	75 mL
1/3 cup	Worcestershire Sauce (page 142) or store-bought	75 mL
1/4 cup	Steak Sauce (page 126) or store-bought	50 mL
1/4 cup	water	50 mL
2 tbsp	apple cider vinegar	25 mL
1/2 tsp	hot pepper sauce	2 mL

1. In a medium saucepan, heat oil over medium heat. Add onion and sauté until softened, about 4 minutes. Stir in ketchup, brown sugar, Worcestershire sauce, steak sauce, water, vinegar and hot pepper sauce and bring to a simmer. Reduce heat and simmer, stirring occasionally, until thickened and reduced enough to coat the back of a spoon, for 25 minutes.

Blackberry BBQ Sauce

**Makes 2 cups
(500 mL)**

*Sweet and spicy this sauce is
perfect for small bites such as
wings or shrimp.*

1 cup	blackberry preserves or jam	250 mL
¼ cup	peanut oil	50 mL
¼ cup	freshly squeezed lemon juice	50 mL
¼ cup	Worcestershire Sauce (page 142) or store-bought	50 mL
¼ cup	dark beer, at room temperature	50 mL
1	clove garlic, minced	1
1 tsp	sea salt	5 mL
1 tsp	freshly ground black pepper	5 mL

1. In a medium saucepan over medium heat, combine blackberry preserves, oil, lemon juice, Worcestershire sauce, beer, garlic, salt and pepper and bring to a simmer. Reduce heat and simmer, stirring often, until thickened, about 5 minutes.

Creole Spicy BBQ Sauce

**Makes 2 cups
(500 mL)**

*Most sauces in Cajun
country are dark brown and
full of flavor. This one is
no different.*

1 tbsp	unsalted butter	15 mL
1	onion, diced	1
5	cloves garlic, minced	5
1	red bell pepper, chopped	1
1 cup	dark beer, at room temperature	250 mL
¾ cup	apple cider vinegar	175 mL
½ cup	light (fancy) molasses	125 mL
½ cup	lightly packed brown sugar	125 mL
1	can (6 oz/175 mL) tomato paste	1
¼ cup	hot pepper sauce, such as Tabasco	50 mL
1 tsp	cayenne pepper	5 mL

1. In a medium saucepan, melt butter over medium heat. Add onion, garlic and bell pepper and sauté until onion is lightly browned, about 8 minutes. Stir in beer, vinegar, molasses, brown sugar, tomato paste, hot pepper sauce and cayenne and bring to a simmer. Reduce heat and simmer, stirring often, until thickened, about 20 minutes.

Double Chile BBQ Sauce

Makes 1 cup (250 mL)

This sauce is so hot with chiles, the chicken will never know what hit it!

1 tbsp	unsalted butter	15 mL
1/3 cup	minced shallots	75 mL
1	clove garlic, minced	1
1/3 cup	liquid honey	75 mL
1/3 cup	dry white wine	75 mL
1/4 cup	Dijon Mustard (page 120) or store-bought	50 mL
2	jalapeño peppers, seeded and minced	2
1	small serrano chile, seeded and minced	1
2 tbsp	chopped Italian flat-leaf parsley	25 mL
1 tsp	sea salt	5 mL
1/4 tsp	freshly ground black pepper	1 mL

1. In a medium saucepan, melt butter over medium heat. Add shallots and garlic and sauté for 2 minutes. Stir in honey, wine, mustard, jalapeños, serrano chile, parsley, salt and pepper and bring to a simmer. Reduce heat and simmer, stirring often, until slightly thickened, for 20 minutes.

Honey Balsamic Mustard BBQ Sauce

Makes 2 1/4 cups (550 mL)

Sweet and tangy, this sauce pairs perfectly with shrimp and scallops.

Tip

This sauce can double as a dipping sauce as the texture is thinner than most barbecue sauces.

1 cup	liquid honey	250 mL
1/2 cup	red wine vinegar	125 mL
1/3 cup	Worcestershire Sauce (page 142) or store-bought	75 mL
1/4 cup	Country Ketchup (page 116) or store-bought	50 mL
1/4 cup	balsamic vinegar	50 mL
2 tbsp	granulated sugar	25 mL
2 tbsp	dry mustard	25 mL
2 tsp	freshly grated gingerroot	10 mL
1 tsp	grated lemon zest	5 mL

1. In a medium saucepan over low heat, combine honey, red wine vinegar, Worcestershire sauce, ketchup, balsamic vinegar, sugar, dry mustard, ginger and lemon zest and bring to a simmer. Cook, whisking often, until thickened, about 20 minutes. Simmer until flavors are blended, about 5 minutes.

Honey Orange BBQ Sauce

Makes 1½ cups (375 mL)

Basted in this sauce, pork ribs never tasted so good.

½ cup	reduced-sodium soy sauce	125 mL
½ cup	pure maple syrup	125 mL
¼ cup	thawed frozen orange juice concentrate	50 mL
¼ cup	liquid honey	50 mL
2 tbsp	dry mustard	25 mL

1. In a small saucepan over low heat, combine soy sauce, maple syrup, orange juice concentrate, honey and dry mustard and heat until simmering, stirring often.

Hot Hot Hot BBQ Sauce

Makes 1½ cups (375 mL)

This is an easy no-cook sauce that's great to brush on meat or fish.

1 cup	Country Ketchup (page 116) or store-bought	250 mL
¼ cup	Spicy Chili Sauce (page 124) or store-bought	50 mL
3 tbsp	liquid honey	45 mL
1 tbsp	freshly squeezed lemon juice	15 mL
1 tbsp	hot pepper sauce	15 mL
½ tsp	hot pepper flakes	2 mL

1. In a bowl, combine ketchup, chili sauce, honey, lemon juice, hot pepper sauce and hot pepper flakes.

Indian Yogurt BBQ Sauce

Makes 1 cup (250 mL)

This creamy yogurt sauce suits lamb or chicken.

- Food processor or blender

1 tbsp	olive oil	15 mL
1	onion, diced	1
2	cloves garlic, minced	2
½ tsp	grated gingerroot	2 mL
½ cup	Roasted Red Pepper Ketchup (page 118)	125 mL
1 tsp	curry powder	5 mL
1 tsp	Hungarian paprika	5 mL
½ tsp	sea salt	2 mL
½ tsp	hot pepper sauce	2 mL
½ cup	plain low-fat yogurt, at room temperature	125 mL

1. In a saucepan, heat oil over medium heat. Add onion, garlic and ginger and sauté until lightly browned, about 4 minutes.
2. Stir in ketchup, curry powder, paprika, salt and hot pepper sauce and bring to a simmer. Reduce heat and simmer, stirring often, until slightly thickened, for 5 minutes.
3. Remove from heat and let cool slightly. Stir in yogurt. Transfer to a food processor or blender and purée until smooth.

Island BBQ Sauce

Makes 1½ cups (375 mL)

Dip pork ribs and chicken wings into this island sauce.

½ cup	reduced-sodium soy sauce	125 mL
½ cup	pineapple juice	125 mL
¼ cup	rum, dark or light	50 mL
¼ cup	liquid honey	50 mL
2 tbsp	dry mustard	25 mL
2 tbsp	lightly packed brown sugar	25 mL

1. In a small saucepan over low heat, combine soy sauce, pineapple juice, rum, honey, dry mustard and brown sugar and heat until simmering, stirring often.

Kansas City BBQ Sauce

Makes 1½ cups (375 mL)

This classic Kansas City barbecue sauce is thick and sweet, with a touch of heat to give it a little kick.

1¼ cups	Country Ketchup (page 116) or store-bought	300 mL
1 cup	water	250 mL
⅓ cup	apple cider vinegar	75 mL
¼ cup	lightly packed brown sugar	50 mL
2 tbsp	liquid honey	25 mL
1 tbsp	onion powder	15 mL
1 tbsp	garlic powder	15 mL
1 tbsp	freshly ground black pepper	15 mL
1 tsp	ground allspice	5 mL
1 tsp	cayenne pepper	5 mL
½ tsp	freshly grated nutmeg	2 mL

1. In a medium saucepan over low heat, combine ketchup, water, vinegar, brown sugar, honey, onion powder, garlic powder, black pepper, allspice, cayenne and nutmeg and bring to a boil. Reduce heat and simmer, stirring often, until reduced by half, about 20 minutes.

Memphis BBQ Sauce

Makes 2 cups (500 mL)

I love the ribs from the Rendezvous restaurant in Memphis. They usually use a dry rub on the cooking ribs, then serve the sauce on the side so you can choose just how much you want.

1 cup	Country Ketchup (page 116) or store-bought	250 mL
1 cup	Bold Chili Sauce (page 125) or store-bought	250 mL
1	large onion, diced	1
1 cup	red wine vinegar	250 mL
¼ cup	Dijon Mustard (page 120) or store-bought	50 mL
¼ cup	lightly packed brown sugar	50 mL
2	cloves garlic, minced	2
1 tsp	hot pepper sauce	5 mL

1. In a saucepan over medium heat, combine ketchup, chili sauce, onion, vinegar, mustard, brown sugar, garlic and hot pepper sauce and bring to a simmer. Reduce heat and simmer, stirring often, until thickened, about 10 minutes.

Mexican Chile BBQ Sauce

**Makes 2 cups
(500 mL)**

*Having a party? Bring on
the spareribs and cover them
in this spicy sauce.*

● **Food processor or blender**

1 tbsp	olive oil	15 mL
1	onion, chopped	1
1	clove garlic, minced	1
1	can (14½ oz /411 mL) diced tomatoes with juice	1
⅓ cup	canola oil	75 mL
¼ cup	red wine vinegar	50 mL
¼ cup	dark Mexican beer	50 mL
2 tbsp	chili powder	25 mL
2 tbsp	granulated sugar	25 mL
2 tsp	sea salt	10 mL
2	serrano chiles, seeded and chopped	2

1. In a medium saucepan, heat olive oil over low heat. Add onion and garlic and sauté until softened, about 3 minutes. Stir in tomatoes, canola oil, vinegar, beer, chili powder, sugar, salt and chile peppers and bring to a simmer. Reduce heat and simmer, stirring often, until slightly thickened, for 10 minutes. Let cool slightly. Transfer to a food processor or blender and purée until smooth.

Strawberry BBQ Sauce

**Makes 2 cups
(500 mL)**

*Here's a lovely sweet-and-
sour sauce to enjoy with
chicken in the summertime.*

½ cup	Worcestershire Sauce (page 142)	125 mL
½ cup	apple cider vinegar	125 mL
½ cup	lightly packed brown sugar	125 mL
⅓ cup	freshly squeezed lemon juice	75 mL
¼ cup	canola oil	50 mL
2 tbsp	corn syrup	25 mL
2 tsp	sea salt	10 mL
1 tsp	garlic salt	5 mL
½ tsp	freshly ground black pepper	2 mL
1 cup	strawberries, slightly crushed	250 mL

1. In a saucepan over medium-high heat, combine 1 cup (250 mL) water, Worcestershire, vinegar, sugar, lemon juice, oil, corn syrup, salt, garlic salt and pepper and bring to a boil. Remove from heat. Stir in berries. Let cool.

Orange Pepper BBQ Sauce

Makes 2 cups (500 mL)

Here's an easy-to-cook sauce that's really tasty with beef.

● **Food processor or blender**

2 tbsp	canola oil	25 mL
1	onion, chopped	1
2	cloves garlic, chopped	2
2 tsp	grated gingerroot	10 mL
1 tsp	freshly ground black pepper	5 mL
½ tsp	aniseeds, crushed	2 mL
1	can (14½ oz /411 g) diced tomatoes with juice	1
1	can (6 oz/175 mL) tomato paste	1
½ cup	orange marmalade	125 mL
¼ cup	hot pepper jelly	50 mL

1. In a medium saucepan, heat oil over low heat. Add onion and sauté until softened, about 5 minutes. Add garlic, ginger, black pepper and aniseeds and sauté for 5 minutes.
2. Stir in tomatoes with juice, tomato paste, orange marmalade and hot pepper jelly and bring to a simmer. Reduce heat and simmer, stirring, until slightly thickened, for 5 minutes. Thin sauce with a little water if it seems too thick.
3. Let cool. Transfer to a food processor or blender and purée until smooth.

Pucker Up BBQ Sauce

**Makes 3 cups
(750 mL)**

*Get vegetables roasting on
the grill, then throw on the
meat — and use this dipping
sauce for the whole works.*

- Food processor or blender
- Preheat barbecue grill to medium

6	Roma (plum) tomatoes, cut in half and seeded	6
½	red onion, quartered	½
2	poblano chile peppers, cut in half and seeded	2
3 tbsp	extra virgin olive oil	45 mL
1 cup	red wine vinegar	250 mL
¼ cup	chopped Italian flat-leaf parsley	50 mL
¼ cup	chopped fresh basil	50 mL
3	cloves garlic, minced	3
3 tbsp	freshly squeezed lemon juice	45 mL
1 tsp	sea salt	5 mL
1 tsp	freshly ground black pepper	5 mL

1. Brush tomatoes, onion and chile peppers with oil. Grill over medium heat, turning frequently, until charred. Transfer to a food processor or blender with vinegar, parsley, basil, garlic, lemon juice, salt and pepper and purée until smooth.
2. Transfer to a medium saucepan over low heat and bring to a simmer. Reduce heat and simmer, stirring often, until slightly thickened, for 20 minutes.

Sun-Dried Tomato BBQ Sauce

Makes 1 cup (250 mL)

This rich sauce is full of intense flavor.

● **Food processor or blender**

8 oz	oil-packed sun-dried tomatoes, drained	250 g
3 tbsp	Worcestershire Sauce (page 142) or store-bought	45 mL
2 tbsp	canola oil	25 mL
1 tbsp	freshly squeezed lemon juice	15 mL
3	cloves garlic, minced	3
2	jalapeño peppers, seeded and minced	2
2 tsp	grated gingerroot	10 mL
2 tsp	chili powder	10 mL
1 tsp	sea salt	5 mL
1 tsp	freshly ground black pepper	5 mL

1. In a medium saucepan over low heat, combine sun-dried tomatoes, Worcestershire sauce, oil, lemon juice, garlic, jalapeños, ginger, chili powder, salt and black pepper and bring to a simmer. Simmer, stirring often, until slightly thickened, for 20 minutes. Transfer to a food processor or blender and purée until smooth.

Sweet and Smoky BBQ Sauce

Makes 1½ cups (375 mL)

This is the fastest sauce ever!

½ cup	Smoked Chili Sauce (page 123) or store-bought	125 mL
⅓ cup	Coarse Brown Mustard (page 121) or store-bought	75 mL
⅓ cup	liquid honey	75 mL
¼ cup	Worcestershire Sauce (page 142) or store-bought	50 mL
½ tsp	sea salt	2 mL

1. In a bowl, whisk together chili sauce, mustard, honey, Worcestershire sauce and salt.

Sweet and Sour BBQ Sauce

Makes 2 cups (500 mL)

Pork and beef ribs are perfect with this sauce.

2 cups	Country Ketchup (page 116) or store-bought	500 mL
1½ cups	lightly packed brown sugar	375 mL
½ cup	apple cider vinegar	125 mL
½ cup	water	125 mL
2 tsp	onion salt	10 mL
1 tsp	celery salt	5 mL
½ tsp	ground cinnamon	2 mL
½ tsp	ground cloves	2 mL
½ tsp	ground allspice	2 mL
¼ tsp	ground nutmeg	1 mL

1. In a medium saucepan over low heat, combine ketchup, brown sugar, vinegar, water, onion salt, celery salt, cinnamon, cloves, allspice and nutmeg and bring to a simmer. Simmer, stirring often, until thickened, for 1 hour.

Tamarind BBQ Sauce

Makes 1½ cups (375 mL)

This spicy sauce livens up lamb and chicken.

2 tbsp	peanut oil	25 mL
¼ cup	minced shallots	50 mL
4	cloves garlic, minced	4
1¼ cups	hoisin sauce	300 mL
½ cup	tamarind concentrate	125 mL
⅓ cup	reduced-sodium soy sauce	75 mL
¼ cup	liquid honey	50 mL
1 tbsp	grated gingerroot	15 mL
1 tsp	hot chili sauce	5 mL
1 tsp	coriander seeds	5 mL
1 tsp	grated lime zest	5 mL
½ tsp	aniseeds	2 mL

1. In a medium saucepan, heat oil over high heat. Add shallots and sauté until lightly browned, about 4 minutes. Add garlic and sauté for 2 minutes. Reduce heat to low. Stir in hoisin sauce, tamarind, soy sauce, honey, ginger, hot chili sauce, coriander seeds, lime zest and aniseeds and bring to a simmer. Simmer, stirring often, until thickened, for 10 minutes.

Whiskey BBQ Sauce

Makes ¾ cup (175 mL)

This is a quick sauce for chicken and pork.

¼ cup	Dijon Mustard (page 120) or store-bought	50 mL
¼ cup	Steak Sauce (page 126) or store-bought	50 mL
¼ cup	whiskey	50 mL
1 tsp	grated lemon zest	5 mL
2 tbsp	freshly squeezed lemon juice	25 mL
¼ tsp	hot pepper sauce	1 mL
¼ tsp	sea salt	1 mL

1. In a bowl, whisk together mustard, steak sauce, whiskey, lemon zest and juice, hot pepper sauce and salt.

Pepper Spice BBQ Sauce

Makes 1 cup (250 mL)

I baste grilled chicken wings with this sauce, just before I serve them.

¼ cup	peanut oil	50 mL
¼ cup	freshly squeezed lemon juice	50 mL
¼ cup	Worcestershire Sauce (page 142) or store-bought	50 mL
¼ cup	reduced-sodium soy sauce	50 mL
1 tsp	sea salt	5 mL
1 tsp	freshly ground black pepper	5 mL
1 tsp	ground white pepper	5 mL
1 tsp	Chinese 5-spice powder	5 mL
1	clove garlic, minced	1
½ tsp	cayenne pepper	2 mL

1. In a bowl, whisk together oil, lemon juice, Worcestershire sauce, soy sauce, salt, black pepper, white pepper, 5-spice powder, garlic and cayenne.

Dry and Semidry Rubs

Rub Chart

In many places, meats are grilled and barbecued with dry spice rubs instead of sauces. Rubs are applied to meat after marinating and before cooking. I often put rubs on roasts or other meat and fish if I am cooking in my oven. The rubs impart so many flavors, and the pan drippings are a good starting point or base for an extra sauce or garnish if you feel inclined to make one. Rubs, on their own, add enough flavor for me, but some people also serve barbecue sauce, for dipping, on the side.

Dry larger cuts of meat with a paper towel before pressing the rub all over them, then place the meat in a resealable freezer bag or glass dish covered with plastic wrap and put it into the refrigerator. Usually 4 to 6 hours will work the magic. Sometimes I coat the meat with the rub in the morning, so it's ready to grill that night, but, if you're in a rush, you can grill it 30 to 45 minutes after you coat it. If the rub won't adhere, spread a little honey or oil over the meat before the rub. Alternatively, you can combine the rub with 1 cup (250 mL) fresh or dry bread crumbs, then pat the mixture onto the meat. Cook the meat according to your recipe or as recommended on the Internal Temperatures for Cooked Meats chart (page 211).

Meat	Rubs
Poultry	
Cornish hens	Citrus Rosemary Rub
	Herbes de Provence Rub
	Peppery Dry Rub
Whole chickens	Ginger Rub
	Porky Porky Rub
	Six-Garlic Rub
Chicken breasts	Brown Sugar Rub
	Citrus Rosemary Rub
	Herbes de Provence Rub
	Six-Garlic Rub

Meat	Rubs
Poultry	
Chicken pieces	Chipotle Dry Rub
	Creole Rub
	Curry Rub
	Jerk Rub
	Tuscan Rub
Chicken wings	Jamaican Rub
	Hot Hot Hot Rub
	Simple Spice Rub
	Six-Garlic Rub
Turkey breasts	Jamaican Rub
	Simple Spice Rub
	Tuscan Rub
Beef	
Roast	Aztec Spice Rub
	Brown Sugar Rub
	Espresso Rub
Ribs	Chile Pepper Rub
	Chipotle Dry Rub
	Kansas City Dry Rub
	Memphis Dry Rub for Ribs
Steaks	Kansas City Dry Rub
	Peppery Dry Rub
Lamb	
Shanks/Legs	Aztec Spice Rub
	Citrus Rosemary Rub
	Curry Rub
	Greek Rub
	Herbes de Provence Rub

Meat	Rubs
Pork	
Chops	Jerk Rub
	North Carolina Rub
	Tuscan Rub
	Six-Garlic Rub
Shoulder	Chile Pepper Rub
	Curry Rub
	Porky Porky Rub
Loin	Citrus Rosemary Rub
	Ginger Rub
	Jerk Rub
	North Carolina Rub
	Porky Porky Rub
Ribs	Chile Pepper Rub
	Creole Rub
	Cuban Spice Rub
	Mexican Rub
	Porky Porky Rub
Fish and Seafood	
Salmon	Cajun Rub
	Cuban Spice Rub
	Orange Dill Rub
	Simple Spice Rub
Shrimp	Greek Rub
	Hot Hot Hot Rub
	Orange Dill Rub
Scallops	Orange Dill Rub
	Simple Spice Rub

Aztec Spice Rub

**Makes 2 cups
(500 mL)**

*This rub feels more like a
paste than a traditional rub
and is easy to massage into
rough cuts of meat such as
brisket or butterflied leg
of lamb.*

• **Food processor**

½ cup	cumin seeds, toasted (see Tip, page 189)	125 mL
6	cloves garlic, minced	6
3 tbsp	kosher salt	45 mL
2 tbsp	unsweetened cocoa powder	25 mL
1 tbsp	cayenne pepper	15 mL
1 tsp	ground cinnamon	5 mL
1 cup	extra virgin olive oil	250 mL

1. In a food processor fitted with a metal blade, process cumin seeds, garlic, salt, cocoa powder, cayenne and cinnamon until powdery, for 1 minute. While motor is running, drizzle in oil through feed tube.

Brown Sugar Rub

**Makes ¾ cup
(175 mL)**

*Here's a sweet rub with a
hint of pepper.*

½ cup	lightly packed brown sugar	125 mL
2 tbsp	kosher salt	25 mL
1 tsp	cayenne pepper	5 mL
½ tsp	Hungarian paprika	2 mL
½ tsp	onion powder	2 mL

1. In a bowl, combine brown sugar, salt, cayenne, paprika and onion powder.

Cajun Rub

**Makes about
¾ cup (175 mL)**

You can create blackened, Cajun-style dishes at home with this rub. Just turn the exhaust vent to high if you're cooking inside.

Tip

Adobe seasoning is a blend of spices with a flavorful, smoked chile taste, but it's not too hot. Look for it in Mexican or Latin American grocery stores or online (see Sources, page 343).

¼ cup	Hungarian paprika	50 mL
¼ cup	kosher salt	50 mL
2 tbsp	freshly ground black pepper	25 mL
1 tbsp	dried thyme	15 mL
1 tbsp	garlic powder	15 mL
2 tsp	dried basil	10 mL
1 tsp	onion powder	5 mL
1 tsp	dried oregano	5 mL
1 tsp	cayenne pepper	5 mL
1 tsp	ground white pepper	5 mL
¼ tsp	adobe seasoning (see Tip, left)	1 mL

1. In a bowl, combine paprika, salt, black pepper, thyme, garlic powder, basil, onion powder, oregano, cayenne, white pepper and adobe seasoning powder.

Chile Pepper Rub

**Makes 1¾ cups
(425 mL)**

With a flavor that's intense and strong, this rub works best with long, slow smoking.

Tip

Use a mini food processor or a spice grinder to grind the dried jalapeños.

• **Food processor**

1¼ cups	lightly packed brown sugar	300 mL
½ cup	chili powder	125 mL
2	dried jalapeño peppers, ground (see Tip, left)	2
1 tbsp	cayenne pepper	15 mL
1 tsp	freshly ground black pepper	5 mL

1. In a food processor fitted with a metal blade, process brown sugar, chili powder, jalapeños, cayenne and black pepper until powdery, about 1 minute.

Chipotle Dry Rub

**Makes 1 cup
(250 mL)**

This rub permeates meat with a wonderful smoky flavor and aroma.

¾ cup	lightly packed brown sugar	175 mL
2 tbsp	chipotle pepper powder	25 mL
1 tbsp	kosher salt	15 mL
½ tsp	dried oregano	2 mL
¼ tsp	smoked paprika	1 mL

1. In a bowl, combine brown sugar, chipotle pepper powder, salt, oregano and paprika.

Citrus Rosemary Rub

Makes 1 cup (250 mL)

A pork loin loves a nice citrus essence.

Tip
You can find dried lemon and orange peel in spice stores and online (see Sources, page 343). You can use fresh zest, instead, but double the amount called for in the recipe.

½ cup	lightly packed brown sugar	125 mL
1 tbsp	minced dried lemon peel (see Tip, left)	15 mL
1 tbsp	minced dried orange peel	15 mL
2 tsp	sea salt	10 mL
1 tsp	dried rosemary	5 mL

1. In a bowl, combine brown sugar, lemon peel, orange peel, salt and rosemary.

Creole Rub

**Makes about
1¼ cups (300 mL)**

This is a wet paste to spread on chicken and ribs just before grilling or cooking.

Tip
Spread a few spoonfuls on top of meatloaf before it goes into the oven.

½ cup	red wine vinegar	125 mL
½ cup	lightly packed brown sugar	125 mL
8	cloves garlic, minced	8
¼ cup	chili powder	50 mL
1	can (6 oz/175 mL) tomato paste	1
2 tbsp	hot pepper sauce, such as Tabasco	25 mL
2 tbsp	coarse kosher salt	25 mL

1. In a bowl, whisk together vinegar, brown sugar, garlic, chili powder, tomato paste, hot pepper sauce and salt.

Cuban Spice Rub

**Makes about
1/2 cup (125 mL)**

This rub is perfect for salmon, pork or ribs.

Tip
Dried chile molido is a dried red chile powder from New Mexico. It can be found in spice stores and the Hispanic section of major food stores in the American West. You can substitute the same amount of chili powder.

- **Spice grinder or food processor**

2 tbsp	cumin seeds, toasted (see Tip, page 189)	25 mL
2 tbsp	dried chile molido (see Tip, left)	25 mL
1 1/2 tbsp	whole black peppercorns	22 mL
1 tbsp	coriander seeds	15 mL
1 tbsp	lightly packed brown sugar	15 mL
1 tbsp	kosher salt	15 mL
1 tbsp	Hungarian paprika	15 mL
2 tsp	minced dried orange peel	10 mL

1. In spice grinder or food processor fitted with a metal blade, process cumin seeds, chile molido, peppercorns, coriander seeds, brown sugar, salt, paprika and orange peel until powdery, for 10 seconds.

Curry Rub

**Makes about
1 cup (250 mL)**

This rub is spicy and flavorful and great to use on short ribs.

Tip
You can control the heat of this rub by using more or less cayenne depending on your heat tolerance.

1/2 cup	lightly packed brown sugar	125 mL
3 tbsp	curry powder (mild or hot)	45 mL
1 tbsp	sea salt	15 mL
2 tsp	dry mustard	10 mL
1/2 tsp	cayenne pepper (see Tip, left)	2 mL
1/2 tsp	freshly ground black pepper	2 mL

1. In a bowl, blend together brown sugar, curry powder, salt, dry mustard, cayenne and black pepper.

Espresso Rub

**Makes about
1 cup (250 mL)**

*This rub adds an attractive
dark look to the meat without
a burnt taste.*

½ cup	lightly packed brown sugar	125 mL
2 tbsp	espresso powder	25 mL
1 tbsp	sea salt	15 mL
1 tsp	hot pepper flakes	5 mL
1 tsp	freshly ground black pepper	5 mL
½ tsp	ground allspice	2 mL

1. In a bowl, blend together brown sugar, espresso powder, salt, hot pepper flakes, black pepper and allspice.

Ginger Rub

**Makes about
⅓ cup (75 mL)**

*I like using this rub with
pork loin.*

¼ cup	lightly packed brown sugar	50 mL
2 tbsp	ground ginger	25 mL
1 tsp	sea salt	5 mL
1 tsp	freshly ground black pepper	5 mL
½ tsp	hot pepper flakes	2 mL
½ tsp	curry powder	2 mL

1. In a bowl, combine brown sugar, ginger, salt, black pepper, hot pepper flakes and curry powder.

Greek Rub

**Makes about
1/2 cup (125 mL)**

*On the Greek island of
Rhodes, I enjoyed a lamb
dish that was cooked with a
rub. Happily for us all, the
restaurant owner was pleased
to share his recipe.*

Tip
The capers make this rub
a little moist, helping the
spices cling to the meat.

- **Spice grinder or food processor**

1/4 cup	sea salt	50 mL
1/4 cup	capers, drained	50 mL
2 tsp	cumin seeds	10 mL
2 tsp	dried dill	10 mL
1 tsp	fennel seeds	5 mL
1 tsp	dried oregano	5 mL
1 tsp	Hungarian paprika	5 mL
1/2 tsp	ground white pepper	2 mL

1. In a spice grinder or food processor fitted with a metal
   blade, process salt, capers, cumin seeds, dill, fennel seeds,
   oregano, paprika and white pepper until powdery, for
   30 seconds.

Herbes de Provence Rub

**Makes about
1 1/2 cups (375 mL)**

*In 1997 I took my first
tour of students to France.
We all fell in love with
herb-crusted lamb, and
devoured it.*

Tip
Coat meat, such as lamb,
with honey, rubbing all
over. Press spice mixture
over honey.

- **Food processor**

1 cup	dry bread crumbs	250 mL
1 tbsp	dried basil	15 mL
2 tsp	dried oregano	10 mL
1 tsp	dried marjoram	5 mL
1 tsp	dried thyme	5 mL
1/2 tsp	dried sage	2 mL
1/2 tsp	dried mint	2 mL
1/2 tsp	dried rosemary	2 mL
1/2 tsp	fennel seeds	2 mL
1/2 tsp	dried lavender	2 mL

1. In a food processor fitted with a metal blade, process
   bread crumbs, basil, oregano, marjoram, thyme, sage,
   mint, rosemary, fennel seeds and lavender until blended,
   about 20 seconds.

Hot Hot Hot Rub

If you want just a little zing, simply sprinkle this on after the meat is cooked.

Tip
You may purchase whole dried arbol and pequín chiles and grind them yourself.

1 tbsp	sea salt	15 mL
1 tbsp	arbol chile powder (see Tip, left)	15 mL
1 tbsp	hot pepper flakes	15 mL
½ tsp	cayenne pepper	2 mL
¼ tsp	pequín chile powder (see Tip, left)	1 mL

1. In a small bowl, combine salt, arbol chile powder, hot pepper flakes, cayenne and pequín chile powder. Use sparingly.

Jerk Rub

This rub provides the perfect balance of hot and spicy for your jerk chicken and pork dishes.

Tip
If you dry your own thyme or your purchased thyme are too large, pulse the leaves or flakes a few times in a spice grinder.

1 tbsp	onion flakes	15 mL
1 tbsp	onion powder	15 mL
2 tsp	ground thyme (see Tip, left)	10 mL
2 tsp	granulated sugar	10 mL
2 tsp	sea salt	10 mL
1 tsp	ground allspice	5 mL
1 tsp	garlic powder	5 mL
1 tsp	freshly ground black pepper	5 mL
1 tsp	cayenne pepper	5 mL

1. In a bowl, combine onion flakes, onion powder, thyme, sugar, salt, allspice, garlic powder, black pepper and cayenne.

Jamaican Rub

**Makes ¾ cup
(175 mL)**

*This rub is hot and spicy,
just like the islands.*

- **Spice grinder or food processor**

¼ cup	unsalted roasted sunflower seeds	50 mL
2 tbsp	ground turmeric	25 mL
2 tbsp	cumin seeds	25 mL
1 tbsp	coriander seeds	15 mL
1 tbsp	ground cinnamon	15 mL
1 tbsp	ground ginger	15 mL
1½ tsp	mustard seeds	7 mL
1½ tsp	whole cloves	7 mL
1½ tsp	hot pepper flakes	7 mL
1 tsp	celery seeds	5 mL

1. In a spice grinder or food processor fitted with a metal blade, process sunflower seeds, turmeric, cumin seeds, coriander seeds, cinnamon, ginger, mustard seeds, cloves, hot pepper flakes and celery seeds until powdery, about 2 minutes.

Kansas City Dry Rub

**Makes 2 cups
(500 mL)**

*This Midwestern city is
known for ribs and large
steaks. Here is a rub that
flavors tri-tip or skirt steak
perfectly.*

- **Food processor**

1 cup	granulated sugar	250 mL
½ cup	Hungarian paprika	125 mL
¼ cup	celery salt	50 mL
3 tbsp	onion powder	45 mL
3 tbsp	chili powder	45 mL
2 tbsp	ground cumin	25 mL
2 tbsp	whole black peppercorns	25 mL
1 tbsp	kosher salt	15 mL
2 tsp	dry mustard	10 mL
1 tsp	cayenne pepper	5 mL

1. In a food processor fitted with a metal blade, process sugar, paprika, celery salt, onion powder, chili powder, cumin, peppercorns, kosher salt, dry mustard and cayenne until powdery, for 1 minute.

Mexican Rub

**Makes about
½ cup (125 mL)**

*Add some south-of-the-border
spice with this great rub.*

Tip
When you use this rub,
make sure your meat is dry
before pressing the spice
mixture into the surface.

2 tbsp	Hungarian paprika	25 mL
2 tbsp	cumin seeds	25 mL
2 tbsp	lightly packed brown sugar	25 mL
2 tsp	freshly ground black pepper	10 mL
2 tsp	dried oregano	10 mL
2 tsp	unsweetened cocoa powder	10 mL
1 tsp	hot pepper flakes	5 mL

1. In a bowl, combine, paprika, cumin seeds, brown sugar, black pepper, oregano, cocoa powder and hot pepper flakes.

North Carolina Rub

**Makes about
1 cup (250 mL)**

*I'll never forget my first
taste of pulled-pork
sandwiches served by a
barbecue joint in North
Carolina, a state that's
famous for its pulled pork.*

¼ cup	Hungarian paprika	50 mL
¼ cup	lightly packed brown sugar	50 mL
2 tbsp	kosher salt	25 mL
2 tbsp	ground cumin	25 mL
2 tbsp	chili powder	25 mL
2 tbsp	freshly ground black pepper	25 mL
1 tsp	cayenne pepper	5 mL

1. In a large bowl, blend together paprika, brown sugar, salt, cumin, chili powder, black pepper and cayenne.

Orange Dill Rub

Try coating jumbo prawns with this zesty rub.

- Food processor

	Zest and juice of 2 oranges	
1	jalapeño pepper, seeded and minced	1
5	cloves garlic, minced	5
2 tbsp	chili powder	25 mL
1 tbsp	extra virgin olive oil	15 mL
1 tbsp	Hungarian paprika	15 mL
1 tbsp	dried dill	15 mL
1 tsp	ground cumin	5 mL
1 tsp	sea salt	5 mL
1/2 tsp	celery seeds	2 mL
1/2 tsp	dried oregano	2 mL
1/4 tsp	ground cinnamon	1 mL

1. In a food processor fitted with a metal blade, process orange zest and juice, jalapeño, garlic, chili powder, oil, paprika, dill, cumin, salt, celery seeds, oregano and cinnamon until a paste, about 2 minutes.

Peppery Dry Rub

Makes about 1/2 cup (125 mL)

Pat this rub on both sides of your steak before grilling it.

- Spice grinder or food processor

1/4 cup	kosher salt	50 mL
2 tbsp	dried thyme	25 mL
3	bay leaves	3
2 tsp	whole black peppercorns	10 mL
1 tsp	hot pepper flakes	5 mL
1/2 tsp	whole allspice	2 mL

1. In a spice grinder or food processor fitted with a metal blade, process salt, thyme, bay leaves, peppercorns, hot pepper flakes and allspice until a fine powder, about 2 minutes.

Porky Porky Rub

Makes about
1 cup (250 mL)

I like to use this on all kinds of pork, from pulled pork to ribs to loin.

- Spice grinder or food processor

3 tbsp	kosher salt	45 mL
3 tbsp	whole black peppercorns	45 mL
2 tbsp	cumin seeds, toasted (see Tip, page 189)	25 mL
2 tbsp	chili powder	25 mL
2 tbsp	lightly packed brown sugar	25 mL
2 tbsp	dried oregano	25 mL
2 tbsp	dried cilantro	25 mL
4	cloves garlic	4
1 tsp	grated orange zest	5 mL
½ tsp	cayenne pepper	2 mL

1. In spice grinder or food processor fitted with a metal blade, process salt, peppercorns, cumin seeds, chili powder, brown sugar, oregano, cilantro, garlic, orange zest and cayenne until blended, for 30 seconds.

Six-Garlic Rub

Makes about
½ cup (125 mL)

The fresh garlic makes this more like a paste than a rub, and helps make it a great coating for meats.

¼ cup	sea salt	50 mL
6	cloves garlic, minced	6
2 tsp	ground cumin	10 mL
2 tsp	dried oregano	10 mL
2 tsp	freshly ground black pepper	10 mL
1 tsp	cayenne pepper	5 mL

1. In a small bowl, combine salt, garlic, cumin, oregano, black pepper and cayenne pepper.

Simple Spice Rub

**Makes about
³⁄₄ cup (175 mL)**

*This is a simple basic rub for
anything.*

3 tbsp	kosher salt	45 mL
3 tbsp	freshly ground black pepper	45 mL
3 tbsp	Hungarian paprika	45 mL
2 tbsp	garlic powder	25 mL
2 tbsp	dry mustard	25 mL
1	bay leaf, crushed	1
1 tsp	hot pepper flakes	5 mL

1. In a bowl, combine salt, pepper, paprika, garlic powder,
   dry mustard, bay leaf and hot pepper flakes.

Tuscan Rub

**Makes about
¹⁄₂ cup (125 mL)**

*Tuscany is a magical place.
I had this flavorful rub on
chicken for one of the meals
I experienced there.*

● **Spice grinder or food processor**

3 tbsp	dried basil	45 mL
1¹⁄₂ tbsp	garlic powder	22 mL
1¹⁄₂ tbsp	kosher salt	22 mL
1 tbsp	dried rosemary	15 mL
1 tbsp	dried oregano	15 mL
1¹⁄₂ tsp	fennel seeds	7 mL
1¹⁄₂ tsp	ground white pepper	7 mL

1. In a spice grinder or food processor fitted with a metal
   blade, process basil, garlic powder, salt, rosemary,
   oregano, fennel seeds and white pepper until powdery,
   for 20 seconds.

Memphis Dry Rub for Ribs

Makes 2¼ cups (550 mL)

Memphis is known for dry-rubbed ribs. I crave them often, so I just created my own rub!

- **Food processor**

1 cup	lightly packed brown sugar	250 mL
⅔ cup	chili powder	150 mL
¼ cup	Hungarian paprika	50 mL
2 tbsp	garlic salt	25 mL
2 tbsp	coarse sea salt	25 mL
1 tbsp	whole black peppercorns	15 mL
2 tsp	mustard seeds	10 mL
2 tsp	granulated sugar	10 mL
1 tsp	ground ginger	5 mL
1 tsp	whole cloves	5 mL
¼ tsp	ground turmeric	1 mL
¼ tsp	onion powder	1 mL
¼ tsp	garlic powder	1 mL
¼ tsp	cornstarch	1 mL

1. In a food processor fitted with a metal blade, process brown sugar, chili powder, paprika, garlic salt, sea salt, black peppercorns, mustard seeds, granulated sugar, ground ginger, whole cloves, turmeric, onion powder, garlic powder and cornstarch until a fine powder, about 2 minutes.

Savory and Fruit Salsas

Savory Salsas

Fresh salsas are not just for chips anymore — you can use salsas for an array of main dishes, such as fish tacos, or use a spoonful on a cooked chicken breast. Let your imagination run wild, but keep in mind that fresh salsas do not last as long as the cooked store varieties and must be eaten within a few days. None of these salsas freeze well, so use them up quickly.

Avocado Gorgonzola Salsa

Makes 2 cups (500 mL)

Chunks of ripe avocado and cheese make this salsa rich.

Tip
The avocado turns brown within 1 to 2 hours, so use all of this salsa promptly.

3	Roma (plum) tomatoes, seeded and diced	3
1/2	red onion, diced	1/2
2	serrano chiles, seeded and minced	2
2	cloves garlic, minced	2
1/4 cup	chopped Italian flat-leaf parsley	50 mL
1 tbsp	extra virgin olive oil	15 mL
1 tbsp	red wine vinegar	15 mL
1 tsp	dried oregano	5 mL
4 oz	Gorgonzola cheese, crumbled	125 g
1	large avocado, chopped	1

1. In a bowl, combine tomatoes, red onion, chiles, garlic, parsley, oil, vinegar and oregano. Let stand for at least 1 hour for the flavors to develop. Fold in Gorgonzola and avocado just before serving.

Black Bean and Roasted Corn Salsa

This dip is very easy; everything is mixed in the food processor.

Tip
If you can't find roasted corn, you can roast 2 cups (500 mL) fresh or thawed frozen corn kernels in a single layer in a dry skillet over medium heat, stirring constantly, until lightly browned.

● **Food processor**

1	can (14 oz to 19 oz/398 to 540 mL) black beans, drained and rinsed	1
12 oz	cream cheese, softened	375 g
1/3 cup	roasted red pepper (about 1 small)	75 mL
2	chipotle peppers in adobo sauce, drained	2
2 tbsp	chopped fresh cilantro	25 mL
1 tbsp	taco seasoning	15 mL
2 tsp	freshly squeezed lime juice	10 mL
1	bag (12 oz/375 g) roasted corn (see Tip, left)	1

1. In a food processor fitted with a metal blade, process black beans, cream cheese, red pepper, chipotle peppers, cilantro, taco seasoning and lime juice until smooth, about 3 minutes. Transfer to a bowl and fold in roasted corn.

Chipotle Chile Salsa

This fast and easy salsa uses only four ingredients!

4	Roma (plum) tomatoes, seeded and diced	4
2	chipotle peppers in adobo sauce, drained and chopped	2
4	cloves garlic, roasted (see Tip, page 33), mashed	4
1 tsp	onion salt	5 mL

1. In a bowl, combine tomatoes, chipotle peppers, garlic and onion salt. Let stand in a covered container in the refrigerator for at least 1 hour for flavors to develop or for up to 2 days.

Cucumber Salsa

**Makes 3 cups
(750 mL)**

*If you have a garden you
can make this salsa
just-picked fresh.*

3	small cucumbers, peeled, seeded and chopped	3
3	Roma (plum) tomatoes, seeded and diced	3
1	red onion, chopped	1
2	small jalapeño peppers, seeded and minced	2
2	cloves garlic, minced	2
2 tbsp	freshly squeezed lemon juice	25 mL
2 tbsp	chopped fresh cilantro	25 mL
½ tsp	dried dill	2 mL
½ tsp	sea salt	2 mL

1. In a bowl, combine cucumbers, tomatoes, red onion, jalapeños, garlic, lemon juice, cilantro, dill and salt. Let stand in a covered container in the refrigerator for at least 1 hour for flavors to develop or for up to 2 days.

Diablo Salsa

**Makes 3 cups
(750 mL)**

*This is a creamy salsa that
you can use as a topping
for fish or shrimp.*

4	Roma (plum) tomatoes, seeded and diced	4
1	red onion, chopped	1
1 cup	sour cream	250 mL
1 tbsp	Worcestershire Sauce (page 142) or store-bought	15 mL
1 tbsp	taco seasoning	15 mL

1. In a bowl, combine tomatoes, red onion, sour cream, Worcestershire sauce and taco seasoning. Let stand in a covered container in the refrigerator for at least 1 hour for flavors to develop or for up to 2 days.

Fast Salsa

**Makes 2 cups
(500 mL)**

*This is a fast salsa made
even faster if you use a food
processor.*

3	Roma (plum) tomatoes, chopped	3
1	clove garlic, minced	1
½	onion, chopped	½
1	jalapeño pepper, seeded and chopped	1
¼ cup	chopped fresh cilantro	50 mL
1 tsp	sea salt	5 mL

1. In a bowl, combine tomatoes, garlic, onion, jalapeño, cilantro and salt. Let stand in a covered container in the refrigerator for at least 1 hour for flavors to develop or for up to 2 days.

Fiery Hot Salsa

**Makes 3 cups
(750 mL)**

*This salsa will put hair on
your chest.*

4	Roma (plum) tomatoes, seeded and chopped	4
½	onion, chopped	½
1	clove garlic, minced	1
½	green bell pepper, seeded and chopped	½
2	jalapeño peppers, seeded and chopped	2
2	banana peppers, chopped	2
2 tbsp	freshly squeezed lemon juice	25 mL
1 tsp	granulated sugar	5 mL
½ tsp	ground white pepper	2 mL
½ tsp	sea salt	2 mL
½ tsp	freshly ground black pepper	2 mL
½ tsp	prepared horseradish	2 mL
¼ tsp	ground cumin	1 mL

1. In a large bowl, combine tomatoes, onion, garlic, bell pepper, jalapeños, banana peppers, lemon juice, sugar, white pepper, salt, black pepper, horseradish and cumin. Let stand in a covered container in the refrigerator for at least 1 hour for flavors to develop or for up to 2 days.

Fire-Roasted Chipotle Salsa

Makes 4 cups (1 L)

This salsa is easy to make if you have a hot grill. I like serving it with margaritas.

- **Preheat broiler**
- **Baking sheet, lined with foil**
- **Food processor**

2 lbs	Roma (plum) tomatoes, cut in half, divided	1 kg
1 tbsp	canola oil	15 mL
1/2	onion, chopped	1/2
4	cloves garlic	4
1/2 cup	loosely packed fresh cilantro	125 mL
4	chipotle peppers in adobo sauce, drained	4
1/4 cup	extra virgin olive oil	50 mL
1/4 cup	red wine vinegar	50 mL
1 tsp	sea salt	5 mL
1 tsp	granulated sugar	5 mL

1. Place tomato halves, skin side up, on prepared baking sheet. Broil until skin is blackened and charred, about 6 minutes.
2. In a skillet, heat canola oil over medium-high heat until lightly smoking. Add onion and sauté until browned, about 10 minutes.
3. In a food processor fitted with a metal blade, process onion, half of the blackened tomatoes and garlic until puréed, about 30 seconds. Add cilantro and chipotle peppers and pulse about 10 times. Transfer to a large bowl.
4. Coarsely chop remaining tomatoes and fold into onion mixture. Stir in olive oil, vinegar, salt and sugar. Let stand in a covered container in the refrigerator for at least 1 hour for flavors to develop or for up to 2 days.

Garlic Ginger Salsa

Makes 2 cups (500 mL)

The roasting of the garlic makes this a sweet, spicy salsa.

4	Roma (plum) tomatoes, seeded and chopped	4
6	cloves garlic, roasted (see Tip, page 33), minced	6
1/4 cup	chopped fresh cilantro	50 mL
2 tbsp	minced fresh gingerroot	25 mL
1 tsp	granulated sugar	5 mL
1/2 tsp	celery seeds	2 mL
1/4 tsp	sea salt	1 mL

1. In a bowl, combine tomatoes, garlic, cilantro, ginger, sugar, celery seeds and salt. Let stand in a covered container in the refrigerator for at least 1 hour for flavors to develop or for up to 2 days.

Green Chile Salsa

Makes 2 cups (500 mL)

I like to spoon this salsa over grilled fish.

2	Roma (plum) tomatoes, seeded and diced	2
1/2	onion, diced	1/2
2 tbsp	minced fresh cilantro	25 mL
1	can (4 1/2 oz/127 mL) chopped green chiles, drained	1
1 tbsp	freshly squeezed lime juice	15 mL
1/2 tsp	garlic powder	2 mL
1/2 tsp	sea salt	2 mL
1/2 tsp	freshly ground black pepper	2 mL

1. In a bowl, combine tomatoes, onion, cilantro, green chiles, lime juice, garlic powder, salt and pepper. Let stand in a covered container in the refrigerator for at least 1 hour for flavors to develop or for up to 2 days.

Guacamole

Since I live in Southern California where most of the world's avocados are grown, I serve this dip often.

Tip

To tell if an avocado is ripe, hold it in the palm of your hand and gently squeeze. It is ready to use if it feels firm yet soft, like a tomato. If it's not, ripen it inside a brown paper bag for a few days at room temperature.

2	ripe avocados , halved and mashed (see Tip, left)	2
2 tsp	freshly squeezed lime juice	10 mL
1/2 cup	finely minced shallots	125 mL
2	Roma (plum) tomatoes, seeded and diced	2
1	jalapeño pepper	1
2	cloves garlic, minced	2
2 tbsp	chopped fresh cilantro	25 mL

1. In a bowl, combine avocados, lime juice, shallots, tomatoes, jalapeño, garlic and cilantro. Use within a few hours as the guacamole will darken.

Heirloom Tomato Salsa

It's become easier to find heirloom tomatoes in your local grocery store. Use them in this colorful side dish for any event.

2 lbs	heirloom tomatoes (use colorful ones), seeded and chopped	1 kg
1/2	onion, chopped	1/2
1/2	red onion, chopped	1/2
1/2 cup	chopped fresh cilantro	125 mL
1 tbsp	red wine vinegar	15 mL
1 tbsp	granulated sugar	15 mL
3	cloves garlic, minced	3
1 tsp	sea salt	5 mL

1. In a large bowl, combine tomatoes, onion, red onion, cilantro, vinegar, sugar, garlic and salt. Let stand in a covered container in the refrigerator for at least 1 hour for flavors to develop or for up to 2 days.

Jalapeño Salsa

**Makes 2 cups
(500 mL)**

*This salsa is very spicy with
a kick.*

- Preheat oven to 400°F (200°C)
- Roasting pan, lined with parchment paper
- Food processor

3	large Anaheim or Cubanelle chiles, cut in half and seeded	3
10	jalapeño peppers, cut in half and seeded	10
½	red onion, sliced	½
6	cloves garlic	6
¼ cup	extra virgin olive oil	50 mL
2 tbsp	freshly squeezed lime juice	25 mL
1 tsp	sea salt	5 mL

1. Place Anaheim chiles, jalapeños, red onion and garlic on prepared roasting pan. Brush with oil. Roast in preheated oven until skins on Anaheim chiles and jalaneños are darkened, about 20 minutes.
2. In a food processor fitted with a metal blade, pulse roasted vegetables 10 times or until desired consistency. Transfer to a bowl. Stir in lime juice and salt. Let stand in a covered container in the refrigerator for at least 1 hour for flavors to develop or for up to 2 days.

Medium-Heat Salsa

You can add as many chiles as you like to get the heat you want, but some people will still find it too hot while others will find it too mild!

5	Roma (plum) tomatoes, seeded and chopped	5
3	cloves garlic, minced	3
1/4	large onion, chopped	1/4
1/2	green bell pepper, chopped	1/2
1 to 2	habanero chiles, seeded and chopped	1 to 2
2 tbsp	liquid honey	25 mL
1 tbsp	thinly sliced fresh basil	15 mL
2 tsp	chopped fresh cilantro	10 mL
1 tsp	sea salt	5 mL
1/2 tsp	ground white pepper	2 mL

1. In a large bowl, combine tomatoes, garlic, onion, bell pepper, chiles, honey, basil, cilantro, salt and pepper. Let stand in a covered container in the refrigerator for at least 1 hour for flavors to develop or for up to 2 days.

Old World Salsa

**Makes 3 cups
(750 mL)**

*This salsa is a favorite of
my guests when I have a
south-of-the-border party.*

Tip
If you would like a smooth
salsa, process the mixture
for a few minutes. If you
would like it chunky, pulse
until it's the desired texture.

- **Food processor**

3	Roma (plum) tomatoes, quartered	3
½	red onion, quartered	½
½	sweet onion, quartered	½
2	cloves garlic	2
½	green bell pepper, quartered	½
½	red bell pepper, quartered	½
4	jalapeño peppers, cut in half and seeded	4
2 tbsp	coarsely chopped fresh cilantro	25 mL
2 tsp	freshly squeezed lime juice	10 mL
2 tsp	freshly squeezed lemon juice	10 mL
¼ tsp	freshly ground black pepper	1 mL
¼ tsp	celery salt	1 mL
¼ tsp	sea salt	1 mL
1	can (8 oz/227 mL) tomato sauce	1

1. In a food processor fitted with a metal blade, process
   tomatoes, red onion, sweet onion, garlic, green and red
   bell peppers, jalapeños, cilantro, lime and lemon juices,
   black pepper, celery salt and salt for 1 minute. Transfer
   to a bowl. Stir in tomato sauce. Let stand in a covered
   container in the refrigerator for at least 1 hour for flavors
   to develop or for up to 2 days.

Olive Salsa

**Makes 3 cups
(750 mL)**

*This is a flavorful salsa based
on olives and peppers.*

- **Food processor**

½ cup	pine nuts	125 mL
1 cup	green olives, pitted	250 mL
1 cup	black olives, pitted	250 mL
1	red onion, quartered	1
1	red bell pepper, quartered	1
1	green bell pepper, quartered	1
4	cloves garlic	4
2	jalapeño peppers, seeded and cut in half	2
2 tbsp	extra virgin olive oil	25 mL
2 tbsp	chopped Italian flat-leaf parsley	25 mL
1 tbsp	red wine vinegar	15 mL
1 tsp	granulated sugar	5 mL
½ tsp	sea salt	2 mL

1. In a skillet over low heat, toast pine nuts until lightly browned, about 4 minutes. Set aside.
2. In a food processor fitted with a metal blade, pulse green and black olives, red onion, red and green bell peppers, garlic and jalapeños until coarsely chopped, about 10 times. Add oil, parsley, vinegar, sugar and salt. Pulse 10 more times. Stir in pine nuts.

Olive Tapenade

Makes 1 cup (250 mL)

I use this spread on top of toasted rounds of baguette.

Tip
If the tapenade separates, stir it with a fork before serving.

- **Food processor**

1½ cups	black olives, pitted and drained	375 mL
2 tbsp	capers, drained	25 mL
2	cans (each 1⅔ oz/48 g) anchovy fillets, drained and chopped	2
2	cloves garlic	2
2 tbsp	white wine vinegar	25 mL
2 tbsp	chopped Italian flat-leaf parsley	25 mL
½ cup	extra virgin olive oil	125 mL
	Sea salt and freshly ground black pepper	

1. In a food processor fitted with a metal blade, process olives, capers, anchovies, garlic, vinegar and parsley until smooth, about 20 seconds. While motor is running, pour oil in through feed tube and process until incorporated. Season with salt and pepper to taste.

Onion Salsa

Makes 3 cups (750 mL)

This is a colorful salsa that looks great on a steak.

1	sweet onion, chopped	1
1	red onion, chopped	1
1 cup	chopped green onions	250 mL
1	small shallot, minced	1
½ cup	chopped fresh cilantro	125 mL
2	Roma (plum) tomatoes, seeded and chopped	2
3	cloves garlic, minced	3
1 tsp	red wine vinegar	5 mL
1 tsp	freshly squeezed lemon juice	5 mL
½ tsp	sea salt	2 mL

1. In a bowl, combine sweet, red and green onions, shallot, cilantro, tomatoes, garlic, vinegar, lemon juice and salt. Let stand in a covered container in the refrigerator for at least 1 hour for flavors to develop or for up to 2 days.

Orange Chipotle Salsa

Makes 4 cups (1 L)

This zesty salsa has a nice smoky bite to it.

6	Roma (plum) tomatoes, seeded and chopped	6
1 tbsp	grated orange zest	45 mL
2 cups	orange segments, diced (2 to 3 oranges)	500 mL
2	chipotle peppers in adobo sauce, drained and chopped	2
1	red onion, chopped	1
1 cup	chopped Italian flat-leaf parsley	250 mL
3	cloves garlic, minced	3
1 tsp	ground ginger	5 mL
½ tsp	sea salt	2 mL

1. In a large bowl, combine tomatoes, orange zest and segments, chipotle peppers, red onion, parsley, garlic, ginger and salt. Let stand in a covered container in the refrigerator for at least 1 hour for flavors to develop or for up to 2 days.

Pico de Gallo Salsa

Makes 2 cups (500 mL)

This condiment is available on every table in Mexican restaurants.

6	Roma (plum) tomatoes, seeded and chopped	6
½	red onion, chopped	½
¼ cup	chopped fresh cilantro	50 mL
2	jalapeño peppers, seeded and chopped	2
1 tsp	freshly squeezed lemon juice	5 mL
½ tsp	sea salt	2 mL

1. In a bowl, combine tomatoes, red onion, cilantro, jalepeños, lemon juice and salt. Let stand in a covered container in the refrigerator for at least 1 hour for flavors to develop or for up to 2 days.

Roasted Corn and Pepper Salsa

Makes 2½ cups (625 mL)

When I have parties I like to serve two different colors of salsa. This flavorful green salsa takes only a few minutes to assemble. Try pairing it with Fire-Roasted Chipotle Salsa (page 264) for your next party.

Tips

Do not run water over the chiles to try to loosen the skins — it washes the flavor away. If the skins are difficult to remove, you need to let them steam longer in the bag.

You can broil the corn, tomatoes and chiles until the skins bubble and the corn is browned, about 10 minutes.

Variations

Use cherry tomatoes instead of Roma tomatoes and you won't have to seed them.

In place of fresh corn, use 1 bag (12 oz/340 g) roasted corn. You can also roast a single layer of fresh corn kernels in a dry skillet over medium heat, stirring to the desired doneness.

● **Preheat barbecue grill to high**

1 tbsp	extra virgin olive oil	15 mL
6	ears corn, husked	6
1 lb	Roma (plum) tomatoes (6 to 8)	500 g
12 oz	New Mexico chiles (10 to 12)	375 g
½	onion, chopped	½
¼ cup	apple cider vinegar	50 mL
1 tsp	granulated sugar	5 mL
½ tsp	dried oregano	2 mL
¼ tsp	sea salt	1 mL

1. Brush oil all over sides of corn, tomatoes and chiles. Grill, turning often, until browned and skins of tomatoes and chiles are blistered. Set aside corn to cool and place tomatoes and chiles in a brown paper bag to sweat for 20 minutes.
2. Scrape corn from cob and place in a bowl. Peel skins from tomatoes and chiles and scrape out seeds. Coarsely chop and place in bowl with corn. Stir in onion, vinegar, sugar, oregano and salt. Refrigerate for at least 1 hour for the flavors to develop or refrigerate in a covered container for up to 2 days.

Roasted Garlic Onion Salsa

**Makes 2 cups
(500 mL)**

*This sweet and hot salsa is
good on grilled chicken as
well as chips.*

2	Roma (plum) tomatoes, seeded and chopped	2
12	cloves garlic, roasted (see Tip, page 33) and smashed	12
½	red onion, chopped	½
¼ cup	chopped fresh cilantro	50 mL
2	serrano chiles, seeded and chopped	2
½ tsp	sea salt	2 mL

1. In a large bowl, combine tomatoes, garlic, red onion, cilantro, chiles and salt. Let stand in a covered container in the refrigerator for at least 1 hour for flavors to develop or for up to 2 days.

Roasted Red Pepper Salsa

**Makes 2 cups
(500 mL)**

*When you use roasted
red peppers you get a
sweeter flavor.*

• **Food processor**

1	jar (7 oz/210 mL) roasted red bell peppers	1
2 tbsp	heavy or whipping (35%) cream, at room temperature	25 mL
4	Roma (plum) tomatoes, seeded and chopped	4
2	cloves garlic, minced	2
2 tbsp	chopped fresh tarragon	25 mL
1 tsp	sea salt	5 mL

1. In a food processor fitted with a metal blade, process red peppers and cream until smooth, about 30 seconds. Transfer to a bowl. Stir in tomatoes, garlic, tarragon and salt. Let stand for at least 1 hour for flavors to develop or refrigerate in a covered container for up to 2 days.

Roasted Tomato Salsa

Makes 3 cups (750 mL)

Tomatoes take on a pleasant, smoky taste when roasted at a high heat.

- **Preheat oven to 400°F (200°C)**
- **Baking sheet, lined with parchment paper**

2 tbsp	extra virgin olive oil	25 mL
8	Roma (plum) tomatoes, cut in half and seeded	8
3	jalapeño peppers, cut in half and seeded	3
1/4 cup	chopped fresh cilantro	50 mL
1/4 cup	chopped Italian flat-leaf parsley	50 mL
3	cloves garlic, minced	3
1/2 tsp	sea salt	2 mL

1. Rub oil on tomatoes and jalapeños. Place, skin side up, on prepared baking sheet. Roast in preheated oven until skins are blistered, 15 to 20 minutes. Let cool. Peel off skins.

2. Coarsely chop roasted tomatoes and jalapeños and transfer to a bowl. Add cilantro, parsley, garlic and salt. Let stand in a covered container in the refrigerator for at least 1 hour for flavors to develop or for up to 2 days.

Roasted Vegetable Salsa

**Makes about
2 cups (500 mL)**

*I roast my vegetables in either
the barbecue or the oven.
It's worth the effort for this
flavorful salsa.*

- **Preheat oven to 400°F (200°C)**
- **Roasting pan, lined with parchment paper**

1	onion, chopped	1
2	large carrots, diced	2
½ cup	radishes, diced (about 8 oz/250 g)	125 mL
1	red bell pepper, chopped	1
2 tbsp	extra virgin olive oil	25 mL
1 tsp	chopped fresh thyme	5 mL
1 tsp	chopped fresh oregano	5 mL
½ tsp	sea salt	2 mL
½ tsp	ground white pepper	2 mL
3	Roma (plum) tomatoes, seeded and diced	3

1. In a large bowl, toss together onion, carrots, radishes, bell pepper, olive oil, thyme, oregano, salt and white pepper. Place in a single layer on prepared roasting pan and roast in preheated oven, stirring occasionally, until lightly browned and tender, 45 to 60 minutes. Let cool to room temperature. Transfer to a bowl. Stir in tomatoes. Let stand in a covered container in the refrigerator for at least 1 hour for flavors to develop or for up to 2 days.

South-of-the-Border Salsa

**Makes 3 cups
(750 mL)**

*This is a very hot and spicy
salsa for chip dipping.*

2 tbsp	canola oil	25 mL
1	can (7 oz/200 g) corn, drained	1
2 tbsp	chopped red bell pepper	25 mL
2 tbsp	chopped green bell pepper	25 mL
1	can (28 oz/796 mL) diced tomatoes, drained	1
1	red onion, chopped	1
½ cup	extra virgin olive oil	125 mL
5	jalapeño peppers, seeded and chopped	5
2	cloves garlic, minced	2

1. In a skillet, heat canola oil over medium heat. Add corn and red and green bell peppers and sauté until roasted, about 4 minutes. Transfer to a bowl. Stir in tomatoes, red onion, olive oil, jalapeños and garlic. Let stand in a covered container in the refrigerator for at least 1 hour for flavors to develop or for up to 2 days.

Southwest Salsa

Makes 8 cups (2 L)

This really should be called "Lots-of-Pepper Salsa," since it's got more than all the other salsas, but the colors make it Southwest.

Tips

There are many varieties of sweet onions available, but I think the Walla Walla variety is best.

This makes such a large batch, you may want to cut the recipe in half.

8	Roma (plum) tomatoes, seeded and chopped	8
1	large sweet onion, chopped (see Tips, left)	1
1	red bell pepper, chopped	1
1	yellow bell pepper, chopped	1
1	green bell pepper, chopped	1
1	orange bell pepper, chopped	1
1/2	red onion, chopped	1/2
4	serrano peppers, seeded and minced	4
4	jalapeño peppers, seeded and minced	4
4	cloves garlic, minced	4
1/4 cup	chopped fresh cilantro	50 mL
1	habanero or Scotch bonnet pepper, seeded and minced	1
2 tbsp	sea salt	25 mL
2 tbsp	freshly squeezed lime juice	25 mL
1 tsp	ground cumin	5 mL
1 tsp	dried oregano	5 mL
1 tsp	chili powder	5 mL
1 tsp	extra virgin olive oil	5 mL

1. In a large bowl, combine tomatoes, sweet onion, red, yellow, green and orange bell peppers, red onion, serranos, jalapeños, garlic, cilantro, habanero, salt, lime juice, cumin, oregano, chili powder and oil. Let stand in a covered container in the refrigerator for at least 1 hour for flavors to develop or for up to 2 days.

Tecate Salsa

Makes 2 cups
(500 mL)

The exciting Mexican border town of Tecate is home to the factory that makes the beer of the same name. I once had the pleasure of eating carnitas topped with this salsa in a crowd of locals at a Tecate food stand.

● **Food processor**

5	Roma (plum) tomatoes, seeded and quartered	5
6	cloves garlic	6
1/2 cup	loosely packed fresh cilantro	125 mL
1/4 cup	light Mexican beer	50 mL
3	drops hot pepper sauce	3
1 tsp	sea salt	5 mL
1/2 tsp	ground white pepper	2 mL

1. In a food processor fitted with a metal blade, process tomatoes, garlic, cilantro, beer, hot pepper sauce, salt and white pepper until desired texture, about 30 seconds. Let stand in a covered container in the refrigerator for at least 1 hour for flavors to develop or for up to 2 days.

Tempe Salsa

Makes 3 cups
(750 mL)

The inspiration for this salsa comes from a small Mexican food stand on the south side of the city of Tempe in Arizona.

8	Roma (plum) tomatoes, seeded and chopped	8
1/2	red onion, chopped	1/2
1 cup	chopped green onions	250 mL
1/2 cup	chopped fresh cilantro	125 mL
1/2 cup	finely chopped celery	125 mL
1/4 cup	balsamic vinegar	50 mL
1/4 cup	extra virgin olive oil	50 mL
3	jalapeño peppers, seeded and chopped	3
4	cloves garlic, minced	4
2	habanero peppers, seeded and chopped	2
1 tsp	sea salt	5 mL
1/2 tsp	ground white pepper	2 mL

1. In a large bowl, combine tomatoes, red onion, green onions, cilantro, celery, vinegar, oil, jalapeños, garlic, habaneros, salt and white pepper. Let stand in a covered container in the refrigerator for at least 1 hour for flavors to develop or for up to 2 days.

Tequila Salsa

Makes 2 cups (500 mL)

A shot of tequila in this salsa gives it an extra spark.

1	can (28 oz/796 mL) diced tomatoes, drained	1
1	onion, chopped	1
1	small avocado, chopped	1
¼ cup	extra virgin olive oil	50 mL
¼ cup	chopped fresh cilantro	50 mL
2	jalapeño peppers, seeded and chopped	2
2	cloves garlic, minced	2
2 tbsp	tequila	25 mL

1. In a bowl, combine tomatoes, onion, avocado, oil, cilantro, jalapeños and garlic. Add tequila. Let stand in a covered container in the refrigerator for at least 1 hour for flavors to develop or for up to 2 days.

Three-Herb Salsa

Makes 2 cups (500 mL)

I have a garden with an abundance of fresh herbs. I love making this simple salsa with the harvest.

6	Roma (plum) tomatoes, seeded and chopped	6
½	red onion, chopped	½
¼ cup	chopped fresh cilantro	50 mL
2	jalapeño peppers, seeded and chopped	2
1 tbsp	chopped fresh tarragon	15 mL
1 tbsp	chopped fresh dill	15 mL
1 tsp	freshly squeezed lime juice	5 mL
½ tsp	sea salt	2 mL

1. In a bowl, combine tomatoes, red onion, cilantro, jalapeños, tarragon, dill, lime juice and salt. Let stand in a covered container in the refrigerator for at least 1 hour for flavors to develop or for up to 2 days.

Tomatillo Avocado Shrimp Salsa

Makes 4 cups (1 L)

This is my all-time favorite salsa! It has a little bit of a bite to it. I can eat the whole batch in one sitting.

Tip
Don't skip washing the tomatillos after husking them. There is a sticky substance on the skins that you need to remove.

Variation
Add ¼ tsp (1 mL) hot pepper sauce to the mixture for more zip.

- Food processor

½	red onion, quartered	½
1 lb	tomatillos, husked, washed and quartered (see Tip, left)	500 g
1	avocado, quartered	1
4 oz	cooked shrimp, peeled and divined	125 g
1	serrano chile, seeded and chopped	1
½ cup	chopped fresh cilantro	125 mL
2 tbsp	freshly squeezed lime juice	25 mL
1 tsp	sea salt	5 mL

1. In a food processor fitted with a metal blade, pulse red onion until diced, about 10 times. Place into a strainer and rinse with water. Return onion to food processor and add tomatillos, avocado, shrimp, chile, cilantro, lime juice and salt. Pulse 10 times or until desired texture is achieved.

Tomatillo Salsa Verde

Makes 4 cups (1 L)

Tomatillos look like green tomatoes wrapped in paper husks. To use them, peel off the husks then wash the stickiness off the skins.

- **Preheat oven to 450°F (230°C)**
- **Food processor**

1½ lbs	tomatillos (see Tip, page 281)	750 g
½ cup	chopped onion	125 mL
½ cup	chopped fresh cilantro	125 mL
1 tbsp	freshly squeezed lime juice	15 mL
¼ tsp	granulated sugar	1 mL
2	serrano peppers, seeded and minced	2
1 tsp	sea salt	5 mL

1. Cut tomatillos in half and place on a baking sheet, skin side up. Roast in preheated oven until skins are darkened and blistered, about 15 minutes. Let cool.
2. In a food processor fitted with a metal blade, pulse roasted tomatillos until chopped, about 10 times. Transfer to a bowl and stir in onion, cilantro, lime juice, sugar, serranos and salt. Let stand in a covered container in the refrigerator for at least 1 hour for flavors to develop or for up to 2 days.

Traditional Salsa

This is an all-purpose salsa that's great with chips, grilled meats or tacos.

Tip
When seeding the chiles wear rubber gloves and discard the seeds. If you get any chile juice on your fingers, don't rub your eyes or you will feel it!

Variation
You can replace the serrano chiles with jalapeño peppers for less heat.

- **Food processor**

1	onion, cut into quarters	1
1 lb	Roma (plum) tomatoes, cored, cut in half and seeded (7 to 9 tomatoes)	500 g
2	serrano chiles, cut in half and seeded (see Tip, left)	2
¼ cup	loosely packed cilantro leaves	50 mL
2 tbsp	freshly squeezed lime juice	25 mL
2 tsp	granulated sugar	10 mL
1 tsp	salt (approx.)	5 mL

1. In a food processor fitted with a metal blade, pulse onion until finely chopped, 10 to 12 times. Place into a strainer and rinse with water. Drain well. Transfer to a bowl and set aside.
2. In the same work bowl of food processor, pulse tomatoes, chiles and cilantro until desired consistency, 15 to 20 times.
3. Add tomato mixture to drained onions with lime juice, sugar and salt to taste. Let stand in a covered container in the refrigerator for at least 1 hour for flavors to develop or for up to 2 days.

Zucchini Salsa

**Makes 3 cups
(750 mL)**

*There are never enough
recipes for homegrown
zucchini.*

4	Roma (plum) tomatoes, seeded and chopped	4
2	large zucchini, peeled and shredded	2
1/2	red onion, chopped	1/2
1	red bell pepper, chopped	1
1/4 cup	white wine vinegar	50 mL
1 tbsp	lightly packed brown sugar	15 mL
1 tsp	sea salt	5 mL
1 tsp	hot pepper flakes	5 mL
1/2 tsp	dry mustard	2 mL
1/2 tsp	garlic powder	2 mL
1/2 tsp	dried cumin	2 mL
1/4 tsp	freshly grated nutmeg	1 mL
1/4 tsp	freshly ground black pepper	1 mL

1. In a large bowl, combine tomatoes, zucchini, red onion, bell pepper, vinegar, brown sugar, salt, hot pepper flakes, dry mustard, garlic powder, cumin, nutmeg and black pepper. Let stand in a covered container in the refrigerator for at least 1 hour for flavors to develop or for up to 2 days.

Fruit Salsas

Just as with the fresh vegetable salsas you must use the fruit salsas within 1 to 2 days. Use the freshest fruit with the best aroma.

Asian Pear Salsa

Makes 2 cups (500 mL)

This is a colorful red, white and green salsa.

2	Asian pears, cored and chopped	2
1	Roma (plum) tomato, seeded and chopped	1
1/4 cup	chopped fresh cilantro	50 mL
1 tsp	sea salt	5 mL
1 tsp	grated lime zest	5 mL

1. In a bowl, combine Asian pears, tomato, cilantro, salt and lime zest. Let stand in a covered container in the refrigerator for at least 1 hour for flavors to develop or for up to 2 days.

Apple Ginger Salsa

Makes 2 cups (500 mL)

I like to top pork chops with this sweet salsa.

2	large Granny Smith apples, peeled and diced	2
1/4 cup	lightly packed brown sugar	50 mL
1 tbsp	minced gingerroot	15 mL
1/2 tsp	ground cinnamon	2 mL
1/2 tsp	sea salt	2 mL

1. In a bowl, combine apples, brown sugar, ginger, cinnamon and salt. Let stand in a covered container in the refrigerator for at least 1 hour for flavors to develop or for up to 2 days.

Apricot Salsa

*This salsa is a nice
accompaniment for spicy ribs.*

4	fresh apricots, diced	4
1 cup	grape tomatoes, cut in half	250 mL
1/4 cup	chopped Italian flat-leaf parsley	50 mL
1	serrano chile, seeded and chopped	1
1 tbsp	liquid honey	15 mL
1 tsp	sea salt	5 mL

1. In a large bowl, combine apricots, grape tomatoes, parsley, chile, honey and salt. Let stand in a covered container in the refrigerator for at least 1 hour for flavors to develop or for up to 2 days.

Cherry Salsa

*This salsa is an excellent
garnish for roast lamb
or pork.*

1 lb	Bing cherries, stemmed and pitted, coarsely chopped	500 g
1/4 cup	loosely packed basil chiffonade	50 mL
1/4 cup	almonds, toasted and chopped (see Tip, page 127)	50 mL
2 tsp	liquid honey	10 mL
1 tsp	salt	5 mL

1. In a bowl, combine cherries, basil, almonds, honey and salt. Let stand in a covered container in the refrigerator for at least 1 hour for flavors to develop or for up to 2 days.

Mango Salsa

**Makes 3 cups
(750 mL)**

*Here's a sweet salsa for
spiced-rubbed pork, fish
or chicken.*

Tip
To tell if a mango is ripe,
hold it in the palm of your
hand and gently squeeze. It
is ready to use if it feels soft,
like a tomato.

3	mangos, diced (see Tip, left)	3
½ cup	chopped red cabbage	125 mL
2 tbsp	chopped fresh mint	25 mL
2 tbsp	liquid honey	25 mL
1 tsp	sea salt	5 mL

1. In a bowl, combine mangos, cabbage, mint, honey and
   salt. Let stand for at least 1 hour for flavors to develop or
   refrigerate in a covered container for up to 2 days.

Mixed Roasted Fruit Salsa

**Makes 2 cups
(500 mL)**

*Here's a versatile salsa to use
with fish, pork or warm Brie.*

● **Preheat oven to 450°F (230°C)**

2 cups	red seedless grapes, cut in half	500 mL
½ cup	strawberries, cut in half	125 mL
½ cup	blackberries, cut in half	125 mL
3 tbsp	extra virgin olive oil, divided	45 mL
2 tbsp	balsamic vinegar	25 mL
1 tbsp	liquid honey	15 mL
½ tsp	sea salt	5 mL

1. On a baking sheet, arrange grapes, strawberries and
   blackberries, cut side down, in a single layer. Sprinkle
   with a few spoonfuls of the oil. Roast in preheated oven
   until liquid expelled from the fruit caramelizes, about
   20 minutes. Let cool on pan on a wire rack
2. Once cooled, the fruit will be darkened and broken up.
   Transfer to a large bowl and add remaining oil, vinegar,
   honey and salt. Lightly toss with a fork. Let stand in a
   covered container in the refrigerator for at least 1 hour for
   flavors to develop or for up to 2 days.

Papaya Salsa

Try this salsa next to a shrimp dish. You will think you are on a beach overlooking the Caribbean.

1	papaya, chopped	1
1	avocado, chopped	1
½	red bell pepper, chopped	½
½	onion, chopped	½
¼ cup	chopped Italian flat-leaf parsley	50 mL
1 tsp	balsamic vinegar	5 mL
1 tsp	granulated sugar	5 mL

1. In a large bowl, combine papaya, avocado, bell pepper, onion, parsley, vinegar and sugar. Let stand in a covered container in the refrigerator for at least 1 hour for flavors to develop or for up to 2 days.

Peach Salsa

Makes 2 cups (500 mL)

Sweet and spicy, the peaches and peppers in this salsa create a twist for your taste buds.

2	ripe peaches, chopped	2
1	jalapeño pepper, seeded and chopped	1
½	onion, chopped	½
½	green bell pepper, chopped	½
1 tsp	grated lemon zest	5 mL
1 tbsp	freshly squeezed lemon juice	15 mL

1. In a bowl, combine peaches, jalapeño, onion, bell pepper and lemon zest and juice. Let stand in a covered container in the refrigerator for at least 1 hour for flavors to develop or for up to 2 days.

Pear Pineapple Salsa

I like to serve this alongside Peach Salsa (page 288) when I'm serving scallops.

2	pears, chopped	2
1	can (14 oz/398 mL) pineapple chunks, drained	1
½ cup	chopped fresh cilantro	125 mL
½ cup	chopped red onion	125 mL
2	serrano chiles, seeded and chopped	2
2 tbsp	chopped fresh mint	25 mL

1. In a bowl, combine pears, pineapple, cilantro, red onion, chiles and mint. Let stand in a covered container in the refrigerator for at least 1 hour for flavors to develop or for up to 2 days.

Strawberry Salsa

This is a very flavorful, colorful and festive fruit salsa. It can be served with fish, beef, chicken or even corn chips.

Variation

You can use raspberries in place of the papaya for an all-red salsa. It's perfect for the Christmas holidays.

4 cups	strawberries, cut into small pieces	1 L
½	papaya, cubed	½
3 tbsp	liquid honey	45 mL
2 tbsp	chopped Italian flat-leaf parsley	25 mL
1 tbsp	port wine	15 mL
½ tsp	sea salt	2 mL

1. In a bowl, combine strawberries, papaya, honey, parsley, port and salt. Let stand in a covered container in the refrigerator for at least 1 hour for flavors to develop or for up to 2 days.

Watermelon Salsa

**Makes 2½ cups
(625 mL)**

I love eating watermelon right off the rind, but I also like to use it in this fast salsa.

2 cups	coarsely chopped seedless watermelon	500 mL
½ cup	chopped red onion	125 mL
2	serrano chiles, seeded and chopped	2
1 tbsp	balsamic vinegar	15 mL
1 tsp	liquid honey	5 mL
1 tsp	sea salt	5 mL

1. In a bowl, combine watermelon, red onion, chiles, vinegar, honey and salt. Let stand in a covered container in the refrigerator for at least 1 hour for flavors to develop or for up to 2 days.

Butters and Cheese Spreads

Compound Butters

Adding compound butters is an efficient way to infuse special flavor just before serving. Thin slices on top of hot steaks, fish or vegetables make them taste like you went to a lot of trouble. This is a good way to enjoy these European-style butters. They are found in specialty shops, and have a slightly higher butterfat content.

To store compound butters, refrigerate them in airtight containers. If a container is not airtight, the butter inside may pick up other flavors and aromas from your refrigerator. These butters will keep to the best-before dates on their original labels.

Maître d'hôtel Butter

Makes ½ cup (125 mL)

For this — the "king" of the compound butters — use the highest quality butter you can find. It was crowned "king" in French cooking by the famous chef Auguste Escoffier in the early 1900s.

Uses
Steaks, steamed vegetables and broiled fish.

- Parchment paper

½ cup	unsalted butter, softened	125 mL
2 tbsp	minced Italian flat-leaf parsley	25 mL
1 tbsp	freshly squeezed lemon juice	15 mL
¼ tsp	sea salt	1 mL

1. In a bowl, using a wooden spoon, mix butter with parsley, lemon juice and salt, blending completely.
2. Place butter on a piece of parchment paper and roll into a log about 4 inches (10 cm) long, twisting ends of paper around butter. Place in freezer to firm up, about 2 hours.

Gorgonzola Scallion Butter

Makes ¾ cup (175 mL)

Here's a flavorful butter with the bite of rich cheese.

Uses
Steamed vegetables.

- **Parchment paper**

½ cup	unsalted butter, softened	125 mL
1 oz	Gorgonzola cheese	30 g
2 tbsp	finely chopped scallions (green onions)	25 mL
1 tbsp	freshly squeezed lemon juice	15 mL
¼ tsp	sea salt	1 mL

1. In a bowl, using a wooden spoon, mix butter with Gorgonzola, scallions, lemon juice and salt, blending completely.
2. Place butter on a piece of parchment paper and roll into a log about 4 inches (10 cm) long, twisting ends of paper around butter. Place in freezer to firm up, about 2 hours.

Tri-Herb Butter

Makes ½ cup (125 mL)

Fresh herbs make the best compound butter, and let you create many combinations to suit yourself.

Uses
Steamed vegetables and broiled fish such as salmon.

Tip
Use only the leaves of the herbs. The fibrous stems won't melt in your mouth.

- **Parchment paper**

½ cup	unsalted butter, softened	125 mL
1 tbsp	finely chopped fresh tarragon	15 mL
1 tbsp	finely chopped fresh thyme	15 mL
1 tbsp	finely chopped fresh dill	15 mL
1 tbsp	freshly squeezed lemon juice	15 mL
½ tsp	sea salt	2 mL

1. In a bowl, using a wooden spoon, mix butter with tarragon, thyme, dill, lemon juice and salt, blending completely.
2. Place butter on a piece of parchment paper and roll into a log about 4 inches (10 cm) long, twisting ends of paper around butter. Place in freezer to firm up, about 2 hours.

Parsley Garlic Butter

Makes ½ cup (125 mL)

This butter is similar to Maître d'hôtel Butter (page 292), but with a bite of garlic.

Uses
Steamed vegetables and steaks.

- Parchment paper

½ cup	unsalted butter, softened	125 mL
2 tbsp	minced Italian flat-leaf parsley	25 mL
2	cloves garlic, finely minced	2
1 tbsp	freshly squeezed lemon juice	15 mL
¼ tsp	sea salt	1 mL

1. In a bowl, using a wooden spoon, mix butter with parsley, garlic, lemon juice and salt, blending completely.
2. Place butter on a piece of parchment paper and roll into a log about 4 inches (10 cm) long, twisting ends of paper around butter. Place in freezer to firm up, about 2 hours.

Hungarian Paprika Butter

Makes ½ cup (125 mL)

Here's a flavorful butter with a reddish brown color from the paprika.

Uses
Steamed vegetables and fish.

- Parchment paper

½ cup	unsalted butter, softened	125 mL
2 tbsp	minced Italian flat-leaf parsley	25 mL
1 tbsp	freshly squeezed lemon juice	15 mL
½ tsp	Hungarian paprika	2 mL
¼ tsp	sea salt	1 mL

1. In a bowl, using a wooden spoon, mix butter with parsley, lemon juice, paprika and sea salt, blending completely.
2. Place butter on a piece of parchment paper and roll into a log about 4 inches (10 cm) long, twisting ends of paper around butter. Place in freezer to firm up, about 2 hours.

Curry Butter

A little of this hot and spicy butter goes a long way.

Uses
Steamed vegetables.

- **Parchment paper**

½ cup	unsalted butter, softened	125 mL
2 tbsp	minced Italian flat-leaf parsley	25 mL
1 tbsp	freshly squeezed lemon juice	15 mL
½ tsp	curry powder	2 mL
¼ tsp	hot pepper flakes	1 mL
¼ tsp	sea salt	1 mL
2	drops hot pepper sauce	2

1. In a bowl, using a wooden spoon, mix butter with parsley, lemon juice, curry powder, hot pepper flakes, salt and hot pepper sauce, blending completely.
2. Place butter on a piece of parchment paper and roll into a log about 4 inches (10 cm) long, twisting ends of paper around butter. Place in freezer to firm up, about 2 hours.

Brandy Butter

This sweet butter makes a nice addition to your brunch table; place it next to the muffins and scones.

Uses
This butter is great on waffles, pancakes or apple muffins.

Variation
Use rum instead of brandy.

- **Parchment paper**

½ cup	unsalted butter, softened	125 mL
½ cup	lightly packed brown sugar	125 mL
6 tbsp	brandy	90 mL

1. In a bowl, using a wooden spoon, mix butter with brown sugar. Add brandy, a spoonful at a time, until blended.
2. Place butter on a piece of parchment paper and roll into a log about 4 inches (10 cm) long, twisting ends of paper around butter. Place in freezer to firm up, about 2 hours. Butter will keep, covered and refrigerated, for up to 2 weeks.

Horseradish Butter

Makes ½ cup (125 mL)

Horseradish is a classic condiment for beef, but get that jar off the table and blend the horseradish with butter, instead.

- **Parchment paper**

½ cup	unsalted butter, softened	125 mL
¼ cup	chopped chives	50 mL
3 tbsp	prepared horseradish	45 mL
	Freshly ground black pepper	

1. In a bowl, using a wooden spoon, mix butter with chives and horseradish, blending completely. Season with pepper to taste.
2. Place butter on a piece of parchment paper and roll into a log about 4 inches (10 cm) long, twisting ends of paper around butter. Place in freezer to firm up, about 2 hours. Butter will keep, covered and refrigerated, for up to 1 week.

Herb and Lime Butter

Makes ½ cup (125 mL)

Here's a zesty butter for steamed vegetables, steak and broiled fish.

- **Parchment paper**

½ cup	unsalted butter, softened	125 mL
2 tbsp	chopped Italian flat-leaf parsley	25 mL
1 tbsp	chopped fresh cilantro	15 mL
2 tsp	grated lime zest	10 mL
	Freshly ground black pepper	

1. In a bowl, using a wooden spoon, mix butter with parsley, coriander and lime zest, blending completely. Season with pepper to taste.
2. Place butter on a piece of parchment paper and roll into a log about 4 inches (10 cm) long, twisting ends of paper around butter. Place in freezer to firm up, about 2 hours. Butter will keep, covered and refrigerated, for up to 1 week.

Nut Butters

Nut butters are more than just puréed nuts. Salt, sugar, and sometimes spices and herbs are added to the nuts, along with all kinds of other good things that you can choose. Once you start making your own, you'll be able to tell the difference between homemade and store-bought. I started making nut butters back in the 1980s during a peanut butter shortage. I experimented with different nuts and came up with many flavorful combinations. Homemade nut butters become rancid fairly quickly, but they will keep in the refrigerator for up to 1 month.

Hazelnut Butter

Makes 1 cup (250 mL)

Dark and rich, this butter is perfect on crackers or piped into large strawberries after they've been hulled.

Tip

To toast hazelnuts: Place nuts in a single layer on a baking sheet in a preheated 400°F (200°C) oven until lightly browned, 8 to 12 minutes. Transfer them onto a damp tea towel, then fold over the towel corners and rub the nuts until most of their skins come off.

Variation

Chocolate Hazelnut Butter: Add 2 tbsp (25 mL) unsweetened Dutch-process cocoa powder when you add the nuts.

- **Food processor**

1½ cups	hazelnuts, toasted with skins removed (see Tip, left)	375 mL
½ tsp	sea salt	2 mL
½ tsp	lightly packed brown sugar	2 mL

1. In a food processor fitted with a metal blade, process hazelnuts, salt and brown sugar until smooth, about 2 minutes.
2. Transfer to a covered container and refrigerate for up to 1 month.

Smooth Peanut Butter

**Makes 1 cup
(250 mL)**

*A little peanut oil makes this
butter smooth.*

Variation
To make this a crunchy
butter, stir ¼ cup (50 mL)
chopped peanuts into the
finished butter.

● **Food processor**

10 oz	unsalted roasted peanuts	300 g
2 tbsp	peanut oil	25 mL
¼ tsp	sea salt	1 mL

1. In a food processor fitted with a metal blade, process
   peanuts, peanut oil and salt until smooth, about 2 minutes.
2. Transfer to a container and refrigerate for up to 1 month.

Chunky Honey Roasted Peanut Butter

**Makes 1 cup
(250 mL)**

*The sweet taste of honey
makes this butter a hit on
toast or crackers. Try using
it in your favorite peanut
butter cookies instead of
regular butter, the next time
you bake.*

● **Food processor**

10 oz	honey roasted peanuts, divided	300 g
1 tbsp	peanut oil	15 mL
1 tsp	liquid honey	5 mL

1. In a food processor fitted with a metal blade, process 8 oz
   (250 g) of the peanuts, peanut oil and honey until smooth,
   about 2 minutes.
2. Coarsely chop remaining 2 oz (60 g) of the peanuts and
   fold into butter. Transfer to a container and refrigerate for
   up to 1 month.

Cashew Honey Butter

**Makes 1 cup
(250 mL)**

*Cashews are very rich and
full of flavor. Try using this
butter, instead of peanut
butter, in cookies.*

● **Food processor**

12 oz	unsalted roasted cashews	375 g
1 tbsp	canola oil	15 mL
1 tbsp	liquid honey	15 mL

1. In a food processor fitted with a metal blade, process
   cashews, oil and honey until smooth, about 2 minutes.
2. Transfer to a container and refrigerate for up to 1 month.

Mixed Nut Butter

Makes 1 cup (250 mL)

This mixed nut butter brims with rich flavors.

Tip
If you can find unsalted mixed nuts for this recipe, then skip Step 1.

- **Food processor**

10 oz	roasted mixed nuts (see Tip, left)	300 g
2 tsp	canola oil	10 mL
2 tsp	granulated sugar	10 mL

1. Rub nuts in a tea towel to get as much salt off as possible.
2. In a food processor fitted with a metal blade, process nuts, oil and sugar until smooth, about 2 minutes.
3. Transfer to a container and refrigerate for up to 1 month.

Sunflower Seed Butter

Makes 1 cup (250 mL)

Aboard a plane bound for the East Coast, I discovered this butter in my $5 meal packet. I loved it, and immediately thought about all the ways I could use it in recipes that called for peanut butter.

- **Food processor**

8 oz	unsalted roasted sunflower seeds	250 g
1 tbsp	canola oil	15 mL
½ tsp	sea salt	2 mL

1. In a food processor fitted with a metal blade, process sunflower seeds, oil and salt until smooth, about 2 minutes.
2. Transfer to a container and refrigerate for up to 1 month.

Pistachio Butter

**Makes 1 cup
(250 mL)**

*This greenish butter
looks and tastes great on
pumpernickel bread.*

● **Food processor**

10 oz	unsalted roasted pistachio nuts	300 g
1 tbsp	canola oil	15 mL
½ tsp	sea salt	2 mL

1. In a food processor fitted with a metal blade, process pistachios, oil and salt until smooth, about 3 minutes.
2. Transfer to a container and refrigerate for up to 1 month.

Almond Butter

**Makes 1 cup
(250 mL)**

*This butter is the perfect
match for bagels or corn
muffins.*

● **Food processor**

10 oz	toasted blanched almonds	300 g
1 tbsp	almond oil	15 mL
½ tsp	sea salt	2 mL
¼ tsp	ground cinnamon	1 mL

1. In a food processor fitted with a metal blade, process almonds, almond oil, salt and cinnamon until smooth, about 3 minutes.
2. Transfer to a container and refrigerate for up to 1 month.

Cheese Spreads

Cheese spreads are so versatile. You can spread one on a bagel for a hearty breakfast, or on toast points or crackers for a party. I refrigerate these spreads in small ramekins so they're ready to serve. The containers need to be covered with plastic wrap to prevent the cheese from developing a crust.

Tarragon Cheese Spread

Makes 1 cup (250 mL)

This herb cheese spread is delectable on hot vegetables.

• **Food processor**

8 oz	cream cheese, softened	250 g
2 tbsp	fresh tarragon	25 mL
1	clove garlic	1
½ tsp	granulated sugar	2 mL
¼ tsp	sea salt	1 mL

1. In a food processor fitted with a metal blade, process cream cheese, tarragon, garlic, sugar and salt until blended, about 20 seconds.
2. Place in a ramekin, cover and refrigerate for 1 hour prior to use.

Port Wine Cheddar Spread

Makes 1 cup (250 mL)

Just a hint of sweet port goes a long way with this Cheddar cheese spread.

• **Food processor**

8 oz	mild Cheddar cheese	250 g
4 oz	cream cheese, softened	125 g
2 tbsp	port wine	25 mL
¼ tsp	sea salt	1 mL

1. In a food processor fitted with a metal blade, process Cheddar cheese, cream cheese, port and salt until blended, about 20 seconds.
2. Place in a ramekin, cover and refrigerate for 1 hour prior to use.

Sharp Cheddar Spread

Makes 1½ cups
(375 mL)

The olives add texture and flavor to this cheese spread.

● **Food processor**

12 oz	sharp Cheddar cheese, cut into 6 cubes	375 g
¼ cup	green olives with pimentos	50 mL
2 tbsp	fresh dill	25 mL
½ tsp	capers, drained	2 mL
¼ tsp	sea salt	1 mL

1. In a food processor fitted with a metal blade, process Cheddar cheese, olives, dill, capers and salt until smooth, about 20 seconds.
2. Place in a ramekin, cover and refrigerate for 1 hour prior to use.

Dill Goat Cheese Spread

Makes 2 cups
(500 mL)

People who don't like goat cheese taste this spread and change their minds!

● **Food processor**

8 oz	cream cheese, softened	250 g
7 oz	goat cheese, softened	210 g
2 tbsp	Italian flat-leaf parsley	25 mL
1 tbsp	fresh tarragon	15 mL
1 tbsp	fresh dill	15 mL
1 tbsp	chopped fresh chives (about 5 stems)	15 mL
1 tbsp	freshly squeezed lemon juice	15 mL
½ tsp	sea salt	2 mL
¼ tsp	freshly ground black pepper	1 mL

1. In a food processor fitted with a metal blade, process cream cheese, goat cheese, parsley, tarragon, dill, chives, lemon juice, salt and pepper until smooth, about 20 seconds.
2. Place in a ramekin, cover and refrigerate for 1 hour prior to use.

Curry Cheese Spread

Makes 1 cup (250 mL)

This spicy spread livens up the flavor of sliced root vegetables.

• **Food processor**

8 oz	cream cheese softened	250 g
1 tbsp	dried onion flakes	15 mL
¼ cup	flaked sweetened coconut	50 mL
1 tsp	curry powder	5 mL

1. In a food processor fitted with a metal blade, process cream cheese, onion flakes, coconut and curry powder until smooth, about 20 seconds.
2. Place in a ramekin, cover and refrigerate for 1 hour prior to use.

Pumpkin Cream Cheese Spread

Makes 1 cup (250 mL)

Try this spread on pumpkin bread or on an apple spice muffin.

• **Food processor**

8 oz	cream cheese, softened	250 g
2 tbsp	pumpkin purée (not pumpkin pie filling)	25 mL
1 tbsp	liquid honey	15 mL
½ tsp	ground cinnamon	2 mL
¼ tsp	freshly ground nutmeg	1 mL
¼ tsp	ground cloves	1 mL

1. In a food processor fitted with a metal blade, process cream cheese, pumpkin purée, honey, cinnamon, nutmeg and cloves until smooth, about 30 seconds.
2. Place in a ramekin, cover and refrigerate for 1 hour prior to use.

Bacon Scallion Cheese Spread

**Makes ¾ cup
(175 mL)**

*Here's a fast cheese spread
with the smokiness of bacon.*

7 oz	goat cheese, softened	210 g
2 tbsp	minced scallion (green onion)	25 mL
1 tbsp	real bacon bits	15 mL
½ tsp	sea salt	2 mL
½ tsp	garlic salt	2 mL

1. In a bowl, using a wooden spoon, mix together goat cheese, scallion, bacon bits, salt and garlic salt until smooth.
2. Place in a ramekin, cover and refrigerate for 1 hour prior to use.

Chive Cheese Spread

Makes 1 cup (250 mL)

*This mild herb spread is
perfect for a scone or
savory bagel.*

8 oz	cream cheese, softened	250 g
1	clove garlic, minced	1
2 tbsp	chopped fresh chives	25 mL
½ tsp	sea salt	2 mL
¼ tsp	ground white pepper	1 mL
¼ tsp	hot pepper sauce	1 mL

1. In a bowl, using a wooden spoon, mix together cream cheese, garlic, chives, salt, white pepper and hot pepper sauce until smooth.
2. Place in a ramekin, cover and refrigerate for 1 hour prior to use.

Herb and Garlic Cheese Spread

**Makes 1½ cups
(375 mL)**

Here's a lighter spread for calorie-watchers who don't want to cut down on flavor.

● **Food processor**

8 oz	Neufchâtel cheese, softened, or light cream cheese (not whipped cream cheese)	250 g
4 oz	feta cheese	125 g
1 tbsp	dried oregano	15 mL
1 tbsp	chopped fresh tarragon	15 mL
1	clove garlic	1

1. In a food processor fitted with a metal blade, process Neufchâtel cheese, feta, oregano, tarragon and garlic until smooth, about 30 seconds.
2. Place in a ramekin, cover and refrigerate for 1 hour prior to use.

Honey Walnut Cheese Spread

**Makes 1½ cups
(375 mL)**

Fresh, firm, sliced pears or apples are delicious combined with this spread.

8 oz	cream cheese, softened	250 g
½ cup	walnuts, toasted and finely chopped (see Tip, page 207)	125 mL
¼ cup	liquid honey	50 mL
1 tsp	maple extract	5 mL

1. In a bowl, using a wooden spoon, mix together cream cheese, walnuts, honey and maple extract until smooth.
2. Place in a ramekin, cover and refrigerate for 1 hour prior to use.

Smoked Salmon Cheese Spread

**Makes 1½ cups
(375 mL)**

I like to pipe this onto water crackers and top it off with fresh dill leaves.

● **Food processor**

8 oz	cream cheese, softened	250 g
3 oz	smoked salmon	90 g
¼ cup	fresh dill	50 mL
2 tbsp	capers, drained	25 mL
½ tsp	ground white pepper	2 mL
¼ tsp	hot pepper flakes	1 mL

1. In a food processor fitted with a metal blade, process cream cheese, salmon, dill, capers, white pepper and hot pepper flakes until smooth, about 30 seconds.
2. Place in a pastry bag fitted with a star tip to pipe on top of crackers.

Wild Berry Cheese Spread

**Makes 2 cups
(500 mL)**

This spread takes plain toast to a colorful holiday special.

8 oz	cream cheese, softened	250 g
¼ cup	blackberries, smashed	50 mL
¼ cup	raspberries, smashed	50 mL
¼ cup	loganberries, smashed	50 mL
2 tbsp	liquid honey	25 mL

1. In a bowl, using a wooden spoon, mix together cream cheese, blackberries, raspberries, loganberries and honey until smooth.
2. Place in a ramekin, cover and refrigerate for 1 hour prior to use.

Jalapeño Cheese Spread

Makes 1½ cups (375 mL)

Jalapeño pepper adds a little bite to this spread.

8 oz	cream cheese, softened	250 g
4 oz	feta cheese	125 g
1	jalapeño pepper, seeded and minced	1
½ tsp	grated orange zest	2 mL
¼ tsp	sea salt	1 mL

1. In a bowl, using a wooden spoon, mix cream cheese with feta cheese until smooth. Stir in jalapeño, orange zest and salt, blending completely.
2. Place in a ramekin, cover and refrigerate for 1 hour prior to use.

Olive and Pimento Cheese Spread

Makes 2 cups (500 mL)

When I was a kid, my father used to buy jars of olive and pimento spread to enjoy with crackers. Here's my version.

- **Food processor**

10 oz	goat cheese, softened	300 g
8 oz	cream cheese, softened	250 g
⅓ cup	green olives with pimento	75 mL
2 tbsp	fresh rosemary	25 mL
½ tsp	sea salt	2 mL

1. In a food processor fitted with a metal blade, process goat cheese, cream cheese, olives, rosemary and salt until smooth, about 30 seconds.
2. Place in a ramekin, cover and refrigerate for 1 hour prior to use.

Light Veggie Herb Cheese Spread

Makes 1½ cups (375 mL)

It's win-win! This spread offers full flavor and fewer calories.

● **Food processor**

2 tbsp	dried red and green bell pepper flakes (see Tip, page 24)	25
1 tbsp	dried oregano	15 mL
1 tbsp	dried tarragon	15 mL
2 tbsp	hot water	25 mL
1	clove garlic	1
8 oz	Neufchâtel cheese, softened, or light cream cheese (not whipped cream cheese)	250 g

1. In a small bowl, combine dried peppers, oregano, tarragon and hot water. Stir until softened.
2. In a food processor fitted with a metal blade, process garlic until finely chopped. Add Neufchâtel and pulse several times to combine. Add herb mixture and process until smooth, about 30 seconds.
3. Place in a ramekin, cover and refrigerate for 1 hour prior to use.

Strawberry Cheese Spread

Makes 2 cups (500 mL)

I like to spread this on lemon scones or orange muffins for a treat.

● **Food processor**

8 oz	cream cheese, softened	250 g
½ cup	strawberry preserves or jam	125 mL
1 tbsp	liquid honey	15 mL
1 tsp	almond extract	5 mL

1. In a food processor fitted with a metal blade, process cream cheese, strawberry preserves, honey and almond extract until smooth, about 20 seconds.
2. Place in a ramekin, cover and refrigerate for 1 hour prior to use.

Sweet Sauces, Coulis and Dessert Fondues

Sweet Sauces

Sweet sauces have many uses. You can decorate a plate for a piece of cake or swirl a ribbon of sauce over a dessert such as a crème brûlée. You can even top ice cream or pound cake. The possibilities are endless.

Before storing it, let the sauce cool down completely, then refrigerate in an airtight container for 1 to 2 weeks. If you want the sauce hot, place it in a microwave-safe bowl and microwave for 15 seconds at a time, stirring after every 15 seconds, until it's the desired temperature.

Fresh Blackberry Sauce

Makes 2 cups (500 mL)

Plump blackberries, fresh from the produce stand, make this a rich, decadent sauce. I use leftovers on pancakes for brunch.

Tip
Use a strawberry huller to remove the hulls of the blackberries, which can create a bitter taste.

1 tbsp	cornstarch	15 mL
2 tsp	cold water	10 mL
1 lb	blackberries, hulled (see Tip, left)	500 g
1/3 cup	granulated sugar	75 mL
1/4 tsp	almond or rum extract	1 mL

1. In a small bowl, combine cornstarch and cold water. Set aside.

2. In a medium saucepan over medium heat, bring blackberries and sugar to a boil. Add cornstarch mixture. Reduce heat to low and whisk until mixture starts to thicken, 2 to 4 minutes. Heat for an additional 2 minutes. Remove from heat and whisk in almond extract. Let cool completely. Store in an airtight container in the refrigerator for up to 1 week.

Fresh Strawberry Sauce

**Makes 3 cups
(750 mL)**

*My dinner party guests
always linger in my kitchen,
watching me prepare stuff.
This flavorful sauce is a
great way to show off in
front of your guests.*

Tips

After heating the liqueur,
you can ignite it with a
match.

If using large berries, cut
them into smaller pieces and
they will cook faster.

1/4 cup	unsalted butter	50 mL
1/2 cup	packed brown sugar	125 mL
4 cups	strawberries, halved	1 L
1/4 cup	orange-flavored liqueur	50 mL

1. In a large skillet, melt butter over high heat. Add brown sugar and cook, stirring, until dissolved, 3 to 5 minutes. Add berries and cook, stirring, until mixture is a brick red color, 5 to 8 minutes. Remove from heat and whisk in liqueur. Serve warm or let cool. Store in an airtight container in the refrigerator for up to 1 week.

Fresh Raspberry Sauce

**Makes 2 cups
(500 mL)**

*Raspberry sauce is a staple
in all pastry kitchens,
including mine. Fold it into
whipped cream for a mousse,
use it as a topping for ice
cream or drizzle it over warm
chocolate brownies.*

Tip

You can use frozen berries
that have been individually
quick-frozen and are not
packed in sugar syrup, but
thaw the berries before
using them.

Variation

Omit the liqueur for a
thicker sauce.

2 tbsp	cornstarch	25 mL
1/4 cup	cold water	50 mL
2 1/2 cups	raspberries	625 mL
1/2 cup	granulated sugar	125 mL
2 tsp	freshly squeezed lemon juice	10 mL
1/4 cup	raspberry-flavored liqueur	50 mL

1. In a small bowl, combine cornstarch and cold water. Set aside.
2. In a heavy saucepan over medium heat, bring raspberries and sugar to a boil.
3. Press raspberry mixture through a fine-mesh strainer to remove the seeds. (You can leave the seeds in, if you prefer.) Return to heat and bring to a boil. Add cornstarch mixture. Reduce heat to low and whisk until mixture has thickened, and is a ruby red color and no longer cloudy, about 2 minutes. Remove from heat and whisk in lemon juice and liqueur. Let cool completely. Store in an airtight container in the refrigerator for up to 1 week.

Truffle Fudge Topping

**Makes 2½ cups
(625 mL)**

*Here's a rich double
chocolate sauce for ice cream
or chocolate cake.*

Tips

You can reheat this topping
in the double boiler, then
use it as a poured glaze.

The chocolate can be a bit
warm when you incorporate
it into the butter. This will
cause the butter to melt,
creating a different texture.

- **2-quart (2 L) double boiler**

12 oz	milk chocolate, chopped	375 g
6 oz	semisweet or bittersweet chocolate, chopped	175 g
1 cup plus 2 tbsp	unsalted butter, softened	275 mL

1. In top of double boiler over simmering (not boiling) water, melt milk and semisweet chocolates, stirring until smooth. Let cool until no longer warm to the touch.
2. In a mixer bowl fitted with whip attachment, beat butter and melted chocolate on medium speed until uniform in color, about 3 minutes. Place bowl in the refrigerator for 10 minutes to firm the frosting. Return to the mixer and beat until fluffy, about 2 minutes.

Fresh Lemon Curd

**Makes 2 cups
(500 mL)**

*This is one of the most useful
mixtures in a pastry kitchen.
Use it in lemon tarts, to fill
cream puffs or a white layer
cake, or spread it over a
cooled cheesecake.*

Variation

You can use Meyer lemon
or tangerine juice if you
like instead of regular
lemon juice.

10	egg yolks	10
¾ cup	granulated sugar	175 mL
¾ cup	freshly squeezed lemon juice	175 mL
½ cup	unsalted butter, softened, cut into pieces	125 mL

1. In a large heatproof glass or nonreactive metal bowl, whisk egg yolks for 2 minutes. Gradually sprinkle sugar over egg yolks while whisking. Whisk in lemon juice. Place on top of a saucepan of simmering water over medium heat, making sure bowl does not touch the water. Cook, whisking constantly, until mixture is thick enough to coat the back of a spoon, about 7 minutes.
2. Remove bowl from saucepan and whisk in butter, a few pieces at a time. Transfer to a cool bowl and place plastic wrap directly on the surface of curd. Let cool completely at room temperature. Cover and refrigerate until chilled, about 2 hours or for up to 2 days.

Cherry Almond Sauce

**Makes 2 cups
(500 mL)**

*While conducting a culinary
tour in Lucca, Italy,
we picked fresh cherries
and made this sauce for
our breakfast.*

Tip

If using frozen cherries, try
to purchase ones that have
been individually quick-
frozen and are not packed
in juice. If the cherries
are packed in juice, drain
before using.

Variation

To create a creamy sauce;
stir in ¼ cup (50 mL) warm
whipping (35%) cream into
the cooked cherries.

1 tbsp	cornstarch	15 mL
2 tsp	cold water	10 mL
12 oz	fresh cherries, pitted and drained, or frozen cherries, thawed	375 g
¾ cup	granulated sugar	175 mL
½ tsp	almond extract	2 mL

1. In a small bowl, combine cornstarch and cold water. Set aside.
2. In a heavy saucepan over medium heat, bring cherries and sugar to a boil. Add cornstarch mixture, reduce heat to low and whisk until mixture starts to thicken, 2 to 4 minutes. Heat for an additional 2 minutes. (If the cherries do not break up while cooking, use a potato masher to slightly smash the fruit.) Remove from heat and whisk in almond extract. Let cool completely. Store in an airtight container in the refrigerator for up to 1 week.

Espresso Cream Sauce

**Makes 1½ cups
(375 mL)**

*This light yet rich cream
sauce is perfect with slices
of angel food cake.*

Variation

Substitute orange- or
almond-flavored liqueur for
the coffee-flavored liqueur.

1 cup	heavy or whipping (35%) cream	250 mL
¼ cup	granulated sugar	50 mL
¼ cup	brewed espresso	50 mL
2 tbsp	coffee-flavored liqueur	25 mL

1. In a small saucepan, heat cream, sugar and espresso over medium heat, stirring, until bubbles form around the sides and sugar is dissolved, about 3 minutes. Remove from heat and stir in liqueur. Serve warm or cold. Store in an airtight container in the refrigerator for up to 2 weeks. To reheat, warm in the microwave for 1 minute on Medium (50%).

Orange Mist Glaze

*Glaze fresh berries on any
dessert to make them shine.*

Tip
I like to spray on this
glaze with a mister, which
coats more evenly than a
pastry brush.

1 cup	granulated sugar	250 mL
¼ cup	water	50 mL
¼ cup	orange-flavored liqueur or rum	50 mL

1. In a small saucepan over medium heat, bring sugar and
   water to a rapid boil. Boil until sugar is dissolved, 5 to
   8 minutes. Remove from heat and stir in liqueur. Transfer
   to a spray mister bottle and use immediately, or store in an
   airtight container in the refrigerator for up to 2 weeks.

Coffee-Flavored Syrup

*This sauce is fast and easy
to make, but your guests will
think you worked all day on
it. Drizzle this syrup over
cake brownies.*

Tip
Make sure that you bring
the sugar and water to a
full boil, then cook it
until the sugar is dissolved.
If you don't, the sugar
may crystallize.

Variation
For a nutty taste, substitute
almond-flavored liqueur for
the coffee-flavored liqueur.

½ cup	granulated sugar	125 mL
¼ cup	water	50 mL
¼ cup	coffee-flavored liqueur	50 mL

1. In a small saucepan over medium heat, bring sugar and
   water to a rapid boil. Boil until sugar is dissolved, 5 to
   8 minutes. Remove from heat and stir in liqueur. Serve
   warm or let cool. Store in an airtight container in the
   refrigerator for up to 2 weeks.

Whiskey Sauce

Makes 1 cup (250 mL)

I like this sauce as a garnish for sweet bread pudding.

½ cup	unsalted butter	125 mL
2 tbsp	lightly packed brown sugar	25 mL
½ cup	dark (golden) corn syrup	125 mL
½ cup	whiskey	125 mL
1 tsp	vanilla extract	5 mL

1. In a medium saucepan, melt butter over low heat. Add brown sugar and corn syrup, stirring until sugar has dissolved, about 3 minutes. Remove from heat.
2. Add whiskey and vanilla and stir well. Serve warm. Stir before using.

Port Wine Berry Compote

Makes 3 cups (750 mL)

This easy compote is so tasty, too! Serve it on top of a berry cheesecake for an added berry punch. I also like to use this on top of shortcakes to make a berry delicious dessert.

Tip

To make superfine sugar, place the amount called for in a food processor and process for 2 minutes.

1½ lbs	berries, such as strawberries, raspberries, blackberries and/or blueberries	750 g
½ cup	superfine sugar (see Tip, left)	125 mL
¼ cup	aged port wine	50 mL

1. Place berries in a large bowl. Add sugar and port; toss to coat. Let stand for at least 30 minutes prior to use. If berries were very fresh, compote will keep, stored in an airtight container in the refrigerator for up to 4 days.

Island Fruit Compote

Makes 3 cups (750 mL)

This compote is a great topping for a lemon cheesecake. If you have any left over, you can use it on cooked chicken breasts.

Tip

To tell if a mango or papaya is ripe, gently squeeze it in the palm of your hand; it is ready to use if it feels soft, like a tomato.

1 cup	diced pineapple	250 mL
1/2 cup	diced mango (about 1 medium)	125 mL
1/2 cup	diced papaya (about 1 medium)	125 mL
1/2 cup	flaked sweetened coconut	125 mL
1 cup	rum	250 mL

1. In a bowl, combine pineapple, mango, papaya and coconut. Add rum and toss to coat. Cover and refrigerate for at least 1 hour prior to use. If fruit was very fresh, compote will keep stored in an airtight container in the refrigerator for up to 1 week.

Maple Pecan Sauce

Makes 2 cups (500 mL)

Large pecan halves in a rich sauce transform any ice cream or simple cheesecake into an elegant dessert.

Tip

Use real maple syrup for full flavor.

Variation

Replace the pecans with any variety of nut.

1 cup	pure maple syrup	250 mL
1/2 cup	heavy or whipping (35%) cream	125 mL
1 cup	pecan halves, toasted (see Tips, page 127)	250 mL
1 tsp	vanilla extract	5 mL

1. In a heavy saucepan, heat maple syrup and cream over medium heat until bubbling, about 4 minutes. Remove from heat and stir in pecans and vanilla. Serve warm.

Pear Sauce

Makes 2 cups (500 mL)

The key to this sauce is using ripe pears for maximum flavor.

Variation
Try substituting the same amount of cinnamon for the nutmeg.

● **Food processor**

6	pears (Bosc or Bartlett), peeled and cubed	6
1 cup	granulated sugar	250 mL
2 tbsp	freshly squeezed lemon juice	25 mL
1 tsp	freshly grated nutmeg	5 mL

1. In a medium saucepan over low heat, cook pears, sugar, lemon juice and nutmeg until pears are tender and softened, about 8 minutes.
2. In a food processor fitted with a metal blade, pulse cooked pear mixture until finely chopped but not puréed, about 10 times. Serve warm or let cool completely before refrigerating. Store in an airtight container in the refrigerator for up to 2 weeks.

Peach Sauce

Makes 4 cups (1 L)

This is great as a garnish for pound cakes or shortcakes.

Tip
To peel a peach: Cut an "x" into the base of the peach with a small paring knife, then submerge the peach in a large saucepan of rapidly boiling water for 45 seconds, to let the water separate the skin from the flesh. Remove it with a slotted spoon, then immediately plunge it into a bowl filled with ice water. You should be able to remove the skin with ease.

1 lb	peaches, peeled and sliced (see Tip, left)	500 g
1/3 cup	granulated sugar	75 mL
1 tbsp	freshly squeezed lemon juice	15 mL
1½ tbsp	rum	22 mL
1 tbsp	cornstarch	15 mL

1. In a medium saucepan over low heat, combine peaches, sugar and lemon juice. Cover and cook until fruit has released a lot of juice, about 5 minutes.
2. Uncover and continue cooking until peach juices are reduced slightly, about 7 minutes.
3. In a small bowl, combine rum and cornstarch. Stir into simmering peach mixture. Continue to cook until thickened, 3 to 4 minutes. Serve warm or let cool completely before refrigerating. Store in an airtight container in the refrigerator for up to 1 week.

White Chocolate Macadamia Midnight Sauce

Makes 2 cups (500 mL)

I named this sauce when I was working late one night. It was close to midnight, and there was a full moon. You can use this sauce on top of a cheesecake or pound cake.

Tips

When purchasing white chocolate, check the ingredients and choose a chocolate made with cocoa butter. Avoid those made with palm kernel, cottonseed or tropical oils, which will give the sauce a coconut flavor.

Do not use the microwave to melt white chocolate. It has a lower melting point than other chocolates and burns easily.

Toasting brings out the natural oils and flavors of nuts. Place nuts in a single layer on a baking sheet and bake in a preheated 350°F (180°C) oven until fragrant, 10 to 12 minutes.

Variation

Substitute hazelnuts or cashews for the macadamia nuts.

- **2-quart (2 L) double boiler**

12 oz	white chocolate, chopped	375 g
1 cup	heavy or whipping (35%) cream	250 mL
½ cup	macadamia nuts, toasted and chopped (see Tips, left)	125 mL

1. In top of double boiler, over hot (not boiling) water, melt chocolate and cream, stirring until well blended. (The steam will melt the white chocolate without the burner being on.) Let cool until lukewarm. Stir in macadamia nuts. Serve warm or cold.

Plum Sauce

**Makes 2 cups
(500 mL)**

*Try making your own plum
sauce for your next take-out
Chinese food.*

• **Food processor**

12 oz	ripe plums, chopped	375 g
½ cup	water	125 mL
¼ cup	minced onion	50 mL
¼ cup	lightly packed brown sugar	50 mL
2 tsp	teriyaki sauce	10 mL
2 tsp	reduced-sodium soy sauce	10 mL
1	clove garlic, minced	1
1 tsp	minced gingerroot	5 mL
1 tsp	sesame oil	5 mL
1 tsp	freshly squeezed lemon juice	5 mL
¼ tsp	hot pepper flakes	1 mL
1 tsp	cornstarch	5 mL
1 tsp	water	5 mL

1. In a large pot, combine plums, water, onion, brown sugar, teriyaki, soy sauce, garlic, ginger, sesame oil, lemon juice and hot pepper flakes and bring to a boil over medium heat. Reduce heat and simmer, stirring often, for 30 minutes.
2. In a small bowl, combine cornstarch and water. Set aside.
3. In a food processor fitted with a metal blade, process cooked plum mixture. Add cornstarch mixture and process for 20 seconds.
4. Return to pot and simmer over low heat, stirring, until thickened, about 4 minutes. Serve warm or let cool completely before refrigerating. Store in an airtight container in the refrigerator for up to 2 weeks.

Rum Raisin Sauce

Makes 2 cups (500 mL)

Here's a rich butter sauce that's laced with dark rum.

½ cup	unsalted butter	125 mL
1¼ cups	lightly packed brown sugar	300 mL
½ cup	dark raisins	125 mL
¼ cup	dark rum	50 mL

1. In a medium saucepan, melt butter over low heat. Add brown sugar and cook until fully melted, about 2 minutes. Remove from heat and whisk in raisins and rum. Store in an airtight container in the refrigerator for up to 2 weeks. Serve hot or cold.

Pineapple Topping

Makes 1½ cups (375 mL)

This topping is delicious on any cake with a tropical flair.

Tip

If you only have chunks of pineapple, you can process them until they're crushed, about 20 seconds.

Variation

Add 1 tbsp (15 mL) rum when you add the pineapple to make a pineapple rum sauce.

¼ cup	cold water	50 mL
3 tbsp	cornstarch	45 mL
1	can (20 oz/567 mL) crushed pineapple in heavy syrup, drained and syrup reserved	1

1. In a small bowl, combine cold water and cornstarch. Set aside.
2. In a heavy saucepan, combine reserved pineapple syrup and enough water to equal 1 cup (250 mL). Heat over medium heat until bubbling, about 3 minutes. Whisk in cornstarch mixture until thickened, about 2 minutes. Remove from heat and stir in crushed pineapple. Let cool completely. Store in an airtight container in the refrigerator for up to 1 week.

Deep Dark Truffle Sauce

**Makes 2 cups
(500 mL)**

*This is one of the darkest
sauces in the book, and
makes a dramatic contrast on
a white cake or vanilla bean
ice cream.*

8 oz	bittersweet chocolate, finely chopped	250 g
2 tbsp	unsweetened Dutch-process cocoa powder	25 mL
1 cup	heavy or whipping (35%) cream	250 mL
2 tsp	unsalted butter	10 mL
1 tsp	vanilla extract	5 mL
1 tsp	coffee-flavored liqueur	5 mL

1. In a heatproof bowl, combine chocolate and cocoa powder. Set aside.
2. In a medium saucepan over medium heat, bring cream and butter to a rolling boil. Immediately pour over top of chocolate. Whisk until smooth. Add vanilla and coffee-flavored liqueur. Serve hot or cold.

Marshmallow Sauce

**Makes 2 cups
(500 mL)**

*Drench a piece of dark
chocolate cheesecake with
this white sauce — pure
decadence. It's also a smooth
sauce for banana splits!*

Tip
You can prepare this sauce
up to 2 days ahead and store
it in an airtight container
in the refrigerator. It will
thicken as it cools, so you
will need to reheat it in the
top of a double boiler on the
stove until it's the desired
consistency.

Variation
Add 1 tsp (5 mL)
peppermint extract for a
minty marshmallow sauce.

3 cups	miniature marshmallows	750 mL
1 cup	heavy or whipping (35%) cream	250 mL
1 tsp	vanilla extract	5 mL

1. In a heavy saucepan, heat marshmallows and cream over medium heat, stirring constantly, until fully melted, about 4 minutes. Remove from heat and stir in vanilla. Serve warm.

Milk Chocolate Sauce

*This is a sweeter sauce for
milk chocolate lovers.*

10 oz	milk chocolate, finely chopped	300 g
¾ cup	heavy or whipping (35%) cream	175 mL
2 tsp	unsalted butter	10 mL
1 tsp	espresso powder	5 mL

1. Place chocolate in a heatproof bowl. Set aside.
2. In a medium saucepan over medium heat, bring cream
   and butter to a rolling boil. Immediately pour on top of
   chocolate. Add espresso powder and whisk until smooth.
   Serve hot or cold.

Double Chocolate Sauce

**Makes 2½ cups
(625 mL)**

*Not one but two chocolates
are used for this decadent
sauce. I like to dip shortbread
cookies into it.*

8 oz	semisweet chocolate, finely chopped	250 g
6 oz	milk chocolate, finely chopped	175 g
1 cup	heavy or whipping (35%) cream	250 mL
1 tbsp	unsalted butter	15 mL
1 tsp	vanilla extract	5 mL

1. In a heatproof bowl, combine semisweet and milk
   chocolates. Set aside.
2. In a medium saucepan over medium heat, bring cream
   and butter to a rolling boil. Immediately pour on top of
   chocolates. Add vanilla extract and whisk until smooth.
   Serve hot or cold.

Espresso Chocolate Sauce

Makes 2 cups (500 mL)

Espresso makes a chocolate sauce seem even richer. You can also use this sauce for fondue.

Variation

You can use a shot (2 oz/60 mL) brewed espresso in place of the powder, if you like.

10 oz	semisweet chocolate, finely chopped	300 g
1 cup	heavy or whipping (35%) cream	250 mL
2 tsp	unsalted butter	10 mL
1 tbsp	espresso powder	15 mL

1. Place chocolate in a heatproof bowl. Set aside.
2. In a medium saucepan over medium heat, bring cream and butter to a rolling boil. Immediately pour on top of chocolate. Add espresso powder and whisk until smooth. Serve hot or cold.

Hot Fudge Sauce

Makes 2 cups (500 mL)

Here's a basic, all-purpose fudge sauce.

10 oz	semisweet chocolate, finely chopped	300 g
1/4 cup	light or golden corn syrup	50 mL
1 cup	heavy or whipping (35%) cream	250 mL
2 tsp	unsalted butter	10 mL
1 tsp	vanilla extract	5 mL

1. In a heatproof bowl, combine chocolate and corn syrup. Set aside.
2. In a medium saucepan over medium heat, bring cream and butter to a rolling boil. Immediately pour over top of chocolate mixture. Add vanilla and whisk until smooth. Serve hot or cold.

Mocha Sauce

Drizzle this sauce on cupcakes or fruit.

¾ cup	strong brewed coffee, preferably double-strength	175 mL
5 oz	bittersweet chocolate, finely chopped	150 g
2 tbsp	coffee-flavored liqueur	25 mL

1. In a heatproof bowl set over a saucepan of lightly simmering water, heat coffee and chocolate, stirring until fully melted. Remove from heat and stir in coffee liqueur.

Bittersweet Chocolate Sauce

Makes 2 cups (500 mL)

Here's a sauce that has a little bitter bite to it. It's great on sweet things such as rich chocolate cake.

8 oz	bittersweet chocolate, finely chopped	250 g
¾ cup	heavy or whipping (35%) cream	175 mL
1 tbsp	light or golden corn syrup	15 mL
2 tsp	unsalted butter	10 mL

1. Place chocolate in a heatproof bowl. Set aside.
2. In a medium saucepan over medium heat, bring cream, corn syrup and butter to a rolling boil. Immediately pour over top chocolate. Whisk until smooth. Serve hot or cold.

Rich Caramel Sauce

I like to ice a cake, then drizzle this sauce on top.

Tips

When heating, the granulated sugar will change from solid crystals to the consistency of wet sand to light amber liquid to dark liquid.

Make sure the cream is not chilled or it will splatter and seize the sauce.

1½ cups	granulated sugar	375 mL
¾ cup	heavy or whipping (35%) cream, at room temperature	175 mL
2 tsp	vanilla extract	10 mL

1. In a small heavy saucepan, heat sugar, stirring constantly, over medium heat until sugar is a dark caramel-colored liquid (see Tips, left). Remove from heat and, while whisking, carefully pour in cream. Stir in vanilla.

Melba Sauce

Makes 2 cups (500 mL)

Melba sauce is a thick topping with a robust berry taste and smell, and it's just the thing for vanilla ice cream. If you have some left over, try spreading some on homemade bread for breakfast.

Tip

For peach Melba dessert, top vanilla ice cream with the sauce, then place a few slices of peach on top, and pour on 2 tbsp (25 mL) rum that you flambé.

2 cups	mixed berries, such as raspberries, strawberries and/or boysenberries, puréed until smooth	500 mL
½ cup	granulated sugar	125 mL
1 tbsp	cornstarch	15 mL
2 tbsp	cold water	25 mL
2 tsp	freshly squeezed lemon juice	10 mL

1. In a medium saucepan over high heat, bring berries and sugar to a boil, stirring occasionally. Reduce heat and simmer, stirring often, until slightly thickened, 10 to 15 minutes.
2. In a small bowl, combine cornstarch, cold water and lemon juice.
3. While berry mixture is simmering, whisk in cornstarch mixture and cook, stirring, until sauce thickens slightly, about 4 minutes. Spoon warm sauce over vanilla ice cream.

Wet Walnut Sauce

**Makes 2 cups
(500 mL)**

*Use this thick and rich sauce
to accompany any chocolate
sauce for ice cream.*

Variation
If you would like to use
your favorite nuts instead of
walnuts, there's no problem.

1 cup	lightly packed brown sugar	250 mL
1 cup	light or golden corn syrup	250 mL
1 cup	water	250 mL
2 tbsp	unsalted butter, softened	25 mL
1 cup	walnuts, toasted and chopped (see Tip, page 207)	250 mL

1. In a medium saucepan over medium heat, bring brown sugar, corn syrup and water to a boil. Reduce heat to low and simmer until reduced by half, about 8 minutes. Remove from heat and stir in butter and walnuts. Serve warm.

Pecan Praline Sauce

**Makes 2 cups
(500 mL)**

*Use the freshest pecans
possible for this decadent,
sauce.*

Tip
You can make Pecan Praline
Ice Cream by adding
this cooled sauce to your
homemade vanilla-based ice
cream during the last few
minutes of churning.

• **Candy thermometer**

1 cup	lightly packed brown sugar	250 mL
½ cup	unsalted butter	125 mL
½ cup	light or golden corn syrup	125 mL
2 tsp	vanilla extract	10 mL
1¼ cups	pecans, toasted and chopped (see Tip, page 127)	300 mL

1. In a medium saucepan over high heat, combine brown sugar, butter and corn syrup and bring to a boil. Reduce heat and boil gently, stirring occasionally, until a candy thermometer registers 210°F (98°C). Remove from heat and stir in vanilla and toasted pecans. Serve warm or cold.

Dulce de Leche Sauce

Makes 1 cup (250 mL)

This is a perfect caramelized sauce. It takes a little time but it's worth it.

1	can (14 oz or 300 mL) sweetened condensed milk	1
1 tsp	vanilla extract	5 mL

1. In a heatproof bowl set over a saucepan of lightly simmering water, heat sweetened condensed milk, stirring occasionally, until light caramel in color and thickened, 60 to 70 minutes. Check water periodically and add more as necessary to keep the water level just below the bottom of the bowl. Stir in vanilla. Serve warm or cold.

Apple Pear Sauce

Makes 3 cups (750 mL)

Sweet apples and pears combine in this sauce that I like to use on muffins and quick breads.

- **Food processor**

4	baking apples, such as McIntosh, Rome, Granny Smith, peeled and cubed	4
3	pears, such as Bosc or Bartlett, peeled and cubed	3
1 cup	granulated sugar	250 mL
¼ cup	lightly packed brown sugar	50 mL
2 tbsp	freshly squeezed lemon juice	25 mL
1 tsp	freshly grated nutmeg	5 mL
1 tsp	ground cinnamon	5 mL

1. In a medium saucepan over low heat, combine apples, pears, granulated sugar, brown sugar, lemon juice, nutmeg and cinnamon. Cook, stirring occasionally, until pears are tender and softened, about 8 minutes.
2. Transfer mixture to a food processor fitted with a metal blade and pulse until finely chopped but not puréed, about 10 times. Serve warm or let cool completely before refrigerating.

Butterscotch Sauce

**Makes 2 cups
(500 mL)**

*I like to top vanilla bean
ice cream with chocolate sauce
and this one, too!*

1¼ cups	light or golden corn syrup	300 mL
1 cup	lightly packed brown sugar	250 mL
1½ tbsp	unsalted butter	22 mL
1 cup	heavy or whipping (35%) cream, at room temperature	250 mL
1 tsp	vanilla extract	5 mL
¼ tsp	rum extract	1 mL

1. In a medium saucepan over high heat, bring corn syrup, brown sugar and butter to a boil. Carefully whisk in cream and bring to a gentle boil. Stir in vanilla and rum extracts. Serve warm or cold.

Crème Anglaise

**Makes 1½ cups
(375 mL)**

*This egg-custard sauce can be
used as a base for ice creams
or just spread on top of a
pound cake.*

3	egg yolks	3
2 tbsp	granulated sugar	25 mL
1 tsp	vanilla extract	5 mL
1 cup	heavy or whipping (35%) cream	250 mL

1. In a small heatproof bowl, whisk together egg yolks, sugar and vanilla. Set aside.
2. In a small saucepan over medium heat, bring cream to a boil. Gradually whisk into egg mixture. Return mixture to saucepan over low heat and cook, stirring constantly, until mixture coats the back of a spoon, about 4 minutes.

Sabayon Sauce

**Makes 2 cups
(500 mL)**

I like to pour this rich wine dessert sauce over freshly cut fruit.

4	egg yolks	4
¼ cup	granulated sugar	50 mL
½ cup	cream sherry	125 mL
2 tsp	grated lemon zest	10 mL

1. In a heatproof bowl set over a saucepan of lightly simmering water (do not let bottom of the bowl touch the water), whisk together egg yolks, sugar and sherry. Cook, whisking constantly, until thickened and frothy, about 10 minutes. Whisk in lemon zest. Serve warm.

Fast Applesauce

**Makes 2 cups
(500 mL)**

Sometimes you have a few apples just about to turn — perfect for an applesauce side dish.

- **Food mill or potato masher**

4	baking apples, such as McIntosh, Rome, Granny Smith, peeled and cubed (about 1 lb/500 g)	4
3 tbsp	water	45 mL
2 tbsp	lightly packed brown sugar	25 mL
1 tbsp	unsalted butter	15 mL
2 tsp	ground cinnamon	10 mL
1 tsp	grated lemon zest	5 mL

1. In a large heavy saucepan or Dutch oven over medium heat, cook apples and water until mushy, about 10 minutes. Stir in brown sugar, butter, cinnamon and lemon zest. Reduce heat and simmer, stirring, until apples break down, for 10 minutes. Transfer mixture to a food mill fitted with coarse plate or use a potato masher to mash all of the fruit to a uniform consistency.

Mint Sauce

**Makes ¼ cup
(50 mL)**

This is not the colored green sauce you find in a jar at the market, but a fresh mint sauce that's perfect for your lamb chops. A little goes a long way.

Tip
Spoon this sauce directly over the lamb.

1½ cups	chopped fresh mint	375 mL
2 tsp	granulated sugar	10 mL
¼ cup	boiling water	50 mL
1 tbsp	white wine vinegar	15 mL

1. In a bowl, combine mint leaves and sugar. Drizzle boiling water over top and let steep for 20 minutes. Add vinegar. Strain and press the liquid from the leaves; discard solids.

Brandy Sauce

**Makes 1 cup
(250 mL)**

Serve this sauce on the side with mincemeat pie.

Tip
I like to use this slightly warm. If you've taken it out of the refrigerator, it will have thickened. Simply put it in a saucepan and warm it up.

1 tbsp	all-purpose flour	15 mL
1 cup	whole milk, divided	250 mL
2 tbsp	granulated sugar	25 mL
2 tbsp	brandy	25 mL

1. In a small bowl, combine flour with 2 tbsp (25 mL) of the milk to make a slurry. Set aside.
2. In a small saucepan over medium heat, bring remaining milk and sugar to a boil. Whisk in flour paste and cook, stirring, until thickened, about 3 minutes. Remove from heat. Add brandy and whisk until smooth. Let cool.

Sticky Toffee Sauce

**Makes 1½ cups
(375 mL)**

*This is a British sauce that
gets sticky as it cools. Enjoy
it with vanilla-bean ice cream
or as a garnish for nut pies
and tarts.*

¾ cup	unsalted butter, softened	175 mL
½ cup	light or golden corn syrup	125 mL
3 tbsp	lightly packed brown sugar	45 mL
½ tsp	vanilla extract	2 mL

1. In a small saucepan over medium heat, bring butter, corn
   syrup and brown sugar to a boil, stirring occasionally.
   Remove from heat. Stir in vanilla.

Lemon Honey Syrup

**Makes ½ cup
(125 mL)**

*I like this syrup drizzled over
a blueberry tart.*

2½ tsp	cornstarch	12 mL
½ cup	cold water	125 mL
⅓ cup	liquid honey	75 mL
1 tbsp	grated lemon zest	15 mL
3 tbsp	freshly squeezed lemon juice	45 mL

1. In a small saucepan, whisk together cornstarch and water
   until smooth. Whisk in honey, lemon zest and juice.
   Bring to a boil over medium heat, and cook, stirring
   constantly, until thickened. Serve warm or cold.

Clementine Sauce

**Makes 3 cups
(750 mL)**

*At holiday time our markets
are filled with clementines
sold by the case. I use any
extras in this sauce that
tops cheesecake or a bowl of
fresh berries.*

● **Blender**

10 to 12	small clementines, peeled and segmented with pith and membranes removed (about 1½ lbs/750 g)	10 to 12
½ cup	water	125 mL
1 tbsp	freshly squeezed lemon juice	15 mL
2 tbsp	lightly packed brown sugar	25 mL
2 tsp	cornstarch	10 mL
2 tbsp	orange-flavored liqueur	25 mL

1. In a large saucepan over medium heat, bring clementines, water, lemon juice and brown sugar to a boil. Reduce heat and boil gently until clementines are softened, 6 to 8 minutes.
2. Transfer mixture to a blender and purée until smooth. Return to the same saucepan over medium heat and return to a boil.
3. In a small bowl, combine cornstarch and liqueur. Stir into boiling fruit mixture and cook, stirring, until thickened, about 3 minutes.

Coulis

Coulis is a thick, puréed sauce that's perfect for decorating a dessert plate with color and a flavor that complements the dish. Put it on before you place the dessert on the plate. If you don't have a squeeze bottle, use a spoon to drizzle on the sauce.

Raspberry Coulis

Makes 2 cups (500 mL)

Place a rich chocolate brownie on this coulis.

Tips

Since this sauce isn't cooked, you need to use it all right away — a good reason to indulge!

You can also make a half batch, if you like.

- **Blender**

2½ cups	fresh raspberries	625 mL
1 cup	granulated sugar	250 mL
2 tbsp	freshly squeezed lemon juice	25 mL

1. In a blender, purée raspberries, sugar and lemon juice until smooth. Press liquid though a fine-mesh strainer to remove seeds. Place in a squeeze bottle. Refrigerate and use within a day.

Brown Sugar Coulis

Makes 1 cup (250 mL)

A rich dark slice of chocolate cake is perfect for this coulis.

Tip

You can also make a half batch, if you like.

- **Blender**

1 cup	lightly packed brown sugar	250 mL
½ cup	sour cream	125 mL
1 tsp	vanilla extract	5 mL

1. In a blender, purée brown sugar, sour cream and vanilla until smooth, about 15 seconds. Place in a squeeze bottle. Refrigerate and use within a day.

Tri-Berry Coulis

Makes 3 cups (750 mL)

Any dessert chocolate or lemon dessert will be enhanced by this coulis.

Tips

Since this sauce isn't cooked, you need to use it all right away.

You can also make a half batch, if you like.

- **Blender**

1 lb	mixed frozen berries, thawed	500 g
1 cup	granulated sugar	250 mL
2 tbsp	berry-flavored liqueur	25 mL
2 tsp	freshly squeezed lemon juice	10 mL

1. In a blender, purée berries, sugar, liqueur and lemon juice until smooth. Press liquid though a fine-mesh strainer to remove seeds. Place in a squeeze bottle. Refrigerate and use within a day.

Sour Cream Coulis

Makes 2 cups (500 mL)

I decorate plates with this coulis and a contrasting sauce such as Raspberry Coulis (page 333).

Tip

You can also make a half batch, if you like.

1 cup	sour cream	250 mL
1 cup	heavy or whipping (35%) cream	250 mL
2 tbsp	granulated sugar	25 mL
2 tsp	freshly squeezed lemon juice	10 mL

1. In a bowl, whisk together sour cream, cream, sugar and lemon juice. Place in a squeeze bottle. Refrigerate and use within a day.

Banana Yogurt Coulis

Makes 2 cups (500 mL)

Here's a fast coulis for any fruit-based dessert.

Tips

If your coulis is too thick, thin it to the desired consistency with milk or cream.

You can also make a half batch, if you like.

● **Blender**

1 cup	banana-flavored yogurt	250 mL
1 cup	sour cream	250 mL
3 tbsp	granulated sugar	45 mL

1. In blender, purée banana yogurt, sour cream and sugar until smooth, about 15 seconds. Place in a squeeze bottle. Refrigerate and use within a day.

Fondue is one of the simplest desserts. You can make the sauce days ahead, then warm it right before serving. Here is a list of ideas for dipping into these sauces: pound cake, fresh berries, clusters of grapes, cookies, marshmallows, pretzels and slices of apple, orange, banana and peach.

You can make the fondue a few days in advance, then store it in a covered heatproof bowl in the refrigerator. Warm it in a double boiler on the stove before serving, stirring to fully blend it. Serve it in a fondue pot to keep your sauce warm (most come with their own rack and heat source).

Dark Chocolate Peanut Butter Fondue

Makes 2½ cups (625 mL)

My mother is fond of peanut butter and chocolate, so this is her favorite fondue sauce.

1 lb	bittersweet chocolate, finely chopped	500 g
½ cup	Smooth Peanut Butter (page 298) or store-bought	125 mL
½ cup	heavy or whipping (35%) cream, at room temperature	125 mL
2 tbsp	hazelnut-flavored liqueur	25 mL

1. In a heatproof bowl set over a saucepan of lightly simmering water, heat chocolate and peanut butter, stirring, until fully melted. Remove from heat. Stir in cream and liqueur. Serve immediately or let cool and cover and refrigerate until ready to use.

Double Chocolate Fondue

**Makes 2½ cups
(625 mL)**

*Here's a fondue with heavy
cream and two types of
chocolate.*

10 oz	milk chocolate, finely chopped	300 g
8 oz	semisweet chocolate, finely chopped	250 g
⅓ cup	heavy or whipping (35%) cream	75 mL

1. In a heatproof bowl set over a saucepan of lightly
   simmering water, heat milk chocolate, semisweet
   chocolate and cream, stirring until fully melted. Serve
   immediately or let cool and cover and refrigerate until
   ready to use.

Almond Crunch Fondue

**Makes 2 cups
(500 mL)**

*I like to use freshly toasted
nuts for flavor and crunch.*

12 oz	milk chocolate, finely chopped	375 g
½ cup	heavy or whipping (35%) cream, at room temperature	125 mL
½ cup	almonds, toasted and finely chopped	125 mL
½ cup	sweetened flaked coconut, toasted	125 mL
2 tbsp	almond-flavored liqueur	25 mL

1. In a heatproof bowl set over a saucepan of lightly
   simmering water, heat milk chocolate, stirring, until
   fully melted. Remove from heat. Stir in cream, almonds,
   coconut and liqueur. Serve immediately or let cool and
   cover and refrigerate until ready to use.

Milk Chocolate Fondue

**Makes 2 cups
(500 mL)**

*Sweet milk chocolate
combined here with rich
cream is the perfect base for
all fondues. See Variations,
below, on how to jazz it up.*

Variation
If you would like to use
a liqueur to change the
flavor of this fondue, you
can use up to 2 tbsp (25 mL)
rum, orange-flavored,
cherry-flavored or
coffee-flavored liqueur.

1 lb	milk chocolate, finely chopped	500 g
¾ cup	heavy or whipping (35%) cream	175 mL

1. In a heatproof bowl set over a saucepan of lightly simmering water, heat milk chocolate and cream, stirring until fully melted. Serve immediately or let cool and cover and refrigerate until ready to use.

Bittersweet Chocolate Fondue

**Makes 2 cups
(500 mL)**

*This fondue looks and tastes
great with marshmallows.*

1 lb	bittersweet chocolate, finely chopped	500 g
1 cup	heavy or whipping (35%) cream	250 mL
2 tbsp	coffee-flavored liqueur	25 mL

1. In a heatproof bowl set over a saucepan of lightly simmering water, heat bittersweet chocolate and cream, stirring, until fully melted. Remove from heat. Stir in liqueur. Serve immediately or let cool and cover and refrigerate until ready to use.

Orange Fondue

**Makes 2 cups
(500 mL)**

*Here's a rich chocolate sauce
with citrus tones.*

8 oz	bittersweet chocolate, finely chopped	250 g
6 oz	milk chocolate, finely chopped	175 g
1 cup	heavy or whipping (35%) cream	250 mL
2 tbsp	orange-flavored liqueur	25 mL
1 tbsp	grated orange zest	15 mL

1. In a heatproof bowl set over a saucepan of lightly simmering water, heat bittersweet chocolate, milk chocolate and cream, stirring until fully melted. Remove from heat. Stir in liqueur and orange zest. Serve immediately or let cool and cover and refrigerate until ready to use.

White Chocolate Fondue

**Makes 2 cups
(500 mL)**

*Using white chocolate with
cocoa butter (see Tip, below)
produces a flavorful,
off-white fondue.*

Tip

Make sure the oil or fat
in the white chocolate is
cocoa butter; if it is tropical
oil, such as palm-kernel or
cottonseed oil, your fondue
will have a different taste.

12 oz	white chocolate, finely chopped (see Tip, left)	375 g
1 cup	heavy or whipping (35%) cream	250 mL
2 tsp	white rum	10 mL

1. In a heatproof bowl set over a saucepan of lightly simmering water, heat white chocolate and cream, stirring, until fully melted. Remove from heat. Stir in rum. Serve immediately or let cool and cover and refrigerate until ready to use.

Caramel Rum Fondue

Makes 2 cups (500 mL)

Eat bananas dipped into this fondue and you will be transported to a tropical isle.

12 oz	white chocolate, finely chopped	375 g
½ cup	warm water	125 mL
1 cup	Rich Caramel Sauce (page 325), or store-bought, warm	250 mL
2 tsp	white rum	10 mL

1. In a heatproof bowl set over a saucepan of lightly simmering water, heat white chocolate and water over low heat, stirring, until fully melted. Remove from heat. Fold in caramel sauce and rum. Serve immediately or let cool and cover and refrigerate until ready to use.

Chocolate Marshmallow Fondue

Makes 2 cups (500 mL)

Here's a gooey, rich sauce that sticks perfectly onto fresh fruits.

6 oz	semisweet chocolate, finely chopped	175 g
¾ cup	heavy or whipping (35%) cream	175 mL
¾ cup	marshmallow cream (fluff)	175 mL

1. In a heatproof bowl set over a saucepan of lightly simmering water, heat semisweet chocolate and cream, stirring until fully melted. Remove from heat. Whisk in marshmallow cream until smooth. Serve immediately or let cool and cover and refrigerate until ready to use.

Salted Caramel Pecan Fondue

Makes 2 cups (500 mL)

This fondue is sweet and salty all at once.

Tip
Fleur de sel is the sweet and white top layer that is harvested from salt ponds in France and Portugal. It is pure and has a clean, crunchy taste. If you can't find it, use coarse kosher salt.

¼ cup	heavy or whipping (35%) cream	50 mL
1½ cups	Rich Caramel Sauce (page 325), or store-bought, warm	375 mL
1 tsp	fleur de sel (see Tip, left)	5 mL
½ cup	pecans, toasted and chopped	125 mL

1. In small saucepan, bring cream to a boil over high heat. Remove from heat. Whisk in caramel sauce, fleur de sel and pecans. Serve immediately or let cool and cover and refrigerate until ready to use.

Browned Butter Maple Fondue

Makes 2 cups (500 mL)

Apple and pear slices are nice with this fondue.

1/2 cup	unsalted butter	125 mL
10 oz	white chocolate, finely chopped (see Tip, page 339)	300 g
1/2 cup	pure maple syrup	125 mL
2 tsp	vanilla extract	10 mL

1. In a medium saucepan, melt butter over low heat. Cook until browned, about 8 minutes. Remove from heat. Whisk in white chocolate, maple syrup and vanilla until smooth. Serve immediately or let cool and cover and refrigerate until ready to use.

Pecan Praline Fondue

Makes 3 cups (750 mL)

Dip butter cookies into this fondue.

1	recipe Pecan Praline Sauce (page 326)	1
8 oz	white chocolate, finely chopped	250 g
2 tbsp	water	25 mL

1. In a saucepan, heat Pecan Praline Sauce over medium heat until lightly bubbling. Remove from heat. Whisk in white chocolate and water until smooth. Serve immediately or let cool and cover and refrigerate until ready to use.

Hazelnut Fondue

Makes 2 cups (500 mL)

This rich nutty sauce pairs well with bananas.

8 oz	semisweet chocolate, finely chopped	250 g
1 1/4 cups	hazelnut spread (such as Nutella)	300 mL
2 tsp	canola oil	10 mL

1. In a heatproof bowl set over a saucepan of lightly simmering water, heat chocolate, stirring, until fully melted. Remove from heat. Add hazelnut spread and oil and blend until smooth. Serve immediately or let cool and cover and refrigerate until ready to use.

Apple Cinnamon Fondue

**Makes 2 cups
(500 mL)**

*Dip cake slices into this
sweet, thick sauce.*

● **Food processor**

4	baking apples, such as McIntosh or Rome, peeled and cubed	4
¾ cup	lightly packed brown sugar	175 mL
1 tbsp	freshly squeezed lemon juice	15 mL
1 tsp	freshly grated nutmeg	5 mL
1 tsp	ground cinnamon	5 mL
½ cup	heavy or whipping (35%) cream, at room temperature	125 mL

1. In a medium saucepan over low heat, cook apples, brown sugar, lemon juice, nutmeg and cinnamon, stirring often, until apples are mushy, about 8 minutes.
2. In a food processor fitted with metal blade, process apple mixture until smooth, for 30 seconds. Add cream and pulse a few times to combine. Serve immediately or let cool and cover and refrigerate until ready to use.

Butter Rum Fondue

**Makes 2 cups
(500 mL)**

*I think pound cake or
gingerbread tastes best with
this fondue.*

½ cup	unsalted butter	125 mL
½ cup	dark (golden) corn syrup	125 mL
¼ cup	lightly packed brown sugar	50 mL
½ cup	dark rum	125 mL
1 tsp	vanilla extract	5 mL

1. In a saucepan, melt butter over low heat. Add corn syrup and brown sugar and cook, stirring, until melted and hot, about 3 minutes. Remove from heat. Stir in rum and vanilla. Serve immediately or let cool and cover and refrigerate until ready to use.